EDUCATING THE CHINESE INDIVIDUAL

EDUCATING

THE

CHINESE INDIVIDUAL

Life in a Rural Boarding School

METTE HALSKOV HANSEN

UNIVERSITY *of* WASHINGTON PRESS | SEATTLE *&* LONDON

Publication of this book was made possible in part by grants from the University of Oslo and the Chiang Ching-kuo Foundation for International Scholarly Exchange.

Portions of chapters 2 and 3 were previously published in "Learning Individualism: Hesse, Confucius, and Pep-Rallies in a Chinese Rural High School" in *The China Quarterly* 213, pp. 60–77. © 2013 the China Quarterly.

Printed and bound in the United States of America
Composed in Minion Pro, typeface designed by Robert Slimbach
18 17 16 15   5 4 3 2 1

University of Washington Press
www.washington.edu/uwpress

Library of Congress Cataloging-in-Publication Data

Hansen, Mette Halskov.
Educating the Chinese individual : life in a rural boarding school / Mette Halskov Hansen.
pages   cm
Includes bibliographical references and index.
ISBN 978-0-295-99408-6 (hardcover : alk. paper)
1. Rural youth—Education—China—History—21st century.
2. Education, Rural—China.
3. Educational change—China—History—21st century.
4. Education and state—China—History—21st century.
I. Title.
LC5148.C6H35   2014
370.9173'40951—dc23   2014007527

CONTENTS

Acknowledgments vii

Introduction
Chinese Education and Processes of Individualization 3

1 | Discipline and Agency
Quests for Individual Space 34

2 | Text and Truth
Visions of the Learned Person and Good Citizen 69

3 | Hierarchy and Democracy
Controlled Rise of the Individual 95

4 | Motivation and Examination
The Making and Breaking of the Individual 128

5 | Dreams and Dedications
Teachers' Views and the Construction of a Generation Gap 151

Conclusion:
Authoritarian Individualization 174

Notes 187
Glossary of Chinese Names and Terms 195
Bibliography 205
Index 219

ACKNOWLEDGMENTS

The research behind this book started with fieldwork at a rural boarding school in Zhejiang in 2008. During the years from 2008 to 2012 I returned several times a year to this and other schools in the area, and each time I stayed for weeks in the private home of a retired teacher, her students, and her relatives. I am profoundly grateful to my dear friends in China who introduced me to this municipality and to the school. The study would not have been possible without this personal introduction to the open-minded leadership of Number Two High, a boarding school situated in a small town whose name is kept anonymous throughout this book. The rector of the school permitted me to do anthropological fieldwork that deepens our understanding of how individualization processes that permeate Chinese society are manifested and evolving in the most important institution for socializing and educating the youth in China: the state school. Every time I returned, the school received me with open arms, and teachers, students, and school superintendents and administrators willingly included me in their daily routines. Spouses of teachers, parents of students, shop owners, fortune tellers, and other inhabitants in the town were friendly and accommodating, opening their doors to me, telling about daily life, their experiences with the education system, or exchanging views on the developments in China, Norway, and the rest of the world.

Obviously, not everyone connected to Number Two High would agree to all my conclusions in this book, and there may well be activities and practices that I interpret in way different than they would have. Nevertheless, I have tried to remain as accurate as possible in my representations of the information, impressions, and insights that I obtained during my time at the school, and I hope that any misunderstandings or misinterpretations on my part will be forgiven.

My fieldwork was made possible by generous financial support from the Faculty of Humanities and the Department of Culture Studies and Oriental Language at the University of Oslo, and by the unconditional support from Dean Trine Syvertsen and Pro-dean Gro Bjørnerud Mo, who approved my research in China even though I had responsibilities at home as a pro-dean member of our team. From 2011 to 2012, the faculty and my department granted me one year of research sabbatical that made it possible to finish the fieldwork and write this manuscript. It also provided my husband and me with the excellent opportunity to be visiting scholars in the Department of Anthropology at the Chinese University of Hong Kong (CUHK) for one year. I sincerely thank the leadership and all the staff members in this department at CUHK. They offered me a great opportunity to become part of a vibrant and stimulating anthropological environment—a scholarly community in which even those who do not explicitly work with or in China have an impressive knowledge of Chinese society and culture and are interested in including it in general anthropology. I am especially grateful to Sidney Cheung, Joe Bosco, Gordon Mathews, Tan Chee Beng, Wang Danning, Chen Ju-chen, Chee Wai-Chee, as well as Li Keping, Eddie Schmitt, and all the postgraduate students with whom I talked during our stay at CHUK. I also benefited greatly from discussions and feedback from many other scholars who were based in Hong Kong at the time, and I especially like to thank Gerry Postiglione, Wang Dan, and their colleagues and postgraduate students working on Chinese education at Hong Kong University, as well as Flora Sapio, Magnus Fiskesjö, and Børge Bakken.

During my work with the manuscript and the articles preceding it, I have been fortunate to have many willing and critical readers. First of all, I thank Stig Thøgersen for so carefully reading and competently commenting on every chapter in the book. I am truly grateful for his willingness to continuously engage in my work. In addition, two of the anonymous readers of the manuscript impressed me with their detailed and highly relevant suggestions for improvements.

Although obviously all mistakes or errors in this book can only be blamed on me, I am grateful to all the other people who have taken time over the years to comment on my work on individualization in the state school, including Björn Alpermann, Marianne Bastid, Peter Cave, Eric Florence, Gilles Guiheux, Christian Göbel, Andrew Kipnis, Richard Madsen, Rachel Murphy, Barbara Schulte, Terry Woronov, Yunxiang Yan, and Dan Smyer Yu.

In the final stages of preparing the manuscript for submission to UWP, Wilford Augustus proved to be an excellent language editor, and Rowan Parry helped with numerous practical tasks. I am sincerely grateful to all the people at the University of Washington Press, including BookMatters, who have worked on the book's production, especially executive editor Lorri Hagman, who has been of invaluable support.

Finally, a special thanks to Cuiming Pang and Koen Wellens, without whom neither fieldwork nor manuscript would have been completed.

EDUCATING THE CHINESE INDIVIDUAL

INTRODUCTION

*Chinese Education and
Processes of Individualization*

"Today I start a new life: I believe in myself! Today I start a new life: I believe in myself!" Imagine five hundred fervent youngsters in rural China bellowing out these words as a collective mantra. The setting is a lecture hall in a regular (non-elite) high school in a township of South China, 2009. This book is based on my ethnographic research in this boarding school and the county in which it is situated. *Educating the Chinese Individual* explores how profound processes of individualization in contemporary Chinese society are shaping educational practices as well as the lives of students and teachers. Which views of the learned individual and moral citizen are promoted through social and educational practices in the school? What kind of individual does the state school set out to produce, and with what results? Finally, what can state-organized high school education tell us about the rise and status of the individual in contemporary Chinese society?

The rural state boarding school in China is in some ways comparable to a miniature version of Chinese society. It is inhabited by people from different generations, genders, and social backgrounds; it embraces top-down, well-structured organizations (such as the Communist Party's Youth League and the student association) as well as bottom-up spontaneous collectives (such as student Internet communities, friendship groups, teacher communities of colleagues and friends, and so on); and although teachers and administrators are supposed to represent state-sanctioned ideologies of education and implement policies accordingly, they are as influenced by other societal trends as are their students. Thus, this book is based on the assumption that "schools are a great site to make explicit ties among the arts and artifices of teaching/learning situations and writ large cultural politics" (McDermott and Raley 2011, 37). I further suggest that the mainstream state school in China is a particularly interesting site for exploring the profound processes of individualization of state institutions, society, and persons that scholars have recently begun to investigate both empirically and theoretically.[1]

The topic of education in China has engaged scholars, journalists, students, and educators all over the world, sparked by the country's remarkable economic growth and the renewed investment in education and research following Deng Xiaoping's reforms in the early 1980s. Many observers of China have wondered how an educational system seemingly built on regurgitation, political indoctrination, and Confucian adherence to social hierarchies could cultivate individuals who have immediately grasped the rising opportunities for creating economic value and have willingly taken risks to secure new and better lives for themselves and their families. The global debates on these issues were intensified in connection with two events. One was the publication in 2011 of Amy Chua's controversial book *Battle Hymn of the Tiger Mother*. Chua was probably the first author writing in English to so explicitly glorify practices of academic drilling and rote repetition. She argued for the need to put heavy pressure on the academic performance of children and adolescents, praising them only for outstanding results and keeping near-total parental control over all their activities. She also claimed that Chinese (and to some extent other Asian) mothers have a long history of successfully raising children in this way, and that it was about time its value be recognized. The book spurred popular debate in Europe and the United States, and the author was interviewed by major media outlets, ranging from the satirical American TV program *The Colbert Report* to the influential German weekly newspaper *Die Zeit*.

An event of longer-term significance took place in 2010, when the results of the 2009 Program for International Student Assessment (PISA) stunned many people outside China by ranking 5,100 fifteen-year-old students from Shanghai highest on a list of sixty-five countries in the fields of reading, math, and science. Although no one, including Chinese authorities, claimed that these Shanghai students were representative of Chinese education as a whole, the mere fact that students from public schools in China scored higher than students from all other countries in Asia (many of which are known for their strong position in natural science education), and higher than students from all Western countries, with only Finland making it to the top five in reading and science, was remarkable in itself.[2] The issue was discussed widely in media outlets around the world, and the stereotypical image of Chinese education as outdated and incompatible with global demands for innovation and creativity had effectively been challenged. Some observers argued that if the Chinese could achieve this in Shanghai in 2009, many more of its schools could follow in the coming years (see, for example, Dillon 2010). Others, such as Andreas Schleicher from the OECD (Organisation for Economic Co-operation and Development) Directorate for Education, argued that Shanghai schools had been so successful precisely because they did not follow established Chinese practices of educational investment. Rather than concentrating its investments only on special elite key schools (*zhongdian xuexiao*), the Shanghai municipality had aimed to raise the overall quality of its educational standards, promising new career opportunities to teachers who successfully transformed poor-performing schools and trying to direct more focus toward student collaboration and creative learning. These factors, Schleicher argued, were the background for the success demonstrated in PISA (see Jiang 2010).

China's profound influence on the world economy, and its ambitions to develop a population not only fit for the labor market of the manufacturing industry but also better able to secure China a future place in the league of innovative countries, are certain to ignite global debates about its education system. Within China, former prime minister Wen Jiabao has already strongly expressed the urgent need for educational reform.[3] Scholars in China have long debated the pros and cons of the current organization of education and the examination regime. Furthermore, many Chinese teachers are frustrated and disillusioned with the fate of educational reforms, such as those to promote "quality education" (*suzhi jiaoyu*) or reduce the burden (*jianfu*) of homework on children. Reforms are doomed to fail, many teachers argue, when a rigid examination system is the major driving factor. This discontent with the failing attempts to change the system of education was also reflected in growing negative views on public education among urban parents, as demonstrated in a Chinese survey released in 2011 (Twenty-First-Century Educational Research Institute 2011).

In Europe and the United States, however, some politicians and academics have used the example of China's rising public investment in education to criticize developments in their own countries, fearing that China might eventually become globally dominant in education and innovation. Others strongly doubt that this is likely to happen.[4] Regardless of position, many have started to ask what will happen when an increasing number of Chinese students develop their competence both at home, in an exam-driven school system with practices of systematic academic drilling, and abroad, in liberal education systems with more emphasis on critical thinking, individual creativity, and learning motivated by personal interest. The overwhelming number of Western publications, web pages, media debates, and reports about issues such as Problem-Based Learning (PBL), empowerment of students, and motivational training, is reflective of the awareness among European and US educational authorities of how best to develop critical thinking and analytic skills in school education. However, some scholars discussing these issues in direct relation to the learning experiences of students studying in Asia argue that Western educational systems, presenting vague ideas of critical thinking as a superior form of learning, fail to acknowledge the quality of learning practices to which students coming from Asia are accustomed (see, e.g., Vandermensbrugghe 2004). It has been argued that Chinese Confucian traditions of education have been unjustly stereotyped and misconceived as preoccupied only with rote learning and unable to foster critical thinking (e.g., Wang 2007; Watkins and Biggs 1996).

All these debates testify to a growing global concern with the development of education in the world's second-largest economy. The aim of this book is to contribute to a deeper understanding of some of the most important social dynamics in contemporary Chinese society by examining in detail the educational practices and lives of teachers and students in a rural high school. I began anthropological fieldwork in a school I call "Number Two High," intending to explore the profound and complex processes of individualization that an increasing number of scholars have started to discuss in other contexts of Chinese society, and that are changing not only people's actions and relations to their families, local communities, or the state but also their perceptions of self.[5] I was truly amazed by the extent to which discussions and negotiations of the role of the individual were at the forefront of so much of the school's culture. Many students saw their parents only a few times a year and were struggling to stay motivated in their studies and to define their purpose in life. Teachers were desperately seeking to instill in students a sense of individual responsibility for both failures and successes. Educational authorities were revising curriculum to promote new visions of the individual, and school administrators were experimenting with what they called "democratic" student elections. My ethnographic data suggested that within the contemporary state school an intensified process of individualization, incorporating Chinese characteristics, was taking place.

Many features of this trend of intensified individualization were recognizable in daily life in the school, including pressure on the individual students to pursue "lives of their own," taking responsibility for individual failure or success without defying authorities. The following analysis shows how profound individualization processes in Chinese education are remaking the Chinese state school from within. My aim is to present an ethnography of Chinese schooling that reveals the ties between the daily drama of education in contemporary Chinese society and global processes of individualization.

The state education system in principle attempts to cultivate learned and skilled citizens who can adapt to the requirements of a China that is governed by what has been described as "late-socialist neoliberalism" (Hoffman 2010, 9). In the process of more than thirty years of economic and political reforms, the Chinese Communist Party (CCP) has adopted both (capitalist) neoliberal and (socialist) authoritarian measures into one regime of governing that the anthropologist Frank Pieke has argued is best understood as a kind of "neo-socialism" rather than late or postsocialism, precisely because it has, at least for the time being, combined a capitalist (reminiscent of neoliberalist) economy with a socialist authoritarian form of governance (Pieke 2009). Pieke argued that unlike the result expected by many scholars and observers from the introduction of market reforms and economic growth, "it has become increasingly clear [since the late 1990s] that the weakening of the Chinese party-state has not happened. Capitalizing on rapidly rising prosperity and continued economic growth, the party-state has reinvented itself, putting the rule of the CCP on an increasingly solid footing both materially and organizationally, and, increasingly ideologically" (Pieke 2009, 4).

This has been achieved because the state has successfully employed a range of techniques through which people have accepted and internalized the elements of a neoliberalist political reasoning that is based on "both economic (efficiency) and ethical (self-responsibility) claims" (Ong 2006, 11). The Foucauldian perspective on techniques of governmentality employed in neosocialist China is relevant also in the context of state education, where, for instance, teachers and school leaders experiment with new techniques for governing students and shaping new subjects, such as student associations or motivational pep rallies. However, in this book the aim is not first of all to show how techniques of governance are employed and developed in the school, but to focus on how broader processes of individualization in Chinese society, including subjective perceptions of the role of the individual, are remaking the state school and its "inhabitants" from within. The book explores and combines objectively observable consequences of the individualization of state education, as reflected, for instance, in textbooks and some aspects of the student association, and subjective dimensions of individualization, as reflected in students' and teachers' ways of acting and perceiving the individual and individualism as a both celebrated and criticized ideology.

CHINESE EDUCATION AND THE INDIVIDUALIZATION OF CHINESE SOCIETY

The global interest in Chinese education is reflected in the abundance of scholarly works on the subject, mainly in the disciplines of education science, history, sociology, and anthropology, often with an emphasis on modern education as it developed from the late Qing dynasty through the twentieth century. China scholar Stig Thøgersen's study of twentieth-century Chinese education as seen through the lens of one county in Shandong, *A County of Culture*, shows how crucial the development of schools and discourses on education were to emerging narratives of Chinese modernization (Thøgersen 2002). Thøgersen's in-depth study of education within one rural county was the first of its kind, and it provided a welcome supplement to other historically oriented studies of Chinese education.[6] These, and other historical works focusing more specifically on pre- and early modern China and on Confucian practices of education (e.g., T. Lee 2000; Elman and Woodside 1994), testify to a profound long-term impact of formal education in China as a path to career, identity, and social status. They have provided insights into the many studies on education that have centered on the period after the establishment of the People's Republic of China (PRC) in 1949.

Studies on education during Mao's era of revolution and class struggle have been well integrated into some of the books mentioned previously (e.g., Thøgersen 2002; Pepper 1996; Cleverley 1991). Other scholars have focused more specifically on the Mao period of political radicalization and modernization, basing their research on texts or interviews with people who had fled the PRC because it was not possible to do fieldwork in Chinese schools at the time.[7] The relaunching of the national university entrance exam in 1977 marked the end of a Maoist education system focused on revolutionary zeal, mass training in literacy, and correct class background as a prerequisite for higher studies. A large number of reforms and changes to the educational system were introduced, while, at the same time, many of the restrictions on social research were gradually lifted, and new opportunities for fieldwork in schools and collaborative research between Western and Chinese scholars emerged.

The result has been a large output of new academic research on a range of different topics in the broad field of education. Studies of educational reforms and social consequences of the modernization of education were now based on ethnographic studies from within schools, and studies of policy documents and curricula in state schools gave basis for new analysis of ideology and political and civic education after Mao.[8]

Similarly, the new options for fieldwork paved the way for ethnographic studies of the social and cultural impact of so-called minority education (*minzu jiaoyu*).[9] In addition, although the vast majority of studies on Chinese education have focused on state academic or "regular" (*putong*) education financed by the state, China has also seen a boom in the number of private schools. Private schools were virtually nonexistent in the late 1980s, but by 2004 they had increased to more than seventy thousand, with 14 million enrolled students (n.a. 2004), and in 2008, there were more than a hundred thousand such schools at all levels of education (China Education and Research Network 2011, 3; see also Mok, Wong, and Zhang 2009).

This increase in private schools, ranging from rural vocational to urban foreign language schools, exemplifies how the government has diversified and decentralized its financing of education. A few early studies (Lin 1999; Peng 1997) have been carried out on private education, but the interest in this increasingly complex and undoubtedly important aspect of education is now growing rapidly (see also Wright 2005).

It is somewhat more surprising that relatively little fieldwork-based research has been carried out within vocational schools in China. Vocational education (*zhiye jishu jiaoyu*) has been an important part of the Chinese educational system since the Republic (1911–1949); but despite the Hu Jintao and Wen Jiabao administration's renewed investment since the early 2000s, this form of education has always been implicitly regarded as education for working or peasant classes and has never been the first choice for officials or intellectual parents, nor for parents who could afford other kinds of schools.[10] Today, for many Chinese parents, including peasants and workers, learning practical skills to qualify for the labor market remains a last educational option for their children. This educational path is often chosen only if the child is unfortunate enough to fail to get into one of the desired regular high schools. Yet, although there are a number of studies on the vocational school system,[11] that is, on its history, structures, financing, and policies, few scholars have studied vocational schools from within, using fieldwork methodologies to better understand not only the ideologies shaping vocational training, but the practices and the popular responses to this educational track. The most notable exception is anthropologist Terry Woronov, whose ethnographic studies of urban vocational schools in Nanjing have shown how students in these schools are not, as commonly expected, accumulating technical skills and knowledge but are rather participating in a mimetic production of a school-like environment, something that allows them to accumulate human capital in the form of education and prepares them for a labor market that requires endurance, docility, and obedience (Woronov 2012). For the vocational students, "school is an endurance test, where value is produced by transforming the students into marketable commodities, and by reproducing the values of human capital accumulation through education" (Woronov 2012, 715; see also Hansen and Woronov 2013).

This work is also reflective of the surge of interest since the early 2000s in applying Foucauldian theory to China, which resulted in a new trend of publications on governmentality, discourse analysis, and audit cultures based on a variety of empirical cases from China.[12] Based largely on written sources rather than fieldwork, the sociologist Børge Bakken was among the first to make a substantial analysis of practices of governmentality in Chinese education, arguing that the combination of disciplinary techniques and educational methods accounts for China being an *exemplary society* (Bakken 2000). This society is based on people learning and being disciplined through exemplary norms and models, and it therefore relies not on "outside" disciplinary techniques as means of ruling, but to a large extent on internal mechanisms of morality and education. Likewise, anthropologist Andrew Kipnis's book *Governing Educational Desires* applies theories of governmentality to China, showing how techniques of discourse and means of "conducting conduct,"[13] are not simply (or always) imports from the West (Kipnis 2011, 7). Kipnis expands the study of governmentality in education by analyzing reasons for the intense educational desires that characterize so much of Chinese society today and drive many people's investments and aspirations for the future. His book is an excellent example of how fieldwork-based studies from within schools and among those who are involved in education (teachers, parents, students, school authorities) may help to deepen our understanding of distinguishable societal traditions and processes of governing and subjects' ways of acting on disciplinary techniques.[14]

Educating the Chinese Individual aims at contributing new perspectives and insights to this existing research in several ways. Building on ethnographic data from the social and educational life of students and teachers within a mainstream Han rural high school, it explores how the Chinese state school, beyond any official educational plan, is a site for intense negotiations of the role of the Chinese individual. The approach of a combination of participant observation, structured interviews, and text studies centered around mainly (though not exclusively) one boarding high school opens up research that is sensitive not only to structures, governmental techniques, and discourses on how to foster a "high-quality" population, but to the behavior and agency of students, teachers, school administrators, parents, and administrative staff. The practices of state schools, like other state institutions, are derived from staffers (Pieke 2004); however, I argue that schools tend to be more complex than most other state-run institutions. First, practices are created and challenged directly from within by the defined objects of the state's education, namely the students. Students belong to a different generation than staff and are not just passive recipients of sanctioned knowledge or norms but also agents of change. Second, strong educational desires permeate Chinese society and create immense expectations of the state's performance with regard to education (Kipnis 2011). Third, the emergence of a global market of education is generating new opportunities for some Chinese schools and students while placing and maintaining others in an increasingly disadvantaged position.

Taking the Individualization Thesis into the Chinese School

By approaching the state school as an institution that, like other state institutions, is part of society rather than separate from it (Pieke 2004), it is possible to make a case-based study of individualization processes as they manifest themselves both in institutional changes at the macro level of state/society and in biographical changes at the micro level of the individual. These aspects of individualization are closely connected. Thus, the case study and analysis presented here integrate three equally important perspectives on how individualization processes are played out in Chinese society, and more specifically in the context of the Chinese state school: the presanctioned and official state vision and ideology of the individual; how individualization and unsanctioned views of the individual are in practice and implicitly taught; how individuals themselves respond to, and help create, processes of societal individualization.

The individualization thesis that makes up a main theoretical framework for this book focuses on structural changes in the relationships among individual, state, and society and is usually credited to scholars such as sociologists Ulrick Beck, Zygmunt Bauman, and Anthony Giddens.[15] Based on experiences from Western Europe during the twentieth century, the individualization thesis argues that during the stages of "late," "high," or "reflexive" modernity (Giddens 1991), also called "second" modernity (Beck 1992) or "liquid" modernity (Bauman 2000), people have tended to disembed from groups and collectives such as family, kinship, class, or gender that once defined their identities and prescribed their behavior and ways of living. In the process of modernization, people lose the traditional security that comes with these identifications, and instead they rely more on modern institutions of welfare and health care, public education, and a liberal labor market. With the global trends of neoliberalism and free market capitalism, most states now strive to decrease the population's dependence on such state-funded institutions, and the individual is increasingly forced to take responsibility for and create his or her own life, facing precarious freedoms, new uncertainties, and risks. The individual rises as a subject in society, experiencing more personal choices and options for decision making as well as an increased legitimacy of individual rights. However, as repeatedly argued by proponents of the individualization thesis, these increased options for personal choice by no means imply that people become "free" from institutional structures. To the contrary, in the process of individualization the person comes to depend on modern institutions that increasingly structure and form his or her experiences, and individuals create and reembed into new forms of collectives and communities (Giddens 1991; Beck and Beck-Gernsheim 2002; Bauman 2000).

Individualization also does not mean that "everyone becomes distinct and unique" (Howard 2007a, 9), and it is clearly distinct from ideologies of individualism.[16] As a reminder of the difference between ideologies of individualism and the societal processes of individualization, Beck writes, "Whereas individualism is commonly understood as a personal attitude or preference, individualization refers to a macro-sociological phenomenon, which possibly, but then again perhaps not, results in changes in attitude in individuals" (Beck 2007, 681). *Educating the Chinese Individual* argues that the macro-sociological processes of individualization are reflected in practices of Chinese state schooling and have an impact on changing attitudes and behavior of individuals—teachers as well as students. It draws on revisions of the theories of individualization that developed from the first decade of the twenty-first century and are based on empirical evidence from societies outside of the Western European/North American sphere, most notably in the countries of China, Japan, and South Korea.[17] Empirical studies of these societies have prompted the redefining of the European model of individualization that assumed at least three basic prerequisites for intensified individualization: first, a developed welfare state providing social security to people that allowed them to disembed from their families; second, a culturally embedded practice of democracy; and third, a historically rooted notion of the individual as autonomous, born with individual rights, and equal to other individuals.

The impact of perspectives from Asia, especially developed in anthropologist Yunxiang Yan's studies of China, is reflected in Beck and Grande's own revisions of the theory of reflexive modernity in a 2010 article in which they go against their own earlier assumption that Europe/North America constitutes a universalist model (Beck and Grande 2010). They still argue that there is a substantial difference between first modernity and second reflexive modernity: "Isn't there a gulf of centuries between the threats, opportunities and conflict dynamics of border-transcending, radicalized modernization in the twenty-first century and the ideas, institutions and structures of industrial capitalism and national state authority rooted in the nineteenth century?" (Beck and Grande 2010, 411). But they go on to promote a modified theory of "cosmopolitan modernities" that emphasizes socie*ties* in the plural—a theory that is capable of grasping the plurality, not only variations or types of reflexive modernities and the paths toward them, *and* their independencies and interactions (412). Individualization is a global trend that is reflected to various degrees in the common features of detraditionalization of societies, disembedding and reembedding of the individual, a compulsory pursuit of a life of one's own (which is not to be confused with genuine individuality), and an internalization of systemic risks (Beck and Grande 2010, 420).

The cosmopolitan approach that moves beyond the European model of individualization inherently calls for research that transcends borders of nation-states. Nevertheless, the modifications to the original theories of reflexive modernities and paths to individualization were, after all, based precisely on studies and theoretical arguments from new *nationally* based case studies from outside of Europe;[18] and there is clearly a need for much more empirical data of this kind in order to support or revise the claims regarding global and local processes of individualization, their impact and manifestation in institutions, and not the least the kinds of individuals that emerge from and help to create these processes. The China case demonstrates how it is possible to undergo a profound process of individualization without the political liberalism, welfare state, and classic notions of autonomy that were regarded as prerequisites for its development in Western European second modernity (e.g., Yan 2010, 508–509).

Individualization in China, unlike that in Europe, was part of an elite strategy of modernization through which the individual would be given more self-responsibility and options for action for the explicit purpose of pursuing national strength and wealth. These ideas were first explored by Chinese intellectuals such as Liang Qichao at the turn of the eighteenth century, and then put into practice at the societal level mainly after the Communist takeover (Yan 2010; Svarverud 2010). Since 1949, the party-state has played, and continues to play, a key role in the promotion of individualization of Chinese society. First, during what Yan calls "partial individualization" under Mao, when people were enabled, and very often directly forced, to disembed from family, kinship, and local communities in order to reembed as socialist subjects into new state-organized redistributive systems (workplaces, communes, etc.); then in a second and intensified stage of individualization, starting with the economic reforms since the late 1970s, when people were gradually compelled and given opportunities to disembed from the Maoist state-controlled communities and were thrown into the new realities of market economy and the ideology of consumerism (Yan 2010). Finally, since the 1990s a number of emerging societal phenomena have been reflective of an intensification of the process of individualization, including the inevitable pressure on individuals to create autobiographies. We see an explosion of autobiographical blogs on Chinese Internet and talk shows in which individuals express personal emotions as entertainment for a large TV audience; a booming popularity of shows such as the Chinese version of *American Idol*, in which people from all over the country vote individually for their favorite artists;[19] and a significant growth of the academic disciplines and practices of psychology and psychiatry (Kleinman et al. 2011).[20]

Individualization has no doubt taken root in China, but it is still being managed by the party-state and is characterized by the absence of culturally embedded democracy, a universalized welfare regime, and shared liberal notions of the individual as autonomous, with innate and institutionalized rights. Thus, China demonstrates simultaneously the premodern, modern, and late-modern conditions: "The Chinese individualization process remains at the stage of emancipation politics of first modernity. Yet individuals in China also live in an environment where a fluid labor market, flexible employment, increasing risks, a culture of intimacy and self-expression, and a greater emphasis on individual responsibility and self-reliance have been created by the globalization of the market economy and an ideology of consumerism" (Yan 2010, 510). These are realities that shape Chinese society and the individuals inhabiting it.

Based on a variety of data collected during my fieldwork, this book shows that the contradictions and dilemmas inherent in the individualization process to a large extent influence educational practices in the contemporary Chinese state school as well as the lives of and interactions among teachers and students. The individualization processes in post-Mao Chinese society are transforming the Chinese educational system from within, regardless of political designs to use the school as an arena for molding youth into neosocialist, morally sound, healthy citizens and collectively responsible learned individuals. Moreover, these processes are also transforming people's ways of thinking about themselves and others as individuals. Therefore, considering the diversity of global experiences of societal and institutionalized individualization, it may be useful to qualify the term *individualization* in order to make it more reflective of the specific conditions of neosocialism under which individualization in China takes place. Thus, the book suggests that China has developed a form of "authoritarian individualization" through which the state consciously, through its education system, promotes the rise of the individual in some spheres while holding it back in others, forcing the individual to experiment with appropriate means to simultaneously make "a life of one's own" and adhere to political authorities.

THE RURAL/URBAN EDUCATIONAL DIVIDE: STATE OF THE ART

The rural middle school that is at the center of this book must be considered in the context of the Chinese government's contemporary education policies and investments, and of the rural/urban distinction that is still maintained in so many discussions of Chinese education and society.[21]

The Chinese 1986 education law instituted a system of nine years compulsory education, with six years of primary school (*xiaoxue*) and three years junior secondary school (*chuzhong*). This was followed by three years of high school (or senior secondary school) (*gaozhong*), as required for entrance into colleges and universities (*daxue*), or by higher secondary or tertiary vocational education (*zhiye jiaoyu*).[22] By 2010 there was officially 99.7 percent enrollment of children nationally into primary school, and the authorities claimed to have largely achieved its ambitious goal of the "two basics" from the mid-1980s: Accomplishing nine years of compulsory education, and the eradication of illiteracy among the younger part of the population (China's Ministry of Education 2011, 1). In the poorest provinces there are still counties and townships where the goals of compulsory education have not been met,[23] and the local governments have had to draw up plans on how to achieve this aim before 2020 (China's Ministry of Education 2010b).

Even with indications that official figures regarding education tend to be exaggerated, especially in the poorer areas and some minority regions,[24] the achievements in Chinese education during the reform period have been considerable. National investment in education has increased over the years, and studies have shown that although educational expenditures in China are unequally distributed, on a whole they have gone up rather than down in the reform period (Kipnis and Li 2010). Critics have pointed out that the growth in public education expenditure has tended to slow down in recent years, and that a number of provinces are now failing to live up to the growth targets set by the national education authorities (Zhou 2011). Nevertheless, especially due to long-term policies of birth control (generally one child in the cities, and two in rural areas if the firstborn is a girl), there are fewer students at all levels except higher education, and some targets, like the rates of students continuing onto the next level of study, are therefore easier to reach (Kuai and Jiang 2011).

The sheer number of students in China is still phenomenal. In 2010, the whole country had more than 99 million students attending the nine years of compulsory education, and nearly 44 percent of all students in junior secondary school were boarding at their schools. In addition, more than 46 million students were attending high school, including regular high schools (*putong gaozhong*) with 24 million students, vocational high schools (*zhongdeng zhiye xuexiao*), and some special adult high school courses (*chengren gaozhong*) (China's Ministry of Education 2011, 3). According to official statistics, about 85 percent of junior secondary school graduates enroll at some point into vocational, adult, or regular high school. In 2010, 17.5 million students graduated from junior secondary school, and 8.3 million enrolled in regular senior high schools (China's Ministry of Education 2011, 1 and 3). In global comparison, some scholars have argued that figures such as these suggest that a country like India, with a population almost as large as China's, lags as much as thirty years behind in terms of the proportion of the population that completes secondary and postsecondary education (Kingdon 2007).

Behind these impressive Chinese figures lie deep discrepancies between educational practices and investments in poorer rural areas and in the richer coastal areas and large cities. According to official statistics from 2010, based on people's household registration (*huji*) as either rural or urban, 720 million Chinese were identified as "rural people" out of a total population of more than 1.3 billion. In addition, approximately 180 million people were registered from rural households but were assumed to have been living for more than a year in a larger city, mostly with a temporary urban household registration. The urban population was estimated at 600 million, up from 400 million thirty years ago, but as much as 27 percent of these were lacking permanent urban residence permits (Jin 2010). According to official figures from 2009, an urban resident earned more than three times that of a rural resident, as shown in the official urban/rural net per capita income gap, which was as large as 3.33:1 (Fu 2010). Furthermore, inequality of distribution has increased considerably during the reform period since 1978. The Gini coefficient is often used to measure development of inequality over time—the closer to zero, the less inequality. Measured in this way, China developed from a low level of inequality, less than 0.30 in the early 1980s, and was up to 0.474 in 2013, with a peak of 0.491 in 2008 (Associated Press 2013). This level is recognized, even in Chinese newspapers, as exceeding the level of inequality at which the risk for social instability becomes considerable (e.g., Chen 2010). According to some studies, inequality in China has surpassed that of the United States and is far larger than, for instance, in India (Naughton 2006, 217–218). Furthermore, for instance John Whalley and Ximing Yue have argued that the real rural/urban distributions gap is larger than suggested by these standard methods of measurement (Whalley and Yue 2009).

The socioeconomic inequalities between regions, and between people from different social categories, create major challenges in the field of education. The reform policies have been successful in creating elite schools and strong new academic programs. However, they have failed to provide equal opportunities and direct sufficient investment toward less-developed rural areas. A brief look at education since 1949 reveals that the late 1970s and early 1980s marked a paradigmatic transition from an education system focused on basic-level schooling and ideological training of the masses to one directed at promoting the modernization of society and supporting the development of a market economy. Education under Mao was much criticized in China in the 1980s and 1990s for having been too concerned with class background and obsessed with fostering "red" citizens rather than "experts." However, it was later recognized that in spite of the failure to develop a highly educated population, rural education during the Cultural Revolution (1966–1976) at least managed to reach and make literate a much higher percentage of the population than ever before in Chinese history (e.g., Thøgersen 2002). With the launching of Deng Xiaoping's policies of opening up and reforming China (*gaige kaifang*), the new focus of education became academic quality and the training of an elite, capable of promoting the modernization of Chinese society through the development of technology and the economy. Consequently, many local and rural schools were closed down. Schools were to do away with exaggerated teaching of "Mao Zedong Thought," and class struggle was replaced with individual tests, exams, and competition regardless of the social background or political stance of students.

The decentralization of administrative and financial responsibility for education in the 1980s was one of the important measures aimed at mobilizing local responsibility for education and stimulating local authorities to attract new non-state financial resources (W. Li, Park, and Wang 2007). The fiscal and administrative education reforms did create new incentives for local governments to serve local needs for education, but they also caused the basis for further inequality in people's access to schools and the level and quality of education they were offered. Richer regions clearly had more options for generating new financial resources than did poorer ones, and up through the 1980s and 1990s inequality in school spending across the provinces increased significantly. By the early 2000s, a primary school student in Shanghai cost ten times as much as a student from one of the provinces that invested the least in primary school education (Tsang 2002 referred to in Hannum, Park, and Cheng 2007, 6). In poorer areas, this also resulted in the rise of miscellaneous and highly unpopular fees that parents had to cover themselves. China had made remarkable achievements in public education and had opened up the market for an expansion of private education, but at the same time the foundation of further inequality had been laid.

Official Chinese statistics suggest that although education has developed rapidly over the past twenty years, a number of challenges have persisted, especially in rural areas. Under the ideological headline of a "harmonious society" (*hexie shehui*), former president Hu Jintao and premier Wen Jiabao therefore launched a number of policies since the year 2002, aimed at developing education in rural areas while at the same time using this as a means to ensure more popular support for the government. The start of these efforts was marked by China's first national conference on rural education in 2003. At this time, popular dissatisfaction with the increased burden of parental fees and expenses was being voiced all over the country. The decentralization of educational management and funding had created problems, especially in rural areas. Government expenditure on education was highly uneven along the urban–rural axis and between different regions (e.g., Mingxing Liu et al. 2009; Mok et al. 2009). According to official statistics, 55.8 percent of the official educational budget in 2003 was allocated to the coastal regions and the major cities of Beijing, Tianjin, and Shanghai—an area that accounted for 41.4 percent of the total population (Mok et al. 2009, 508). On a national basis, there was an average of 1,420 students per 100,000 inhabitants, but while there were as many as 6,240 students per 100,000 inhabitants in the capital of Beijing, there were only 985 students per 100,000 inhabitants in the poor Anhui Province. Although there might be demographic explanations to some of these differences, scholars nevertheless found that the tendency of large inequalities was indisputable (see also Brock 2009).

Family finances is one of many factors that create disparities. Since the beginning of the third millennium, many rural parents have continuously complained that in spite of government regulations against them, a number of educational fees have remained in practice, and isolated cases about abuse of child labor in order to create income for village schools continue to emerge. Nevertheless, policies since 2002 have been moving in the right direction for those hundreds of millions of rural parents who want to ensure that their children get at least the basic compulsory education. In 2007, all fees for the nine years of compulsory education were abolished, with the exception of some of the fees necessary for children boarding and lodging at schools. The responsibility for financing teachers, which had been a major problem for many townships and villages, was transferred up to the county level in 2001, and from 2009 a minimum wage equivalent to those of local civil servants (which differ considerably between provinces and regions) was guaranteed for all teachers (n.a. 2009). Another necessary change in policies came into play in 2006, when new regulations acknowledged that a large and ever-increasing number of rural children were turning urban because their parents migrated to the cities, and that they therefore also needed admission into urban schools (see also Murphy and Johnson 2009).

A set of policies that media and scholars have tended to pay less attention to, but that plays an important role in urban as well as in rural areas, concern the decisions to increase the number of students in vocational schools and make the vocational road to education more attractive to students, and, not least, to their parents.[25] In spite of political intentions and will to invest, at the bottom line, one of the main challenges facing the goal to develop good, attractive vocational education lies in the fact that society, parents, teachers, students, and policy makers alike still tend to regard it as an inferior kind of education, not as the most desired "real" education (Woronov 2012; Hansen and Woronov 2013; Shi and Wu 2011). Despite all the government and school representatives' recommendations to establish more vocational schools and classes, few parents fail to notice that people in power, people with higher educations, or people who are connected to the local or national elite will do almost anything to ensure that their own children make it into an ordinary or, even better, an elite class or school. In many people's minds, the vocational path is reserved for those who fail to achieve access to regular high school or higher education.

In tertiary education, unlike in primary and secondary schools, the number of students continues to increase. In 2010, there were more than 22 million students studying at undergraduate levels in colleges and universities, and 5.7 million students graduated from these schools (China's Ministry of Education 2011, 4). All key universities are in the larger cities, and every year 9 to 10 million students compete in the national exams to get into these and the other approximately two thousand colleges and universities around the provinces of China. Getting into the most attractive universities in China has always been the privilege of a few, and especially rural students who come from less-educated families, have parents with fewer means to support extracurricular activities, and have graduated from secondary schools with fewer resources and less qualified teachers tend to be at a disadvantage in the fierce competition to gain access to the best university educations.

Several observers have expressed great concern because of recent trends in the proportion of rural students in major universities going down rather than up. As widely reported in Chinese newspapers in 2011, more than 60 percent of students sitting for the national university entrance exam were registered as being rural. However, whereas approximately 30 percent of students in Peking University between 1978 and 1998 were from rural areas, the figure was down to around 10 percent by 2005. In the prestigious Tsinghua University, the number was less than 15 percent in 2011, and in the Agricultural University, which traditionally has had a larger proportion of rural students, the number of students with rural backgrounds was down to 30 percent in 2011 (e.g., Yin 2011). In spite of explicit political aims to create more equal opportunities in the access to higher education, twenty Chinese scholars raised their concerns regarding this issue in 2010 in an open letter directed to Wen Jiabao and the minister of education, Yuan Guiren. These scholars argued that policies allowing universities to give preference to students with household registrations from within their own cities had resulted in some national universities almost turning into "local universities" (*difangxing daxue*) (Guo et al. 2011, 320). Such policies have caused many people to express their dissatisfaction with the unequal opportunities for accessing the best higher education, and they have also encouraged rural parents with sufficient finances to do everything they can to get their children registered as inhabitants of a city. The authors of the open letter called for government action to secure more fair competition among students regardless of their geographical household registrations, while maintaining the preferential policies for disadvantaged students from ethnic minority and border areas. They also called for all decisions regarding university quotas of students and means of recruitment to be public and transparent (322). In this way, they indirectly commented on the widespread popular concerns about corruption and abuse of power among people at different levels in the education system. Phenomena ranging from direct bribing to the pulling of connections (*la guanxi*) in order to have a child enter a desired school, not through the legal official entrance system but by illegal or semi-legal ways (widely known as the practice of "opening back doors," *kai houmen*) are well known among the Chinese public and are frequently discussed openly among teachers and parents in the schools.

It is in this political and economic context that Number Two High, the field site of *Educating the Chinese Individual*, operates. Its form and content of education are framed by the policies of the party-state and the available resources, financial as well as human. However, even with the national curricula, the exam system, and other effective means for creating a uniform and standardized education system across the country, there is room for schools and their staffs to create and implement educational practices based on local conditions and preferences, abilities, and experiences. In Number Two High, one of the favorite topics of discussion among teachers and administrators concerned the immediate and long-term future of the government's education policies and how they might—or might not—be able to direct practices within their own school.

The Chinese political authorities since 2013, headed by President Xi Jinping and Prime Minister Li Keqiang, will undoubtedly continue efforts to build a globally competitive, elite educational system while expanding the level of education and possibilities of accessing secondary and tertiary education among its less-privileged inhabitants. A plan has been recommended in the "National Outline for Medium and Long-Term Education Reform and Development (2010–2020)" (China's Ministry of Education 2010b). The plan is broad and ambitious, and requires considerable investment in education. Although it is detailed on a wide range of subjects, ranging from the national examination system to the education of disabled children, it remains unclear how the government will ensure that the goals are achieved. The outline largely repeats and strengthens focus on issues well known from earlier reform plans, but it also emphasizes the need for continuously increasing investments in education and the need to use the reforms to create real changes in the organization of education through, for instance, local experiments. Reforms, according to the plan, should be driven by the need to create a modern (*xiandai*) education system with emphasis on higher quality, not merely quantity. Every aspect of education, from organization to content and form of schooling and administration, should be improved and modernized. At the same time, the education system should become fair and just, providing equal opportunities to children regardless of place of origin or family finances. Unlike most earlier educational reform plans, the 2010–2020 plan has gone through a comprehensive process of public hearing. According to the Ministry of Education, two periods of public hearing resulted in fourteen thousand letters received and 2.1 million proposals to the government

(China's Ministry of Education 2010a). This response reflects the fact that there is immense pressure on the government from the population to succeed, and the government is aware of it.

In Number Two High, many of the teachers hoped, but not really trusted, that future reforms as outlined by the government would provide better resources to rural schools such as their own, whose technical and other equipment was better than in the poorest provinces but still a far cry from many middle schools in other rural areas, for instance, Zouping in Shandong as described by Kipnis (2011). Number Two High's students and teachers also found themselves to be at a disadvantage because of the rapidly growing trend of children going abroad to study. It was regarded as an option mainly for affluent or well educated parents, mostly from urban areas, who knew how to identity educational institutions abroad, apply to them, and organize safe living conditions for their children. Since the early 2000s, the combination of popular desire for education and the growth of an urban middle class with more means to spend on children's education has been reflected in an increasing number of Chinese students going abroad to study at the university level, and more and more often at the high school level. Urban students and their parents invest heavily in study in developed countries (usually Australia, Europe, Japan, New Zealand, North America, and Singapore), not necessarily because the students want to stay abroad but because they hope that their experiences will bring better jobs, greater happiness, higher social status, and more flexibility of citizenship, enabling them to master life in both China and the developed world (Fong 2011).

In 2010 alone, more than 280,000 Chinese students went abroad, and according to the Chinese Ministry of Education there was a total of about 1.27 million Chinese students studying in foreign countries in 2011 (Chen 2011). By 2010, the more than 128,000 Chinese students in the United States had taken over the position as the largest group of international students in US colleges and universities, and while the number of Japanese students abroad was declining, Chinese, Indian, and Korean students together had come to make up nearly half of international student enrollment in US higher education (Institute of International Education 2010).[26] There was evidence of a new trend of students enrolling at undergraduate levels, and in the academic year 2009–2010 the number of Chinese undergraduates in the US increased by 50 percent, to nearly 40,000 students, compared to the year before (Levin 2011). The development of a rapidly increasing number of Chinese parents investing in their children's education abroad is likely to also have an impact on reforms of form and content of education within China in the years to come, although as yet it is far from clear how and to which extent.

What seems certain is that rural students and parents affiliated with schools such as Number Two High will not be able to join this trend for a long time to come. In general their life choices and opportunities are constrained not only by economy and presence at home of one or more siblings whom parents also have to take care of, but by a lack of the social capital that is needed to consider studying abroad, identifying possibilities, applying, and so forth. Not only do rural Chinese have a kind of citizenship that is less desirable than that of urban Chinese, but the process of changing their household registration from rural to urban within China has been comparable to the process of an urban Chinese seeking to become a naturalized citizen of another country (Fong 2011, 34).

RESEARCH

Most of the data that form the basis for the analyses and discussions in this book stem from fieldwork in the period from 2008 to 2012 in Number Two High in the township we here call Gaoshan, in Zhejiang Province, in South China.[27] Doing fieldwork in a state institution in an authoritarian state can be an arduous task that requires a large degree of flexibility as to choice of field site and ethnographic methodologies, combined with a sensitivity to the potential problems research can create for the people who are part of the institutions studied (Heimer and Thøgersen 2006). Therefore, many of the choices that I have made have necessarily been pragmatic, often a matter of grasping whatever opportunity occurred—an approach that has both advantages and disadvantages.

My interest in Chinese education goes back to the mid-1990s when I was doing fieldwork (for one year from 1994 to 1995) for my PhD dissertation about ethnic identity and minority education (published in Hansen 1999). Having completed that project, other interests took me through a study of Han migrants and colonization in minority areas (Hansen 2005) to perceptions of family and individual among rural Han youth who had fallen out of the education system (Hansen and Pang 2010; Hansen and

Svarverud 2010). In 2008, I returned to the topic of education and socialization and the methodology of doing participant observation inside schools. I initially hoped to do a comparative study of an elite urban high school and a mainstream rural high school. However, I quickly experienced some of the same barriers as in my earlier projects: imagining ideal places and contexts for doing fieldwork was not productive. Like so many other social science researchers doing fieldwork in China, I had to rely on good personal connections and individual goodwill in order to get access to a field site, in this case a state school. I modified expectations and decided to conduct research in whatever high school was willing to let me follow classes, socialize as freely as possible with students and teachers, follow social and educational activities, and engage with anyone interested in talking to me. Number Two High was such a school. Unfortunately, however, none of the urban, higher-status schools I approached in different cities in China could agree to this research approach. Therefore, because of coincidence rather than choice, fieldwork was carried out mainly in one school only, and comparisons with other schools were based on my own (limited) fieldwork in schools in the same region, on my fieldwork in Yunnan minority schools in the mid-1990s, or, of course, on other people's work.

Zhejiang, where Number Two High is found, is one of the wealthiest provinces of China. The provincial government itself describes Zhejiang as an administrative unit that economically was based on agriculture but has developed its industry during the past twenty years to the extent that it has now "entered the middle or later stage of industrialization" (Zhejiang Provincial Government 2011, 1). Measured in gross domestic product, Zhejiang, with its 47 million population, is among China's four richest provinces, and among the provinces with most foreign export and highest disposable income per capita. In 2009, the yearly disposable income of the 60 percent urban population of Zhejiang was ¥24,611, although it was less than half, ¥10,008, for the rural population (Zhejiang Provincial Government 2011). By 2011, Zhejiang had the second-highest average disposable income (second only to Shanghai) at ¥18,802, while in comparison the poorest province in the country, Qinghai, had an average disposable income of less than ¥8,000 (Wang X. 2012).

The municipality (*zhen*) where Number Two High is situated is among the poorer ones in the province. The whole town area (*zhenqu*), which we call Gaoshan, has a population of fewer than 130,000. Largely an agricultural area, it has limited industries, a shortage of workplaces for young people, and less tax revenue to spend than many other townships in the province. In 2008 the yearly average income for the population of Gaoshan was less than ¥6,000, considerably lower than the average of the rural population of the whole province, but obviously much higher than that of the rural population in poor provinces of China.

Like in the rest of Zhejiang, education is quite developed in the county where Gaoshan is situated. By 2009 compulsory education had long been in place for all children of school age, and as much as 94 percent of children completed fifteen years of education.[28] Approximately half of these students graduated from regular high schools, and the other half from vocational high schools. This represents a major change compared to thirty years earlier, when only about 30 percent of junior secondary school graduates in the county where Gaoshan is situated continued into higher secondary—something that was at that time a relatively high percentage compared to many other rural areas of China.

The county now has several high schools with provincial key school (*zhongdian xuexiao*) status, which receive extra funding and attract the best teachers. Number Two High is not one of those. Number Two High mainly recruits children from the surrounding villages, or children with parents from the township who themselves do not have educations beyond high school, or for the great majority, not beyond junior secondary school. Number Two High is certainly not the school that parents prefer that their children attend. To the contrary, most parents with educations or strong ambitions for their children's education hope for results in the high school entrance exam that will secure their offsprings' admission to at least Number One High in Gaoshan, or even better, to the most prestigious high school in the county capital, which has by far the best educational resources in the county, and is comparable in equipment to richer high schools in Europe. Number Two High, with its fifteen hundred students (down to twelve hundred in 2012) and 120 teachers and administrators, is considered to be at the mid-level in a rather fierce competition among schools in the county to produce graduates, and especially candidates with success in the national university entrance exam. Therefore, although there are indeed many examples in China of urban parents looking for good rural boarding schools for their children, mainly because of their tight managing of children's studies and discipline (see, e.g., Kipnis 2011, 42), those parents would not be interested in Number Two High. Number Two High's record in the university entrance examination is not very good, its facilities lag far behind those of the best county schools and most urban regular high schools, and its disciplinary practices are less strict than the more elite Number One High in Gaoshan township and the more prestigious Number One High School in the county capital.

About 80 percent of students board at Number Two High, and it was therefore convenient for me to do fieldwork from early mornings to late evenings. In 2008, I began following two classes who had just started grade 1. One was a regular high school class, while the other was one of five newly started experimental vocational classes. After the first year, students would split up and continue in different classes. From grade 1 to grade 2, the main reasons for splitting up were twofold: First, students were divided according to who would specialize in natural science (*like*) and who would continue studying humanities (*wenke*). Second, responding to pressure from parents, and because of the school's lack of capacity to offer specialized vocational training, the best approximately 20 percent of students from the experimental vocational classes were allowed to transfer to regular classes. This policy was highly appreciated by parents and endorsed by the students themselves. Students split up again, based on their academic records, when starting grade 3. The students whom teachers regarded as most likely to be successful enough in the university entrance exam to continue on to a full bachelor education (*benke*) were gathered into one class, getting the best teachers and training that the school was able to offer. The rest would remain in regular classes for students who aimed at specialized, shorter university training (*zhuanke*).

The school authorities let me approach students and teachers freely, and I largely adapted to their daily schedules, organizing fieldwork activities accordingly. Students in regular high schools (especially boarding schools) have tight schedules from morning till evening, and it was relatively easy for me to follow their activities, communicating with them mainly during short breaks, during hours set aside for individual homework, or on weekends or holidays. I was met with a very open attitude from practically everyone at the school, as well as from other inhabitants in the town where I lived and whom I was able to talk to outside of school. Most teachers were willing to let me follow their classes and other activities, and they invited me to join their various social activities outside the school. They included me in their daily communication, for instance, while we were all busy working at our desks in one of the common teachers' offices. Up to fifteen teachers shared such an office, and throughout the day they were busy preparing lessons, evaluating student assignments, talking to student cadres (students holding officials positions in the school, as I return to later) about issues ranging from the day's homework to yesterday's breaches of regulations, or simply socializing and updating each other on the latest private and public news and rumors. Student cadres and students from the student association often came into the offices to talk to their teachers, who sometimes summoned individual or groups of students who had breached regulations, or just behaved inappropriately, for a reprimand in the office. Sometimes a student feeling unwell stayed for a while in the office, and in general there were many occasions when students and teachers spent time together outside the classrooms.

My interest in how processes of individualization manifest themselves in Chinese state education—not merely in official discourse and textbooks, but just as much in the organization of daily life, teacher practices, student activities, and creations of autobiographies—required a highly diverse ethnographic methodology. I therefore collected data using different approaches, trying not to give too much preeminence to any given methodology.

First, over the period of fifteen weeks I spent at the school between 2008 and 2012, I sat in on fifty classes, mainly in two courses: Thought and Politics (*sixiang zhengzhi*) and Language and Literature. I observed how teachers interacted with students in the classroom and how students acted in class. I also was present during short breaks when students often stayed in the classroom and socialized with each other, and sometimes with me.

Second, I carried out participant observation by following, observing, and taking part in as many activities related to the school as possible. This included student association elections, activities organized by the student association or by other student groups, pep rallies to encourage students to study harder, excursions, dinners for teachers, activities in teachers' offices, training lectures for teachers, student breaks, and the like. I also gave a few lectures in a combination of English and Chinese, presenting issues especially from Northern Europe that were of interest to students in grade 3. Through these and other activities in the town and villages surrounding the school, I talked informally and at some length with about fifty current teachers, one hundred students, and a large number of other townspeople and villagers, including parents,[29] former teachers in Number Two High and other schools in the county, relatives of students and teachers, and other people with whom I became acquainted. During all my periods of fieldwork I stayed in a private home, and at times my host had between three and five students boarding in her house as well. This gave me insight into a number of issues related to the life and thoughts of students boarding not in schools but privately with retired teachers.

Third, I read and analyzed a number of texts in the disciplines of the two courses I sat in on, focusing on chapters that I found especially relevant to understanding official representations of the individual and ideals of the moral, learned individual and citizen, or focusing on chapters that were taught in the classes I followed. I read teachers' guidebooks and other written relevant material regarding, for instance, the Party's Youth League (*Gongqingtuan*), student associations, educational regulations, or sometimes students' homework.

Fourth, I conducted a small-scale survey of students in two classes to get more systematic information on their social backgrounds. It would have strengthened the study methodologically if I had been able to also include at least one larger survey among students and teachers. This was not possible, so I constructed a general picture of this kind of information on the basis of the small survey, the specific data transmitted to me during interviews with students, homeroom teachers' insights into the backgrounds of their students, and my general knowledge of Gaoshan municipality.

Fifth, for the purpose of comparison, and to gain more insight into the general educational situation in the county, I paid visits to schools in other places, including private and vocational schools. Here fieldwork was mainly in the form of informal talks and more organized interviews with headmasters or teachers.

Sixth, in addition to the large number of informal conversations and chats, I conducted about thirty longer formal interviews with teachers, and about fifty with students. None of these individuals had ever been interviewed before, but I had talked informally to most of them several times previously during my visits to the school. The primary aim of those interviews was to study how students and teachers themselves would create and present autobiographies with a focus on educational experiences, and how they would present and view their own experiences in the light of what they knew about other generations' lives (such as students, teachers, parents, grandparents). This method of interviewing and expecting people to talk at length about themselves and their own experiences is in itself an expression of the individualized society that I, as a European researcher born in the early 1960s, grew up in. Therefore, I agree with scholars, such as Paul Atkinson and David Silverman, who have warned against the tendency in some ethnography to make interviewing the prime, sometimes sole, methodology of qualitative research, privileging life stories and biographical narratives with a unique status compared to other data. Researchers easily come to comply with the contemporary "interview society" in which any person is expected to be able to account for his or her own experiences and private emotions (Atkinson and Silverman 1997; Atkinson 2005). Studying processes of individualization, also at the level of individual biography, I found interviews to be one—but only one—important part of the qualitative research behind this book.

Seventh, and last, since the early 1990s and up to 2008, when my project in Gaoshan started, I had done fieldwork and collected data in villages and towns in the provinces of Yunnan, Gansu, Sichuan, Fujian, and Shaanxi. Even in periods when I did research on other topics than education, I often talked to teachers, people working in educational administration, or students, and I visited a large number of schools at all levels, especially within the rural areas of these provinces. Throughout this book I draw on these earlier experiences and field data for purposes of comparison over time, across regions, and more in-depth understanding of social life and education in China.

All the different types of data collected through this variety of methodologies play some role in each of the following chapters and in the general analyses. At the same time, the topic of each chapter reflects different priorities of research methodologies and an organization of the types of data collected. The book begins by exploring how the physical environment of the boarding school, its organization of space and time, and its regulations aim at producing an individual who submits to discipline and concentrates on studies. This forms a basis for the further discussions of how visions of the learned person and good citizen are promoted through textbooks and classroom teaching, and how the school is governed both through hierarchical arrangements of students in a cadre system and through new experiments with participatory student associations and pep rallies aimed at motivating the individual student to study harder. The book is focused on life—not merely formal education—in the Chinese school, and it therefore also includes a longer analysis of how teachers, who are themselves children of the era of intensified individualization, struggle with interpreting political expectations and putting them into practice. Data collected largely through participant observation show that it is in the practices of political and educational training in schools that the dilemmas and contradictions of the broader societal individualization process, both at the subjective level of the individual and at the objective level of structural changes, are most clearly expressed.

The book concludes that the shift in Chinese popular discourse and moral practice from an authoritarian, collective ethics of responsibilities and self-sacrifice toward a new, optional, and individualistic ethics of rights and self-development (Yan 2011, 40) is reflected in the state school even while it is one of the most prominent institutions for promoting socialist collective ethics and morals to young people and combat so-called selfish, hedonist, and unfilial behavior. The contemporary Chinese high school and its curriculum do not ask for complete submission of the individual to the party-state, nor does it promote a unidimensional political vision of the moral individual and its role in society. In practice, the school experiments with a range of governing techniques aimed at building a neosocialist individual who is submissive to party rule and accepts dominant behavioral norms but is at the same time potentially capable of innovating and creating economic value through self-assertive behavior. Notwithstanding any political plans to use the school as an arena for changing social behavior of youth according to the vision of a socialist, morally sound, healthy citizen and collectively responsible learned individual, the authoritarian individualization processes in post-Mao Chinese society are transforming the Chinese educational system from within. This happens just as much through teacher and student practices as through official discourse expressed in textbooks and the structural organization of education. The individual who comes out of the neosocialist high school today has implicitly learned to do what he or she is asked, not for the sake of the country, or lineage or clan, but basically for himself or herself. This does not necessarily imply that youth are proponents of extreme utilitarianism or egoism. It may as well help to explain why so many rural people who have a high school education but are not part of a local elite or participants in growing middle-class consumption refuse to accept unjust behavior by local officials in cases when it directly threatens their own interests (e.g., O'Brien and Li 2006).

DISCIPLINE AND AGENCY

Quests for Individual Space

Young people who grow up in rural areas in China, where most people seek employment in cities far from their home towns, are increasingly disembedded from both the constraints and the security provided by their families. Many of the students at Number Two High saw their parents only a few times a year; students would stay with grandparents, be alone in their parents' houses from Friday evening to Sunday afternoon, or have meals with other relatives, spending their free time with friends. Most of their time, with holidays the only exception, was spent in school.

The stereotypical image of a Chinese high school is of a cohort of young people buried in books and individual homework, driven by immense pressure from parents and teachers, obsessed with scoring well in the national university entrance exam, and trying to live up to their parents' and society's expectations. There is some truth to this image, as publications, documentaries, and media reports have testified. Yet not all Chinese students are willing participants in the race for educational success; and even when they are, students create loopholes and time and space for alternative individual and collective social activities. Schoolteachers and school leaders experience different kinds of pressure from students and parents; they respond not simply by enforcing discipline, but also by employing creative modification and adjustment of their ways of correcting and advising students, often based on their own intuition and experiences as well as on state-approved educational planning.

Students' ways of challenging the organization of time and space in school to create more opportunity for themselves are reflective of the broader processes of individualization in Chinese society. Students, as well as the youngest of their teachers, have been brought up in a post-Mao moral landscape in which the very meaning of life has been redefined through the shift away from collective moral experiences of responsibility toward an emphasis on individualistic rights and responsibilities (Kleinman 2011b, 10). In Gaoshan, the profound socioeconomic changes since the early 1980s have resulted in new strategies of child rearing that both reflect on and reinforce the disembedding from family, the transformation of personhood, and the quests for individual space that are among the characteristics of an individualizing society.

Within the school structure, there is limited room for students to exert influence on any aspect of the organization of their lives and studies. However, students find subtle and sometimes effective means of demonstrating agency to create room for individual interests and establish communities among themselves. These actions should not be interpreted as a direct form of resistance to education or educational authorities, but rather as a means of negotiating self and self-interests within the context of the tightly organized state school. Disharmony between ethical aspirations and moral actions is a common experience of many Chinese people today, but individuals are not "heroes" who reform their local worlds because of such disharmony (Kleinman 2011b, 26–27); nor do morally based forms of protest and resistance necessarily grow out of a hatred of authorities or deep political discontent. Likewise, students' ways of creating and negotiating space for individual agency within the confines of the state boarding school were not framed as anti-authoritarian actions with intended political outcomes. Rather, students were implicitly challenging educational authorities without putting themselves at too great a risk. This subtle challenging of authority may have far-ranging consequences, because it allows students to build collective networks while strengthening their ability to acquire space and promote change.

STUDENTS' BACKGROUNDS AND PARENTS' STRATEGIES

Like a growing number of children and young people in Zhejiang, approximately 80 percent of students at Number Two High had lived in boarding schools or teachers' homes since the beginning of junior secondary school, when they were around thirteen years old, and 18 percent had lived for some period of their junior secondary education in private teachers' homes. Of the 1,123 students in Number Two High in 2012,[1] 17.7 percent, or almost one out of five, had lived for one or several years in teachers' homes already during primary school. Those children who grew up in mountain villages had no choice but to board at their schools, but even parents who were not compelled to send their children to boarding school (including teachers who were parents) would sometimes chose to do so. Thus, parental strategies related to children's education and parents' own work situations had profound consequences for the remaking of the rural family as a social unit and for the disembedding of rural youth from it. Students did not lose contact or emotional bonding with their closest family members by living away from home, but, according to my interviews and conversations, many were not able to discuss, on a regular basis, matters of concern in their daily lives or pressing issues relating to their future with their parents or siblings.

My survey from 2012 of the total student body,[2] combined with a survey of two classes in 2008 and numerous interviews with school administrators and homeroom teachers (*banzhuren*) who were familiar with the backgrounds of their students, reveals that only a small fraction, fewer than 3 percent, of the students in Number Two High had parents with educations beyond high school. Mothers had slightly lower education than fathers; 85 percent of the mothers and 75 percent of the fathers had a maximum of nine years of junior secondary education. Thirty-nine percent of fathers were shopkeepers (*kai dian*) and 29 percent were manual laborers (*dagong*); among mothers the equivalent figures were 35 percent and 25 percent respectively. The third most common job among parents was in agriculture, with approximately 7 percent of mothers as well as fathers working in this sector. Generally in Gaoshan, as in other rural areas of China, it was common that people who worked outside the state sector had multiple job experiences, including part-time work in agriculture, some years of employment in a company before opening a private shop or business, some years in a factory, or combination of several part-time jobs, such as taking care of children and selling private insurance. Sometimes mothers did not work at all, or worked part time in order to care for younger children or older relatives at home. Nine percent of the mothers and fewer than 2 percent of the fathers did not work at all at the time of the survey. Approximately 43 percent of the students' fathers lived in Gaoshan or nearby, and these students saw their fathers every weekend or more often, while 58 percent of students saw their mothers during weekends or more often. The rest of the students saw one of their parents between one and six times a year, and more than 25 percent of students' parents lived outside the province.

Only a minority of 21 percent of students in Number Two High were singletons; 62 percent had one sibling; 13 percent had two; and 3 percent had three siblings. Since the late 1970s China has practiced a family policy restricting the number of children of each couple. While this policy has become known abroad as the "one-child policy," members of ethnic minorities have always been allowed to have at least two children, and in areas such as Gaoshan, parents with rural household registrations are now allowed to have two children if the first is a girl. It was well known in Gaoshan, and frequently mentioned by students, that couples would go through many ordeals, such as paying fines or having abortions, to secure at least one son in the family. It was also common, though a breach of regulations, that couples would have several children even if the first-born were a son. People in Gaoshan talked rather openly about this and did not make a great deal out of it. Students had no problems saying that they had more than one sibling, and there seemed to be a high degree of social tolerance toward people who broke these regulations. This was quite unlike the situation reported among urban citizens where policies of birth control have been much more strictly enforced, but maybe also to higher extent internalized or at least accepted (Milwertz 1996; Fong 2011, 159; Greenhalgh 2010, 48).[3] It was even considered a sign of strength in Gaoshan to have more children. Because I have three daughters, people would often joke with me, asking when I would have a son, or whether they could somehow help me get one.[4] On one such occasion in 2008, when I was chatting with a group of neighbors, some of the men started to tell me how "most people" in Gaoshan wanted two or three children, though normally not more than that. "It is easy," one successful businessman explained. "You just pay ¥16,000 for number two and ¥30,000 for number three!" "Oh yes, indeed," another man added grumpily. "Those who have a lot of money can indeed manage to get more children!" "Or," another neighbor interjected, "you just have to be a party secretary!" He pointed to the local party secretary in the group and laughingly explained that this man was so powerful that he had been able to have four children and still get this political position. While everybody was still laughing, another man joined in, saying, "Yes indeed, he has four children, but it is *not* because he is a party secretary that he managed this; he became the party secretary *because* he has four children!" This comment was greatly applauded, and the talk continued about how it was a sign of both masculine and financial strength that a man in rural China could bring four children into the world and raise them properly without getting into trouble with the birth control authorities. A man like this deserved a position with power, the group laughingly agreed.

It was expensive, though, in Gaoshan as elsewhere in China, to have several children. A child needed education; a son should preferably own a house or flat before getting married; and a daughter had to bring gifts and money into her marriage. Nevertheless, people in Gaoshan with several children and at least one son were considered to be fortunate. In this respect parents in Gaoshan were no different from parents in other rural areas of China (with some ethnic minority areas as the exception): the wish to have a boy remains strong, as the demographic statistics on gender balance in China have long confirmed.[5] However, in conversations many people in Gaoshan emphasized the social and emotional advantages of having at least one daughter. Daughters were supposed to be more affectionate, well behaved (*guai*), concerned about their parents, and better than boys at adapting to the schools' demands for diligence, obedience, and patience (see also, e.g., Fong and Kim 2011, 336–337; Johnson 2004).

Such gender comparisons were often brought up in people's discussions about the prospective futures of their children, and the advantages and disadvantages of having children going into businesses and taking financial risks or becoming white-collar workers with more job security but lower income. One of the best scenarios that a pragmatic couple with no higher education themselves could realistically hope for, many parents and teachers told me, was to have a daughter who attended college and got a secure (*wending*) job in the state sector (usually as a teacher), and at least one son who was in business (*zuo shengyi*). This combination of different career paths for children of different genders was regarded as advantageous, for some even ideal, not just because of parents' wishes to secure financial support for themselves at an old age but because they were worried about the futures of their daughters. Many would vividly tell stories about local girls who had jumped into marriages with lazy or incapable men or had been left alone with children and no steady income. People in Gaoshan whose children or grandchildren had not yet married were often worried about the changes in society that suggested a growth in "naked marriages" (*luohun*), wherein young people would marry without first having secured themselves materially.[6] There were also deep concerns about the rising divorce rates and the risk of unemployment for young people. Parents saw these phenomena as being socially and financially more risky for daughters than for sons. The best way to secure a daughter's future in this rapidly changing social environment, many people in Gaoshan thought, was to give her an education and encourage her to continue into a job that provided long-term security and a basic income. A job as a teacher was ideal, and its cumulative effects considerable. In addition to financial security, it provided status and face (*mianzi*) in Gaoshan, and it was believed that a teacher in the family would later help children to be more successful in education than their parents. With a son in business, the family would hope to secure a higher income and greater financial benefits to the entire family.

One of the main concerns for Gaoshan people who did not have comprehensive educations seemed to be ensuring that their children would not follow in their own educational paths. Indeed, by being in a regular high school, most students in Number Two High were attaining higher education than did their parents, and they were, in principle, already en route to different careers. In reality, after graduation from high school or college, many of them might enter the same professions as their parents or even accept insecure or low-paying jobs. Nonetheless, for a period of time, while students were attending regular high school and preparing for the national university entrance exam, they were at the center of their parents' *hope* that they would be able to get higher educations, better jobs, and higher social status.

Consulting fortune-tellers was a popular way for parents to predict and, they hoped, secure their children's success. Fortune-tellers in Gaoshan were mostly blind men who were making hundreds of yuan every day (people paid on a voluntary basis) predicting whether a business deal would be beneficial, whether a marriage would be successful, or which rituals to perform at which hour at the opening of a new store. According to interviews with some of the most successful among an abundance of fortune tellers in Gaoshan, the most frequent questions asked by people—including even teachers and government officials—was whether or not a child would be successful in an upcoming exam and which job he or she might eventually be able to find after completion of school. There was no doubt in the fortune-tellers' minds that Gaoshan parents' aspirations for their children's successful education were strong, and every year when children started to prepare for the examinations, fortune-tellers were kept busy searching for clues about how their customers' children would fare.

Consulting fortune tellers was just one of several strategies to take precautions in order to predict and hopefully secure children's success. At the end of the school year, I observed in Number Two High hopeful parents trying to mobilize whatever personal connections (*guanxi*) they had with people in the education administration in the hope of increasing their children's chances for enrollment. Parents whose children scored relatively well on the high school entrance exam but not well enough to secure free admittance to the regular high school were willing to pay fees of up to ¥20,000 to purchase places in the school. To the embarrassment of some teachers, parents would sometimes bring them fruit or other snacks, using any occasion to mention the name of their sons or daughters. This was a fairly innocent way of approaching teachers by parents who had neither sufficient financial or social capital to really "use the backdoor" (*zou houmen*) or "pull connections" (*la guanxi*). However, everyone inside and outside of the education system was highly aware that the combination of parents' strategies to promote their children's education and the limited number of seats in the most popular regular high schools created serious cases of corruption and irregular admission of students.

While parents wanted their children to have an education, many also needed someone to take care of their children while they were working out of town. Gaoshan was a rural town with long business traditions and was relatively affluent. Many people could afford to integrate their own work practices with strategies to enhance their children's chances to succeed in education, and this laid the groundwork for the surge in the late 1990s of a private market for children boarding in homes of teachers.[7] This practice was both a reflection of, and served to further reinforce, the transformation of the meaning and functioning of the family that takes place under the process of individualization (Yan 2003, 2009). Rural people ages thirty to fifty had changed their perceptions of members of the older generation, who used to be regarded as the natural caretakers of children when parents were away, but who were now seen as inadequate for this primarily because of their lack of formal education.[8] One of the teachers who had been among the first to establish a private boarding home for schoolchildren in Gaoshan, explained the reason behind his expanding business success: "Grandparents are of no use anymore!" He meant that most grandparents were unable to help their grandchildren do homework, and he noted that many parents were explicitly looking for teachers who were also able to teach their children discipline, not the least self-discipline. Although most parents, in this teacher's experience, were looking for someone who would make sure that their children spent most of their time studying, quite a few others were merely using this argument to cover over the fact that they, or the grandparents, were unable to keep their children under control themselves. Parents who worked far away, he claimed, often spoiled their children, and grandparents did not understand the psychology and needs of children in today's society.

The choice of parents to send their children to the homes of teachers may be interpreted as an expression of strong educational desires, but it was also related to practical needs for organizing family life in new ways because of the changing demands of the labor market. What started in Gaoshan as an isolated phenomenon of a few teachers taking children of relatives or friends into their homes to provide a solution to parents who worked far away had ten years later developed into a large private market, with teachers and families competing for boarding students and pupils below the high school level. In 2008, when I first came to Gaoshan, most teachers who had children boarding in their homes did this privately, without public advertising. Only a handful of teachers had put up signs outside their houses, openly offering their services of full- or part-time boarding (*quantuo bantuo*), and academic assistance to children of all ages, including preschool. However, in 2009, about 18 percent of students in Number Two High had lived in teachers' or retired teachers' homes, either during primary or junior secondary school; and by 2012 a quick walk through the main streets of Gaoshan revealed more than twenty signs of different sizes and colors, all designed to attract new customers. Some teachers had up to forty, or in a few cases fifty, children lodging in houses furnished especially for the purpose, hiring helpers to cook and wash. Others had only a couple of children boarding with them, doing the housework themselves or having a spouse or relative doing the cooking and organizing the daily life for children. Parents were paying around ¥7,000 per semester for full-time boarding and lodging in 2008, and around ¥10,000 per semester in 2012. It was impossible for me to ascertain the full scope of this phenomenon, simply because there were so many individual teachers (mostly retired ones) who were engaged in the business but did not openly advertise it or want to talk about it. The increasingly negative publicity given to this kind of business in provincial media, and the local government's attempts to limit the practice to retired teachers only, were deterrents to such openness.

However, I did visit two teachers, each of whom had more than ten students living in their houses, and I stayed for several weeks with a retired primary school teacher who for several years had between two and six junior secondary students boarding with her. She explained that she had not advertised, but like many retired teachers, she had been approached by relatives or villagers who knew her as a diligent and hardworking person "with education and good manners" (*suzhi*). People trusted her to take good care of their children. It added further to her credentials that her own son had become a teacher in the best junior high school in town, and after several requests she agreed to board students. In her own explanation, her motivation for taking children into her home was, first of all, that she, like other female teachers, had been forced to retire at the age of fifty-five, and she was looking for something useful to do. In addition, having her own income made her more "independent" from her second husband (the first had died), and it prevented her from becoming a burden to her son and daughter-in-law because she could easily sustain her own living. She chose to live in her own house where she could have students boarding without the interference of her husband, who stayed in their house just a few blocks away. Her attitude and ways of organizing her life were in themselves a reflection of the individualization processes that are changing not only the lives and outlooks of youth but of the older generations as well (Thøgersen and Ni 2010).

All students had the right to board at school from the level of junior secondary education upward, but among parents who could afford it, the private option in teachers' homes was more and more often preferred because it was seen as providing better living conditions and more personal attention to their children's individual studies. Although dormitories in all the junior high schools were free, they were insufficient to house the entire student population, and by 2011 often two students would have to share a single bed. Food in the canteens had a bad reputation, and parents were concerned that their children did not get proper food and sleep. Finally, but not of least importance, boarding part or full time in a private home ensured that a professional teacher would be in charge of a child's discipline and would aid him or her personally with homework. Parents preferred to have their child board with his or her homeroom teacher, but this was increasingly difficult because of provincial regulations established to prevent working teachers from making tenfold their regular income by privately tutoring students who were boarding in their homes. Rules were established to regulate the number of children teachers were allowed to take in, and to prevent working teachers from engaging in a business that could easily lead to preferential treatment of those students who were staying in the teachers' homes.

The issue of discipline of children growing up in a society in which parents worked out of town and the authority of grandparents had weakened was brought up by the teachers who were boarding students. One of them had, for instance, sent an eleven-year-old boy back to his parents because he refused to do his homework, quarreled with the teacher and his wife, and made a mess in the room he shared with three other boys. This boy had already stayed with several other teachers before coming to this one, who was known for being especially good in maintaining discipline, but, said the teacher, the boy was impossible to manage (*guan*) and he was having a bad influence on the other children. As an example of how spoiled (*guanhuai*) the teacher found this boy to be, he told how the boy's parents took him to the county capital to celebrate his birthday in an expensive restaurant. "Why?" the teacher rhetorically asked. "When this is totally unnecessary?! I myself never got treatment like that as a child, and it is not going to help him at all in his education." I talked to this boy before he moved out, and he said that he was "used to staying with teachers, but did not like it." His parents were locally regarded as rich, and every two or three months they took him out to expensive dinners in in the county capital or they sent him presents, he told me. Apart from this, he rarely had contact with them, and he did not know where he would be staying after leaving his current "teacher's home." He was hoping to go back to his grandparents.

This was just one of many sad stories regarding children and adolescents who were, to different degrees, suffering from little contact with parents and other close relatives, living lives that were structured by the demands for schooling and in which daily emotional support and contact depended on their peers or on the personalities of the teachers with whom they were staying. The psychological effects on students who boarded with teachers were brought up by teachers themselves. The retired female teacher I knew best, who had decided to have between two and six students staying in her home, was determined at the beginning to take in only boys. She pointed out that staying in somebody's private home full time was quite different from being a student attending classes and boarding within the same organized school environment. Therefore, although she found that girls were generally more diligent and well behaved, they were more difficult to handle in everyday life at home. They had their monthly periods, were more moody, and could be very stubborn and self-absorbed. She was the mother of a son and a daughter, and she believed that as a female teacher it would be too difficult to step into another family's teenage girl's life and demonstrate the personal and scholarly authority that was needed to make the girl accept and adapt positively to life outside her own family or outside a more organized school environment. In spite of these reservations, by 2012 the retired teacher was boarding one girl out of four students, and another girl came on weekends, when children boarding in the junior secondary school had to return home.

From Gaoshan parents' perspective, to have a child boarding in a teacher's home or at school was expected to increase the child's possibility of getting into a better, and preferably a regular rather than a vocational, high school, and to solve the problem of child rearing that parents working outside the municipality were facing. Although no systematic studies have yet been carried out about the psychological effects of such expanded practices of having children boarding at teachers' homes from a young age, medical studies of rural youth who grow up without close, regular contacts with parents suggest that this could lead to a range of new social and psychological challenges among rural youth (Gao et al. 2010; Ye and

Lu 2011; Ye 2005). By 2012, this issue was often discussed among teachers and other adults in Gaoshan. Within that year, three students in the first year of junior secondary school in the county had tried to commit suicide; two of them died, and the third was paralyzed. This was a shock to everyone, and because it was not publicly reported, all of those I talked to assumed that similar cases would occur in other counties.[9] Teachers were not in doubt that these suicides (in families who, of course, were well known in the small township) were a result of educational pressures that were widespread. They all knew cases of children developing psychological problems, for instance, losing complete interest in their studies and friends, or becoming introvert and unwilling to communicate with either teachers or parents because of too high a level of individual pressure. There were no psychologists or psychiatrists to help them, and consequently such students dropped out of school, stayed at home, and received no professional help. Such cases were not reported at Number Two High, where everyone emphasized that although there was certainly a lot of pressure on students, especially from the heads of their families (*jiazhang*), the worst cases came from the more prestigious schools.

Extreme cases of psychological problems or suicide were rare, and they had been largely unknown in the area until around 2005. By 2012, however, they were creating worries and concerns, especially among parents. Notwithstanding, because of the needs of parents to make ends meet and at the same time have their children attend school and be taken care of, compounded with the growing expectations for their children' future success, most children were sent to boarding schools or private homes from the age of twelve or younger. When reaching the high school level, the vast majority of students were long accustomed to the tight organization of space and time that characterized boarding schools at all levels, including the private homes.

THE ORGANIZATION OF DAILY LIFE
AND BOTTOM-UP COMMUNITIES

Like most other regular secondary schools I have visited in rural China, Number Two High was designed to make its students stay within the confines of the school and remain focused on their books and studies. Its buildings are situated on the outskirts of the town, and it has only one gate, which is continually guarded, making it inconvenient for students to escape either for window shopping or for quick visits to the local snack or Internet bars. Both the location and architectural outline of the school symbolize its separation from the busy life of the township market and its myriad small-scale traders. The buildings convey the message that its temporary inhabitants are required to concentrate on formal learning in the classroom. A large red banner on the white wall greets the students at the entrance to the school, reminding them that it is up to the individual to prove himself or herself on the final examination: "For a decade I have ground my sword for this one fight; in June's test the bell of war will reveal my true self." As a public space, the school embodies tacit cultural assumptions about the classification of people and things, about professional transactions, and about political processes and citizenship (Atkinson 2005, 7). Likewise, the architectural design and physical outline of each high school in Gaoshan County are reflective of political and cultural assumptions about what is required to raise each generation to be willing and able to "eat bitterness" (*chi ku*) and live simple lives while studying, focusing on their books, and immersing themselves in knowledge in order to pass the final test and emerge as learned and cultivated persons.

The state of the buildings and equipment is, of course, also reflective of the degree of funding from the government: the more elite, the more investments, the better equipped. Compared to the local county elite school, Number Two High does not receive a lot of public investments in buildings and technical equipment, and unlike the best county school it is not designed to impress the outlying society with modern tiles, towers, or beautiful gardens. It is minimalistic, with all the basic necessities in place, such as a canteen, dormitories, a small library, sports area, classrooms, and offices, but with little else to offer to students or teachers to look at, to get distracted by, or to encourage their socializing or relaxation.

For at least ten hours a day, students sit on their simple metal stools (without support for their backs) behind their desks, expected to study individually or pay attention to the teachers and respond to their questions. In their short breaks they stay in their classrooms, hang around the outdoor areas close to the classrooms or playground, or walk the short path to the school shop that sells snacks, stationery, and daily necessities such as soap and shampoo. Except in the leadership offices, the school has no heating for the cold winter days, and no air-condition for the very hot and long summer periods. Walls are barren except for some standard high school posters of famous foreign scientists, or Chinese founders of the nation or poets, in the corridors. Piles of garbage in unused classrooms and teachers' offices testify to numerous failed attempts to give cleaning campaigns a lasting influence beyond the occasional half-day of obligatory collective efforts. All students attend classes at the same time, and everywhere and throughout the day the classrooms are ringing out with students reciting texts together, teachers lecturing, or students individually memorizing texts by mumbling to themselves in low voices. This sound stage changes instantly when the school bell rings for a break, and the corridors become filled with loud noises of young people chatting, teasing each other, running, shouting, and laughing.

When, in 2009, I brought my nineteen-year-old daughter to visit Number Two High, one of her biggest surprises was how happy students appeared to be even though they were living under physical conditions and a time regime that she, with her background from the liberal Scandinavian education system, compared to a prison. Her school life at home was characterized by a much shorter school day, less examination pressure, and more spare time that was not supervised by parents or other adults. She could not imagine being at a school like Number Two High, and yet she observed that the students of approximately her age did not seem to be more unhappy, or less engaged in social life, than she and her friends were at home. During my returning visits to Number Two High, I was often struck by a similar impression. I knew that some students felt anxious or lonely at the school, and some had told me devastating stories of how they suffered psychologically because of divorcing parents, ill siblings, lack of close friends, or strained economic conditions at home. Teachers also told me that there were students who had more serious psychological problems, but like most other rural schools, Number Two High did not have the resources, nor employees with sufficient training, to deal with such issues. As a consequence, students with more serious psychological or social problems usually dropped out, as mentioned previously.

Most students at Number Two High emphasized that the social atmosphere at school was quite good, and many found they had teachers who were considerate and who demonstrated a good degree of understanding of students' ways of thinking and their life situations. Like my two teenage daughters and their friends in Norway, students at Number Two

High strongly emphasized the importance of friendship among peers, and many would tell stories about new friends in Number Two High who helped them to handle the pressures of parental expectations, fears of failing, and lack of regular contact with parents and other close relatives. As a group of girls in grade 3 (the twelfth year of schooling) explained to me while practicing speaking English, "We all hate to study, but as soon as classes are over and we are outside or in our dormitories, we have a really good time together; then we are happy; we are very good friends!" In the short breaks and during activities such as meals, sports classes, washing clothes, or cleaning dormitories, the majority of students could be seen talking, laughing, playing, and socializing. I witnessed several occasions when a student, or a small group of students, tried to comfort a friend who was crying after failing exams, getting low grades, or having personal problems, and teachers recounted many such stories of friendships and mutual support among students.[10]

Yet I was met with strong objections when, during a lecture in Sweden whose audience included a group of Chinese graduate students, I said that although students in Number Two High were often vocally critical of the Chinese school system, they nevertheless did not seemed more or less "happy" in their interactions among each other than did the many high school students I knew in Norway and Denmark. Several of the Chinese students in the class reacted against this; they told me that though I generally had a correct understanding of teaching and daily life in the Chinese high school, I had completely misinterpreted the students' emotions if I thought they were not feeling really miserable in school. They recalled their own time in high school as overwhelmingly depressing, working day and night under constant psychological pressure, much like in Zouping, with its "system that pushes students to the edge of what is humanly possible" (Kipnis 2011, 43). After more discussion, however, the Chinese students in the class also told me that strong friendships in high school had helped them overcome some of the most negative aspects of the pressure, and that they were now grateful for having been given the opportunity to study during high school and continue the road of prestigious education and indeed study abroad.

Obviously, individual students may experience life within the same school and disciplinary system in very different ways, and there is no doubt that many have predominantly negative memories of their time in high school. In China, this was often confirmed in talks with students from other schools and provinces. Reports in Chinese media regarding the rising need for psychological counseling, and an increasing number of suicides among students, also suggest that many students do suffer during their time in school, although these phenomena cannot simply be explained by a strictly organized educational system based on high expectations.[11] In addition to the many obvious differences among reactions, there seems, however, to be a number of structural differences between elite schools and average or below average high schools in the levels of study pressure, expectations, and discipline. The better academic reputation a high school has, the more competition there is to get into the school, and expectations to perform well are consequently higher for students, teachers, and administrative leadership. In comparison, millions of youth who are students in the least prestigious vocational schools are under much less pressure than their peers (Hansen and Woronov 2013), and they often spend their days in school pretending to be studying while keeping themselves busy with unrelated activities or simply learning how to handle boredom (Woronov 2012). Pressures at Number Two High were not as great as at schools in Shandong (Kipnis 2011) and Shanghai (Ako 2003), or at the more elite urban schools in Zhejiang that I visited or at which I interviewed students. And yet, the pressure that many students experienced at home made it almost impossible for them to imagine how they would ever be able to live up to it, as shown in this quote from a girl in grade 3 (speaking in English): "If I test number two in the class, my parents ask why I did not test number one. If I test number one in the class, they ask why I did not test number one in the whole grade. And if I would ever test number one in the whole grade . . . something that is not going to happen [everybody around her laughs in support] they will ask why I did not test number one in the whole county. I do my best. I want to study hard. But it is so difficult."

One of the factors that seemed to be of crucial importance to the well-being of any individual who that took part in the education and daily life at the school was the school's ability to create feelings and experiences of community among students and teachers, and between students and teachers who were so obviously divided in terms of age, status, and power. Here the leadership of the school was very influential, and many teachers in Number Two High who were familiar with the elite schools in the county referred to their school as fortunate to have a relatively relaxed and open-minded leadership.[12] Most of the younger teachers lived in small rooms or flats on campus, and they developed close friendships, helping to look after children, getting together informally during evenings, and sometimes cooking together. Even couples who had apartments off campus would sometimes rent rooms on the campus to serve as homeroom teachers, checking in on students every evening and often in the mornings.

For students who rarely saw their parents, siblings, or other close relatives, and who spent most of their lives within the confines of the school, the importance of school communities should not be underestimated. Communities of different kinds were consciously created by the school, but they also emerged because of students' own agency and social engagement. The boarding school attempted to build and create feelings of community and identification with the alma mater (*muxiao*), with a larger imagined community of high school students and schools in the province, and ultimately with the nation.

LESS ELITE, MORE FREEDOM: RULES AND REGULATIONS

The daily schedule of students in Number Two High was not different from that of most other high school students in the country: it was tight and well managed, leaving a minimum of time for spontaneous activities or even for inactivity. Students woke up at 5:45 AM to start the most dreaded activity of all, the obligatory daily running exercise. They then followed a daily schedule that was divided into more than twenty units, including fifteen to twenty minutes for meals in the canteen, classes of forty-five minutes each, short breaks, classes scheduled for individual homework (under supervision of a teacher or fellow student), cleaning the dormitory, washing clothes, evening homework in the classroom, daily information meetings with news or instructions from the school leadership, along with gymnastics to music outside for the entire student body. Every day and every hour, students knew exactly what they were supposed to do, and they learned to very efficiently exploit short breaks and unexpected moments without surveillance to socialize, play around, check sports or other news on their mobile phones, talk with friends in the class, or send text or Internet messages on the widespread instant messaging software service known as QQ.

Formally, there were strict rules regarding student behavior and dress code. No slippers allowed, no long hair for boys, no earrings or other jewelry, no short trousers or skirts, no dyed hair, no mobile telephones at school, no reading material allowed except what was available in the small school library, no chatting after lights out at 9:45 PM, no eating or drinking of any kind in the schoolyard, no intimate relationships between boys and girls, and no students permitted to leave the school unless they lived outside its grounds. Obviously, drinking alcohol, fighting, gambling, and other illegal activities were prohibited as well. Both the time regime and the set of regulations used to govern students were largely similar to those of other high schools in China (and, indeed, in many other countries). However, comparing *practices* of discipline in different regular high schools in Gaoshan, it was clear that the more prestigious high schools (those with the highest levels of local graduates with top scores in the university entrance exam, and the highest entrance criteria for students from the high school entrance exam) also enforced the strictest discipline in practice among their students. Other research from average schools in cities (Fong 2011), and better equipped rural schools in the North (Kipnis 2011), support the impression that nationally the most prestigious schools require the strictest practices of student discipline, while the vocational high schools at the other end of the school hierarchy are by far the most relaxed in their discipline of students (Hansen and Woronov 2013).

In Number One High, the best high school in Gaoshan, teachers would, for instance, immediately call upon students who broke regulations on campus. A student in uniform would stand guard outside classrooms when students had "self-study" classes, and it was practically impossible for students to leave the school area without permission. Unlike Number Two High, Number One had also efficiently banned its 1,800 students from using of mobile telephones on campus. The use of mobile phones had become increasingly frequent among students throughout Gaoshan from around 2006, and already at that time, the school authorities in Number One High had written letters to all parents informing them that mobile phones were banned on campus. Nevertheless, very much like at Number Two High, the following years continued to see a rapid upsurge in the number of students sending text messages, phoning, or accessing Internet on campus. Although teachers were largely able to control the use during daytime hours, their main problem became the nights, because 85 percent of students at Number One High were boarding. Consequently, in 2010 Number One High decided to ban mobile phones. They set up telephone booths on campus and gave each student a phone card with which the student could effectively call his or her parents. If any mobiles were found on campus, penalties were harsh. One of the teachers from the political office in charge of discipline, the student association, and the Youth League in this local elite school explained, "The phone will be confiscated, parents contacted, and worst of all for the student, a remark about this breach of discipline will follow his or her file [*dang'an*]." The main problem with students' use of mobile phones, according to teachers in this school's political office, was that it weakened self-discipline and prevented them from concentrating on their studies. A teacher in the political office of Number One High remarked:

A mobile phone is basically a good thing. It is good for communication; it is a useful tool for finding information on the Internet. The problem is not the mobile phone as such, but the fact that students lack self-discipline. They cannot control their own usage of the phone, and it keeps them awake until two or three at night. This has a negative impact on their studies. We've got to make sure this practice does not continue to occur. We have explained this in a meeting to the students. Most of them understand that we do it for their own sake, although some of course complain about it. The parents are all very happy, though!

In Number Two High regulations were in principle largely similar to those of Number One High. The main difference was that more rules and regulations were bent or broken occasionally or continually. Some teachers complained that Number Two High was too relaxed toward students who broke the regulations, but many other teachers emphasized that because students in Number Two High would likely not go to elite colleges, there was no need to enforce these regulations strictly. They argued that as a rural school that mainly recruited students from families with backgrounds in agriculture or other kinds of manual labor, it was not only useless and impossible to enforce a too-strict disciplinary regime, it was counterproductive. These students were unable to perform above average in the competitive school system. Furthermore, most teachers did not want to continually correct and discipline their students. Many

had—and wanted to maintain—good relationships with their
and they saw no need for enforcing disciplinary rules too rigidl
ways, students and teachers had a shared interest in buildin
community where the more than a thousand people who spena most or
their days within its walls got along reasonably well and shared an identity as "Number Two High teachers and students." Teachers and students
would sometimes discuss explicitly, or throw in occasional comments,
about how Number Two High's students and/or teachers, while sharing
the fate of being disadvantaged compared to the elite schools and their
students, at least had in common that they were hardworking (*nuli*) rural
children (*nongcun de haizi*). They presented themselves as "commoners"
standing united in the face of those elite schools that were admired and
envied because of their academic achievements.

This exemplifies how teachers and students in different contexts emphasized Number Two High's aim of building a school community that students
could identify with and nurture a positive image of. Like the international
Chinese students in Vanessa Fong's (2011) study, who regarded their home
country with affection but not uncritically—many of the teachers and students at Number Two High regarded their school as a community they
defended with affection when it was stigmatized by others but that they
would criticize in other contexts. As a social setting and form of organization in which people live closely together under disciplinary rules and share
a common purpose of work or mission, the boarding school structure created a community of the people who were part of it. Students and teachers
lived within it over a prolonged period of time, and in a relatively secluded
physical confinement, relating to the same rules of behavior and organization of time, sharing at least in principle the same mission and purpose of
work. To the extent that a community spirit in Number Two High existed
(and it was indeed sometimes severely challenged), it evolved from this
practical organization of the school and from its students' and teachers'
shared interests in defending it when it was depicted as a low-status institution with "bad" students and "average" teachers. The hierarchy of high
schools in Gaoshan mirrored that of provincial and national levels, and the
popular recognition of this hierarchy was strong. Few people in Gaoshan,
especially those who had educations beyond junior secondary school, were
in doubt about which local schools were at the top.

Broadly recognized social hierarchies of schools may strengthen feelings of identification with an alma mater either because students are highly aware that they are all selected as exclusive members of an elite school, or, in the case of Number Two High, because they tend to unite in response to their experience of being in a more stigmatized position. Number Two High was able to create a sense of community among its students and teachers because of its tight organization as a boarding school, its ways of governing time and space, its position in the local school hierarchy, and its combination of these aspects with a relatively flexible approach to discipline and an ability to create a good atmosphere. Therefore, quite a few teachers regretted the pressure from parents that prevented them from initiating activities that would be positive for the students' psychological and physical development, even if the activities did not directly benefit examination results. For instance, teachers were not allowed to organize football games for students because parents were afraid that this type of sport entailed risk of physical injuries that could put a halt to a child's studies. Equally, teachers were not allowed to take students outside of the school for excursions because the risk of injury was considered to be too high.

The strengthening of a unified school community was also challenged by the internal reproduction of national social hierarchies of education. As in other high schools, from the second year the regular high school students in Number Two High were divided into the two tracks of humanities (*wenke*) and natural sciences (*like*). In addition, special classes were organized in year 3 for those students whom teachers assumed had the best chances to pass the final examination with sufficient points to get into a four- to five-year undergraduate study (*benke*), rather than the specialized two- to three-year undergraduate study (*zhuanke*) that did not qualify for a master's program and that was often of a vocational nature. For the most part, 10–15 percent of approximately three hundred yearly graduating students from Number Two High would pass the exam for *benke*. These students were normally those who had been in the "elite classes." They would, for instance, go to teacher training college. Approximately 10 percent of the graduates would continue with private courses in order to retake the university entrance examination the following year, hoping for better results, and a few stopped studying altogether and went into the job market immediately after graduation. However, the majority graduated with results that would allow them to continue with *zhuanke* studies, mostly in the College of Professional Technology (Zhiye Jishu Xueyuan), where they would specialize in auto repair, livestock management, tourism, and the like. The "university" in the expression "test into a university" (*kao daxue*), used so often by both students and parents to express the goal of high school education, included colleges such as this one. Some parents clearly nurtured hopes that their children would qualify for a university of a more academic nature. However, according to students themselves, many parents "did not understand these things" (*bu dong shi*) because they themselves had attended only primary or junior secondary school. They were often unaware of the distinctions between *zhuanke* and *benke* and between different types of universities (beyond those at the national top level) that were all called *daxue*.

However, one hierarchy of study options was clear to everyone, including parents: the division between vocational (*zhigao*) and regular (*pugao*) high schools and classes. In the period from 2008 to 2011, when the vocational classes at Number Two High were gradually dismantled, this division created a student hierarchy that resulted in the formation of subcommunities within Number Two High. This hierarchical division was strengthened by parents' active involvement—an involvement that not only reflected their educational ambitions for their children, but also a dominant perception in Chinese society of an inseparable link between level of formal education (including the moral "quality" or *suzhi* of a person), and the need to provide children with proper role models to avoid what is seen as "polluting" influence from less successful, and thereby implicitly less civilized, peers.

INTERNAL HIERARCHIES AND THE VOCATIONAL OTHER

In the early 2000s, the Chinese central government began to launch a number of new policies aimed at strengthening vocational education in urban as well as rural areas. This expansion of vocational education has been presented by Chinese policy makers as necessary for the creation of a solid base for the evolving knowledge economy and as the key to technical innovation. The Ministry of Education further considers it to be a useful instrument to "satisfy the need of the society's members for pluralistic learning and holistic development" (Ministry of Education, quoted in Schulte 2013, 1). Thus, with the aim of responding to the population's demand for education for their children, and the labor markets' growing interest in recruiting workers with technical skills, the government has increased its investment in vocational schools and education. In provinces and counties alike, local authorities have been asked to increase the number of students attending vocational schools and to improve both the quality and scope of this education.

A major challenge, though, is parents' lack of enthusiasm for their children pursuing vocational rather than academic areas of study. Vocational education was introduced in the late nineteenth century as an alternative form of education within an already existing social hierarchy, and it did not constitute any real option for social mobility of the majority of the Chinese people (Schulte 2013). Although there is no generic vocational education track, but rather a variety of technical, agricultural, financial, and other specializations, its general status remains persistently low, stigmatized in rural as well as urban areas (Hansen and Woronov 2013). At the same time, vocational education is seen by most parents as a better alternative than no education, and society's demand for a skilled workforce has contributed to the government's request that all provinces and counties establish more and better vocational education within a relatively short time span.

Because of a lack of specialized vocational schools with the capacity to quickly take on more students, a number of counties in Zhejiang were asked, in the mid-2000s, to offer vocational classes *within* regular high schools. This was not supposed to be a permanent solution, but instead a temporary policy while educational authorities were working to expand the "real" vocational schools sufficiently to fill the required quotas of students. The leadership in Number Two High was therefore able to attract some additional financial support to their school by agreeing to participate in an experiment with new vocational classes, and in each of the years 2008 and 2009, four new vocational classes were started up simultaneously with eight regular grade 1 (the tenth school year) classes. Admission to these vocational classes was based entirely on the examination results from the high school entrance examination. Students with sufficient points got into regular classes; students who lacked just a few points could pay ¥20,000 and get admission to regular classes; and a group of approximately two hundred students with insufficient points to make it to the regular classes were admitted into the new vocational classes. As a result, students in Number Two High's vocational classes were no different from most students attending "ordinary" vocational schools in rural as well as urban areas (Woronov 2011): Students did not attend these classes because of conscious choice or special wishes regarding their professional futures, but because of their lower examination results after their first nine years of schooling. One of the teachers bluntly explained the differences in status of regular and vocational, and state and private education, in the following way: "Our Number Two High students in the regular classes are not good; those who get into our vocational classes are even worse; but those who only get into the private vocational high school are the worst!"

The different social status of regular and vocational education in the eyes of students, parents, and teachers became evident when observed within one school that offered both tracks. Students from both tracks were in the same corridors, dormitories, and canteen; they largely followed the same curricula (although the curriculum was reduced for the vocational students); and they had the same teachers. However, the vocational classes were made up of a clearly delimited group of students who everybody knew had enrolled with much lower grades than their peers. To the dismay of several homeroom teachers, parents of students in regular high school classes raised collective complaints during the first year's meeting with the "the heads of families" (*jiazhang*) about vocational classrooms that were next to their own children's classrooms. They demanded that vocational classes be moved to a separate corridor because of the presumed bad influence these "low-quality students" (*suzhi di de xuesheng*) would have on their own children's study morale and behavior. The school gave in to this demand, and classrooms for vocational classes were segregated from the regular classes.

Half a year later, to the great satisfaction of their parents, the school administration decided that the best 20 percent of the vocational students should be transferred to regular high school classes. At the same time, many teachers found that their jobs were becoming more difficult than before, because they did not know how best to teach the required academic curriculum to the students who remained in vocational classes. There developed a widespread understanding that vocational students were "bad students," and therefore implicitly "bad people": "The students in these classes are of really low quality [*suzhi zhende hen cha*]: they have low marks; their educational level is definitely very low compared to the regular students; they fight, they gamble, and they smoke!," one teacher complained, though he was quick to add that these problems were caused only by a smaller group of students influencing the entire study environment. Many teachers (though not all) agreed that vocational students were more difficult to deal with than the regular students. After two years, these students were presented with the option to transfer into a vocational track in a college, which would offer different types of vocational, technical, or other kind of specialization, not merely the "regular high school classes light" that Number Two High was able to organize. After three years of experimenting with vocational classes, the programs within Number Two High and other regular schools in the region were gradually dismissed, and by 2012, only two vocational classes remained. They followed the same curricula as regular classes, preparing specifically for the *zhuanke*, and the "vocational" students took part in the national university entrance exam on equal footing with the other students. In practice, the government's attempt to establish more vocational training in regular high schools within a very short period of time had failed.

Prevalent societal perceptions in China of hierarchies of types of study had been strengthened rather than weakened with the dual establishment of regular and vocational tracks within Number Two High. The vocational students within this regular high school were clearly in a different position than students in the "real" vocational schools, who were offered different kinds of specialization aimed at preparing them for the workforce, despite the low quality of education and motivation among students known from vocational schools also in urban areas (Woronov 2011). For the vocational students in Number Two High, the ability to live up to academic expectations became almost equivalent to being a morally solid and socially well-adapted individual.

In the process of setting up vocational classes and then later dissolving them, the school and its teachers gained a lot of experience. They saw that parents whom they had found to be difficult to engage in their children's everyday lives and well-being were willing and able to unite in collective action when they thought that their children's options for social mobility would be threatened. They also suffered from a sense of powerlessness when facing what many of them thought were reasonable complaints from students who had expected vocational training to be something other than regular academic education, not simply a downgraded version of it. For a high school such as Number Two High, with scarce resources and pressures on teachers to ensure that their students performed well in the university entrance exam, this was an almost impossible situation, and stereotypes of "low-quality vocational students" flourished. The vocational students had a reduced curriculum, they were under less pressure than other students, and they took part in fewer mock examinations. Consequently, they had more time and opportunities within the school to create social networks, to socialize, and to engage in activities other than studying. This, again, made them more exposed to moral judgments and labeling as selfish (zisi) and self-absorbed youth who lacked proper concern for their families and the nation.

Although this was a predominant perception, there was an alternative view of the vocational students and their social behavior within Number Two High. The three students who made me aware of this were regarded as successful and diligent students, and they even referred to themselves as "good students" (hao xuesheng), a term that implied good grades, disciplined behavior, and a friendly and respectful attitude toward other students and teachers. They had been so-called student cadres (xuesheng ganbu), with special responsibilities for maintaining discipline among peers, communicating with the homeroom teacher, collecting homework, and so on, and they were members of the student association (xueshenghui). Through these activities, which often crossed boundaries of school classes, they had made friends with vocational students. During one of our conversations about their social environment, these "good students" from the regular classes mentioned their vocational peers as a special group. They believed that vocational students were stigmatized, and they pointed out that this was the reason vocational students stuck together and supported each other to a larger extent than did regular students. They highlighted their own longing for what they called "unity" (tuanjie)[13] among students. They believed that the pressure to study was counterproductive to the development of a positive social environment. Where many teachers and parents saw undisciplined and incapable vocational students, they saw peers who to a larger extent than themselves were able and willing to support each other.

This perception of the vocational students' ability to stick together

Students v parents attitudes → Vocational high Students

in the face of widespread discrimination was confirmed by the ways in which the vocational students talked about the social environment in their school. They were painfully aware that they were unwanted by fellow students' parents as neighbors to their children in regular classes, and the topic was uncomfortable for many students to discuss. On the rare occasion when the topic did arise, or when I would inquire about it, they would often look away, laugh embarrassedly, or quickly change the subject. At times I would garner a response such as this one received from a grade 2 female student: "Their parents think we are bad influence on them. . . . What can we do, other than ignore it . . . !?" There were friendships across vocational and regular classes, but because of the physical reorganization of classes, and the social prevalent stereotypes, most vocational students found their best friends within their own classes or among the other vocational students. The topic of friendship was central for students in vocational as well as regular classes, and it was brought up again and again in talks about daily life in the school. Practices of friendship and community building were displayed through students' agency and creativity, aimed at expanding their means of communicating and socializing, even when it involved serious breaches of disciplinary rules. Through action rather than speech, they demonstrated how quests for individual space and room for collective community were raised in daily life, continually negotiating the limits of the tight social organization that constituted the state boarding school.

STUDENTS' QUESTS FOR INDIVIDUAL SPACE

Since the implementation in 2009 of new policies that were aimed at forcing schools and parents to reduce student study load, students in the two lower grades were allowed to leave Number Two High on Friday afternoon and return on Sunday afternoon. Unlike their peers in larger cities, these students were hardly ever enrolled in extracurricular activities or classes during the weekend. Apart from the homework they had been assigned, which demanded several hours of work on Saturday and on Sunday morning, they were largely free to do what they wanted to do, or what parents or relatives at home would allow them to do. In Gaoshan, there was not a large offering of extracurricular activities, such as piano or violin lessons, reading of classical texts, math, English, or the like, which are common in many cities. A number of teachers privately organized extra help for homework, but only a few students I talked to at Number Two High took such private classes during the semester; some had been to extra classes paid for by their parents during summer holidays.

What then did students do in their spare time? They did many of the things that they were not allowed to do while staying at the boarding school, such as getting up late, playing Internet games, chatting on QQ, watching movies, reading popular youth journals and light (mainly romantic or action) literature, going to cafés, browsing in shops, and spending time together with friends. In other words, their spare time was spent the same way many other teenagers do throughout the world.

What was new and surprising, though, to the teachers at Number Two High, was that students now dared to bring more of these activities into the school.[14] "It keeps surprising me," twenty-seven-year-old female teacher Li said, "that these students who are not that much younger than me, and who attend a school which is very similar to the one I myself used to attend, have so much more nerve [danzi hen da] than we had!" Students challenged authority in a subtle way, without direct confrontation, to create room for themselves without getting into trouble, and teachers like Li seemed to be annoyed, puzzled, and impressed by the courage that these students displayed when challenging the authorities. Again and again, I heard teachers, and other people in Gaoshan who were thirty or older, repeat that the students of today had "a lot of nerve."

This "nerve" or "courage" reflects a rise of the individual among the rural student body in the state boarding schools. Some teachers interpreted it as a form of selfishness and lack of respect, but others regarded it as a reflection of changes in society that logically led to students being more assertive and explicit about their own needs and interests. These teachers did not necessarily see it as a sign of selfishness, but rather as a trend toward following one's own interests, as one male teacher in his late twenties explained. However, among all teachers I talked to, the general consensus was that it was difficult to counter this trend in schools such as Number Two High because the students were academically weak and less motivated and capable of studying as hard as students in the more elite schools. The students at Number Two High were often seen as lacking purpose and direction; and their parents, many teachers found, were not very helpful because they themselves did not have the experience of studying. They were too busy working, and they often were not able to influence the activities of their children whose lifestyle and expectations were so different from their own: "We really cannot do much about it; we are just their teachers, not their parents!," teacher Gao, a man in his forties, argued. He went on to explain, "Our society has changed so quickly. The rural students today just have so many opportunities that we could not even have imagined. Just look at how they use mobile phones."

Indeed, more than anything, it was mobile phone use among students that symbolized intensified modernization of the rural boarding school, the students' growing demand for individual space, and the weakened trust in authorities. Teachers did not simply or exclusively perceive this development as a threat to their own authority or as a proof of the degradation of moral standards among youth. In many ways, they were struggling just as hard as their students with defining the role of the individual and its moral obligations, and making sense of it in a society that increasingly required personal initiative, economic risk taking, and unquestioned adherence to political authority—all in a context in which there was no clear trajectory of a common ideology, morals, or faith binding people together. In their role as teachers, though, they had to prove that they could guide their students through the examinations, and in this process simultaneously improve students' moral standards in accordance with the Chinese government's goal of a "harmonious society" (*hexie shehui*). Therefore, when dealing directly with student breaches of discipline, teachers often expressed one view when talking about these issues privately, and outside the school, and another when confronting the students and taking action against their attempts to expand individual space for communication and socialization.

This was, for instance, characteristic of the handling of the issue of mobile telephones on campus. Starting around 2007, nearly everyone at Number Two High had cheap and convenient Internet access through mobile telephones. Within a short period of time, it created an entirely new space for communication and social activity. Students used it to establish and maintain long-term social networks, to keep contact with friends inside and outside of their school, and to play games and access information, especially about popular sporting events, music, or movies.

In 2008, when I asked students in two classes (without teachers present because this was a somewhat touchy issue), nearly 70 percent indicated that they brought their mobile phones to school, with nearly all admitting to using them on a daily basis. Five years later, in 2012, I was providing English conversation classes to a grade 3 class, and students wanted to take pictures with me. When I asked how we could do it without a camera, they quietly said (the teacher being outside) that we could use one of their mobile phones. I asked the teacher, and she agreed. We split into groups taking the pictures, and, suddenly, not one, but about fifteen mobile phones with cameras emerged during each of the group sessions.

Students only occasionally (some said "rarely") talked to their parents on the phone, but they had almost daily contact with friends by chatting on QQ or text messaging. As an example of how students did not restrict this communication to their spare time, I observed during an ordinary school day that two girls and three boys in the same class were each spending, on average, more than twenty minutes reading or writing on their mobile telephones during each of their eight teacher-led classes that day. Outside classes, during breaks, self-study sessions, meals, and especially in the dormitories in the evenings, many more students were actively communicating on their phones.

Students were, of course, regularly caught in this act, mainly because the assigned student cadres (who were in charge of anything from discipline to drawings on the blackboard in their classes) were obliged to report them, or because they used them freely in obvious sight of teachers. This did not put a halt to the activity, and most student cadres were themselves active users of the phones and saw no reason to be too strict toward their peers. Although the school would strike hard at those few who were caught using their mobiles to cheat during examinations or play games for money, teachers were largely resigned to and mostly ignored the students' growing use of the phones. The scope of the use, and the important role they played in their students' social lives, made it impossible for school authorities and teachers to effectively implement the ban on mobile usage. This meant that students at Number Two High, who experienced less study pressure than their peers in the elite schools, without taking new more drastic measures were better able to organize themselves in virtual communities of classmates and other friends and maintain contact during the week, when they were mostly confined to the school area. And the school did not have to impose new, more drastic measures. Thanks to their individually owned mobile phones, students had managed to collectively expand their room for communication far beyond what was possible only a few years ago. With the help of cheap mobiles, students organized networks that had both a physical dimension, because they included a majority of students who also met within the school, and a virtual dimension, because friends outside the school were drawn into them. Additionally, communication continued during longer holidays when students were spread around the different cities where their parents worked.

Occasionally, the school authorities and individual teachers tried to exert stricter controls on students' use of mobile phones. As of 2012, these attempts had failed miserably, because of substantial, though unorganized and uncoordinated, pressure from the vast majority of students who simply continued their practices despite regulations and renewed attempts to enforce them. As one teacher exclaimed, "Students are inseparable from their mobile phones [*xuesheng libukai shouji*]!" Another teacher explained in more detail just how important the mobile phone was for some of students, who simply would not agree with their parents to study unless they provided them with a phone:

> Some of the worst students just have the attitude that as long as they have their mobile they can get through the three years in high school. They use it to access the internet and play games. They think that "if you just give me a mobile I can sit in this classroom and go through the years of study. If you do not give me one, I do not study!" The mobile phone becomes the main thing in his life, a thing he cannot live without. Without his mobile, he is like a fish without water, he really cannot survive without it.

In the course of their daily lives, the vast majority of students (and not only the "worst" students as mentioned by this teacher) had quietly insisted on continuing and expanding this kind of communication among themselves. Occasionally, students were caught reading illegitimate science fiction or romantic magazines. However, the need for smuggling this kind of reading material into Number Two High was seemingly waning, as mobile phones offered ever more opportunities for diverse collective and individual activities.

Students' self-organized online communities did not necessarily have a specific aim or purpose beyond the social aspects, but they were on the rise, like so many other forms of online communities that extend into "real-life" communities (see also Pang 2011). It is possible (though too early to know) that students will eventually develop these communities further and employ them to promote collective *interests*, for instance, by channeling them through the student association or by forming less formal "grassroots" student collectives, though at the moment this seems unlikely. Another possible development, of course, would be for the school (with support from parents) to emulate the more elite Number One High and step up the pressure on students by more efficiently imposing a ban on mobile phones. This, of course, would not in itself put a halt to students' online communities, because they would still have access outside the school. At the time of this study, some teachers wanted to enforce such a ban, but younger teachers especially argued strongly against it. Looking ahead, they knew that the Chinese state school needed to continuously and more rapidly adapt to a changing society. It needed to develop new means to engage students in their studies without preventing them from developing socially through responsible use of the same kind of technology that everybody outside the school was using, and that political authorities often praised.

The boarding school system that governs students' educational and social lives through a tight organization of time and space has been globally tested in different settings, ranging from British schools for the affluent elite to missionary schools for Native Americans.[15] In China, a majority of rural students especially become acquainted with this system from early in their lives. The system enjoys widespread support from parents as a form of education as well as socialization. Boarding schools are practical arrangements for rural parents who work far away from the school, and they provide safe and predictable social and educational environments that many parents find are better for their children's studies and careers than what they, or their children's grandparents, could offer.

Of course, even with such a pervasive desire for education (Kipnis 2011), counter-discourses and reactions emerge. During my research in Yunnan in the mid-1990s, many rural parents (most of them ethnic minorities) by far preferred to have their children enroll in vocational secondary education rather than in regular high schools because practical considerations of getting a job and a steady income were much more important than aspirations for higher academic education (Hansen 1999). In Zhejiang, some teachers and parents also recalled that, in the late 1980s and early 1990s, increasing opportunities for doing business drew many young people away from schooling. Many parents at the time found that education beyond junior secondary school was unnecessary when the aim was to get into business and make as much money as quickly as possible. This trend was also noticed nationwide and was critically referred to by journalists and scholars as "the view that studying is of no use" (*dushu wuyong lun*).[16] Ten to fifteen years later, in the first decade of the twenty-first century, some scholars have argued that, especially in poor areas of the country, this view still has a stronghold (Yu and Zhang 2006). In Zhejiang, though, this view seems to have largely faded despite the province's history of its inhabitants engaging in business and business-related migration (e.g., Mallee and Pieke 1999). In the first decades of the 2000s, poorer as well as richer parents in Gaoshan seemed to unite in the hope that at least one of their children would be successful in the academic education system. They wanted their children to test into a university or college and eventually get a stable nonmanual job with social benefits. This was perceived as the only gateway to status, privilege, security, and nonmanual work.

Not all students saw this as a desirable or realistic road. Some wanted to follow in the footsteps of older siblings who were working in business, and others dreamed of being the first one in the family to create a small private company. However, having entered high school, the regular high school students were already following the prepared path to college, and most were either determined to pass the final examination with as good a result as possible, or they simply saw no other options. Many emphasized that they tried to live up to their parents' expectations because it would bring them "a better life." What and where to study was not something students in Number Two High spent much time thinking about. They were aiming at the first goal, the national university entrance examination, which they hoped would turn out to be an entrance to money, stability, status and, possibly, their parents' satisfaction and admiration. Just a few months before graduation, two boys in grade 3 spoke in English when they explained their view to me: "You ask where we would like to study.

We do not think about this. We think about the examination. It does not matter what we study. The goal is a good life *after* studying."

Focusing on the final test, however, did not prevent students from challenging the school's organization of daily life in their attempts to create more space for activities and communication beyond the sanctioned school and extracurricular work. This could, of course, be interpreted as student resistance against authorities, the disciplinary school regime, and unbearable pressures from parents, teachers, and society at large. On a small and very local scale, I found that students' actions contained elements of "hidden transcripts," by which subaltern subjects manifest their resistance against the state (or other authorities) without explicitly exposing it or making it publicly known (Scott 1992). At the same time, I found that students in Gaoshan to a large extent had internalized their parents' goals of advancing their families through their children's educational achievements. Consequently, students would conduct themselves with this in mind. They employed subtle means of challenging their immediate authorities, not in explicit or outspoken defiance of the content, or even form, of their education, but in order to negotiate more room for themselves *within* the system.

The notion of the divided self is relevant in this context. In contemporary China, personal "transcripts," or manifestations of implicit protest, are not necessarily or primarily about acts of resistance, but just as much about acts of accommodation and collaboration that "enable ordinary people to negotiate China's social reality in such a way as to open or protect the individual's space while getting on with life lived in an authoritarian society" (Kleinman 2011a, 286). This may help to explain actions and perceptions of students in the rural high school. They display agency in order to negotiate individual space and more options for creating their own communities while trying to accommodate to the demands and expectations that structure their daily lives. Students and teachers (as we will see in chapter 5) displayed many signs of the divided self's burdens of "contradictions, compromise and irony" (Kleinman 2011a, 286); and in different situations during their school lives students and teachers struggled to define the role of the individual and test the limits to individual agency. At the same time, viewing the individual from the perspective of the contemporary authoritarian state, the Communist Party and government aim at creating subjects that are precisely able to integrate into an "undivided whole" what may seem to be contradictory demands on the self. It may be argued that the government, through its curriculum and organization of education, is attempting to foster "neo-socialist" (Pieke 2009) subjects with precisely the ability to uncritically accept political authorities while making the choices and taking the risks that the increasingly individualized society requires.

CHAPTER 2

TEXT AND TRUTH

Visions of the Learned Person and Good Citizen

The individualization of Chinese society and the political and moral concerns with changing duties, rights, and obligations of the individual are reflected in the past thirty years of changing state school curriculum.[1] Curriculum is still largely centralized and standardized, and a formal control system ensures that all textbooks and local adaptations remain in line with official policies and guidelines. As in the 1980s and 1990s, there are few substantial differences between textbooks studied in schools such as Number Two High in Gaoshan and elite schools in Shanghai or Beijing. School curriculum, especially that of moral and political education, literature, and history, offers a good insight into ideologically sanctioned visions of the Chinese individual, and they shed light on some of the apprehensions that political authorities have about the consequences of an individualizing society. Especially since the student demonstrations in the spring of 1989, individualist values among the younger generations of students have been perceived as a potential threat to social stability; and a renewed and revised focus on moral education in schools at all levels is one of the major tools with which the government and party hope to change the mentality and behavior of the coming generation.

The authorities draw on long historical traditions in China of promoting models and rewarding model behavior as means to correct moral misbehavior and immoral mentality (see Bakken 2000). Studies of changes to curriculum since the 1980s by, for instance, Edward Vickers and Alisa Jones confirm that educational authorities have continued to believe in the transformative power of exemplary models, although the form and content have been adapted to both societal and ideological changes. Since the 1980s, textbooks have gradually shifted their focus from revolutionary models and hard-core socialist ideology to state-centered patriotism, citizen training, and a discourse on individual well-being and morality.[2] The educational reform in 2001 for the first time set standards for the integration of moral issues into *all* school subjects, and a selection of moral qualities were explicitly mentioned as goals to be pursued, including, for instance, the ability of each student to "think independently" (Zhu 2006). Obviously, there is not necessarily a direct positive connection between the curriculum's aim of building a sanctioned socialist morality among students and the students' perceptions of state, party, and self. There is a need for more research into the actual relationship between Chinese schooling and students' identities and values, but there are, at the same time, sufficient indications that when textbooks and their ideologies are in concordance with more broadly accepted discourses (as, for instance, in the case of nationalist sentiments), they may have a significant influence on students' attitudes (Vickers 2009a).

Visions of the neosocialist moral individual are presented to students, especially in the courses Language and Literature and Thought and Politics, by teaching both Chinese classical and Western modern texts, by building perceptions of the individual's rights and obligations in society, and by appealing to students' emotions. This shows how the official content of schooling and campaigning by political and educational authorities aims at confronting some of the challenges that the individual in China faces, and through the content of textbooks, educational authorities attempt to construct and offer to the students and teachers an alternative to the tension and dilemmas of the "divided self" (Kleinman 2011b) that emerge from lives with increased possibilities for expanding individual space and simultaneous demands to submit to authoritarian rules and practices. There are, in fact, no real political or societal dilemmas, according to official curriculum, mainly individual ones; and because there is always a correct way of solving these, the teaching material provides the answers, even if students are first encouraged to consider possible alternatives. The educational authorities would like to foster in Chinese students the kind of initiative, boldness, and innovative spirit that they see as a positive outcome of many Western education systems, but they are equally keen to disconnect these attributes from the liberal-democratic ethos of the societies in which these systems have arisen (Vickers 2009a, 65). Seen in an even broader perspective, the party-state may be said to envision a population of neosocialist moral individuals who are fully capable of integrating into a whole and undivided self the ability to act innovatively and take economic risks, while at the same time endorsing socialist authoritarian rule and uniting in a patriotic feeling of universal Chinese cultural community.

IDEALS OF THE LEARNING INDIVIDUAL

Textbooks studied by all grade 1 high school students in China include these two passages:

> Confucius said: "If three men are walking together, there is undoubtedly one of them who could be my teacher. Thus, a student is not necessarily inferior to a teacher, and a teacher not necessarily more talented and virtuous than a student. The difference is just that one may have learned the doctrine before the other, and each of them masters different skills." (From "Discourse on Teachers" [Shi shuo] by Han Yu [768–824])[3]

> Real education is not for any specific purpose. Rather like any other efforts to improve one self, it has a meaning in itself. The pursuit of the perfection of education, like that of the mind or the spirit, does not follow a difficult track towards any kind of narrow goal, but is rather a strengthening and expansion of our self-consciousness which enriches our lives and allows us to experience even more happiness.[4] (From The Way to Acquire Education [Huode jiaoyang de tujing], an adapted textbook version derived from two articles by Hermann Hesse [1877–1962])[5]

In the subject of language and literature, where these two texts are studied, curriculum has become less politicized in comparison to the 1980s and 1990s, and students are introduced to more foreign literature as well as acquiring a firm basis in Chinese classical and early modern texts.

The curriculum revisions from 2007 especially marked a break with the revolutionary canon, and new texts were included with the aim of appealing more to students' interests and their daily experiences (Vickers 2009a). Students now study a variety of texts ranging from excerpts from *Zhuangzi*, the Confucian *Analects* (Lunyu), and *Mengzi*, to Martin Luther King Jr., *The Diary of Anne Frank*, novels about love of the motherland, and Chinese modernist literature by, for instance, Lao She and Lu Xun. Testifying to the modernization of literature curriculum, Lu Xun's well-known essay "Grabism" (*Nalaizhuyi*), about conscious and selective cultural borrowing from the West, is now taught together with a text by the contemporary ethnologist Weng Naiqun about contemporary globalization and the transformation of McDonalds restaurants in China.

In the language and literature classes I followed in Number Two High, the teacher was doing her best to make these texts as relevant to the students as possible to encourage students to be more engaged in the classes. That proved to be a very difficult task. The teacher wanted to extract the politically correct moral messages from the texts and have students acknowledge and accept them. She did this by asking each student to reflect on his or her own position in relation to the messages conveyed by the texts, but she was mostly met by a wall of silence. In classes where she taught Lu Xun's novel, none of the students was able—or willing—to answer questions such as "What is the conclusion in this text?" or "What does the term 'send-ism' [*songquzhuyi*] [as opposed to the term 'grabism'] refer to in the text?" Therefore, the teacher decided to illustrate the gist of Lu Xun's essay by having students instead consider their own ways of making conscious choices related to consumption, their use of mobile phones, and the Internet: "Let us instead learn from the text how our own attitude [*taidu*] ought to be. Have you yourself thought about which things are actually useful for you, and which are not? You should think carefully about that. The things you buy or get from others . . . you should think about if they are at all useful, and useful for what. For instance, a mobile telephone or the Internet . . . give me some concrete examples of how the Internet is useful?!"

The response came promptly from a few shouting and laughing boys: "For playing PC games!" This was clearly not the proper answer, and consequently it was ignored by the teacher. She asked the whole class again, but no other students were willing to stand out and answer, so the teacher herself summed up the text and gave a final advice to the students: "Think carefully about the choices each of you make, and be sure that they are of use to you!" Other texts in the curriculum were clearly attempting to speak to the consumerist tendencies among youth or approach their interest in idols and heroes in order to promote politically correct moral views and behavior. In a textbook interview with China's first astronaut, entitled "Being Regarded as an Idol" (*zuowei ouxiang*), Yang Liwei gives his advice as a national hero to the young people of today, telling them that they need what he calls the "spaceship spirit" (*hangtian jingshen*). With this special kind of agitated spirit, many difficulties in their studies, as well as later work, could be overcome and solved (Yang Liwei in Ding et al. 2008a, 89). This is one of the numerous brief pieces of advice that texts provide to students on how to improve their personal attitudes and behavior in the process of becoming learned.

The cases examined here were taken from classes in which both regular and vocational first-year students were studying literary texts, including those by Han Yu and Hermann Hesse quoted earlier. Both these texts examine in different ways the value of learning, and in the context of schooling they aim to foster in students an "inner motivation" for studying—an alternative to the utilitarian motivation generated by external, mainly examination, pressures. Both texts are concerned with the individual's role in attaining general knowledge and becoming learned, though obviously they were written in very different cultural and historical contexts. One is from twentieth-century Europe by the German-Swiss Nobel Prize-winning author Hermann Hesse (1877–1962), the other is one thousand years older, from the famous Chinese scholar Han Yu (768–824), who was a spokesman for the cultural traditionalism later known as neo-Confucianism during the Tang dynasty.[6] Both texts are required reading for the final examination in Language and Literature. They are on a similar topic, but they play different roles in the curriculum. "Discourse on Teachers" is especially important because of Han Yu's position as a celebrated intellectual in the long historical trajectory of Chinese Confucianism.[7] Students have read the text for centuries, and high school students today still learn it by heart. The text by Hesse, however, serves as an example in the curriculum of how modern foreign or Western literature may emphasize some of the very same values regarding learning and the learned individual that Chinese Confucianists stood for more than a thousand years earlier—values that the party-state in principle wants to promote today. The fact that Hesse has won a Nobel Prize is mentioned in the textbook, and it serves as a proof to students of his international standing and authority.[8] The selective way of presenting Hesse's authorship and the ways in which the two very different texts are taught to students illustrate some of the key contradictions that students face when learning about morals as specifically connected to the duties of being "a learned individual" in contemporary Chinese society.

The teaching of Han Yu's "Discourse on Teachers" was mostly straightforward when I observed classes in Number Two High in 2008. It was difficult for the approximately fifty students in the class to read this crucial classical text (even though it was presented in simplified characters and with annotations), and the teacher had to spend most of the time testing whether students really understood the words and were able to recite the whole text. About eight to ten students, more or less equally divided between boys and girls, were not following the teaching at all. They were sleeping, staring out of the window, playing with their mobile phones, or reading small popular magazines under their desks. During class, the young female teacher emphasized to all the students that they would definitely be asked to cite parts of the text in their final examination, and that they in any case needed to study this text carefully because it constituted a vital example of China's Confucian heritage. In the text, Han Yu argues for the importance of lifelong learning and warns against the kind of learning that is only for the sake of passing an exam (at that time, the civil service examination). Referring to Han Yu and Confucius, the teacher explained that "wise people learn from their teachers," and that "a teacher" may be any person regardless of rank and official title. Even Confucius himself would learn from whoever had something to teach him, as the earlier quote suggests. Students studied this message by memorizing and reciting Han Yu's text; the irony of this did not go unnoticed by the teacher herself. After one of the classes she was shaking her head in dismay, explaining to me that although she in principle found the content of the text very good, it was simply "too difficult for rural students to understand what the author really meant"; contrary to what the text was telling them, "at the end of the day, they anyway simply need to learn this and the other texts *precisely and only* for the sake of the exam."

"Discourse on Teachers" was part of a selection of texts that students studied about the value of learning and the duties of the learned individual. Moreover, it was among the classical texts and poems that they were required to know by heart. Therefore, even when the intense lessons regarding "Discourse on Teachers" were completed and new texts were introduced, teachers in literature and language would continue to require that students occasionally start out by reciting together Han Yu's text a few times and then move on to the reading of other texts in the collection—for instance, the text by Hermann Hesse entitled "The Way to Acquire Education."[9] Searching for the original German version of this text, I was surprised to find that what the Chinese students studied was a combination of selected excerpts from two different articles by Hesse that had been translated into Chinese and published in two different issues of the Chinese literary magazine called *Dushu*.[10] These two articles in *Dushu* were in themselves translations of selected parts of *A Library of World Literature* (Eine Bibliothek der Weltliteratur) from 1927, and of *The Magic of Books* (Magie des Buches) from 1930.[11] Comparing the textbook version with Hesse's German original, it seemed likely that the educational authorities' primary aim of composing a text based on extracts from two translated articles (that were already abstracts from the originals) and placing them under a new headline was to clarify how students should ideally acquire knowledge and become learned. The article was not taught in any specific context of European cultural history. Rather, like the much older text by Han Yu, it was presented as a text containing a universally true and indisputable message about how to learn; about what a truly learned individual is and should be, regardless of cultural or historical context.

The selection of bits of text, and the context in which they were taught, created a discourse on learning that emphasized the ideal of an autonomous learning individual, while stressing the need for this individual to submit to discipline. From Hesse, students learned that genuine education (*zhenzheng de jiaoyang*) should not be for a specific purpose. According to Hesse, learning has a meaning in itself, and as such it helps to build self-confidence and create happiness, as the quote at the beginning of this section of the chapter shows. In order to emphasize that learning had a meaning in itself for each individual regardless of external pressure to study, the teacher raised the following question to students in class: "What then is *genuine* education?" and students repeated more or less exactly the words from the text, saying that "genuine education does not have a purpose in itself. . . ." The teacher continued, "What is then the *real* purpose of education?" Students again repeated several times, according to the text, that the purpose was to perfect oneself (*ziwo wanshan*). At this point the teacher started to get frustrated, because she had wanted students to "use their own words," as she explained to the class, but students were unable or unwilling to attempt anything apart from the verbatim expressions from Hesse's text. After a long sigh, she explained that an educated person (*you jiaoyang de ren*) was not necessarily one who got good grades or good results on the exams, but rather someone "who knows his own limitations, who loves nature, who learns from others, and who loves to study and to read."

This ideal, extracted from Hesse's text and reformulated by the teacher, concerned the individual learner and was related to a strong moral lesson that the text was teaching and that contradicted students' own experiences: namely, that one should not force children to limit their reading to certain genres. By doing so, one risks, according to Hesse, extinguishing young people's natural desire to read, thereby also blocking the road toward subsequent learning from the masterpieces. Instead, "each and every one of us should start reading what we are able to comprehend and to love," because "reading without love, knowledge without reverence, education without the heart, is one of the worst sins against the soul," Hesse writes (Ding et al. 2008b, 41). These views on the power of learning and the ultimate motivation for it were studied by high school students who were themselves not allowed to bring any reading material into the school apart from their schoolbooks because they were required to concentrate only on reading material of direct relevance to the final examination.

Although the Chinese textbook version of Hesse's writings did not include much of his original views on the value of reading different genres as a doorway to more challenging forms of literature, it did contain another short moral paragraph that Hesse wrote in 1920s Europe. This section was probably included because it fit well into the contemporary Chinese discourse on youth as hedonists lacking the will to study for the sake of true learning. Hesse's disappointment with youth in Europe between the First and Second World Wars, because of their presumed lack of interest in reading and worrisome pursuit of pleasure, resonates with concerns that many Chinese teachers and educators have today:

In today's world [referring to Europe in the 1920s], the literature is already somewhat despised. Among many young people it seems as if they find it ridiculous and unworthy to immerse themselves in reading, rather than in a happy life. They find that life is too short and precious for this, although they do manage to go to the coffee bar six times a week and to spend time on the dance floor. Well, regardless of how lively it is in "real life" in the universities and workshops, at the stock market and places of pleasure, can this really bring us closer to genuine life, than if we spend one or two hours a day reading the works of wise people and poets from the antique? (Hesse in Ding et al. 2008b, 41–42)[12]

The Chinese official vision of the learned and learning individual, as taught through these examples from textbooks, is laden with moral judgments about the real meaning of studying and the individual's responsibility for following the true way. Literary texts, such as the one by Hesse, are subject to interpretations that transform them into condescending statements of indisputable moral truth. Implicitly, those who do not live up to these moral standards are not learned or able to become truly learned persons; their *suzhi* is low, even if they manage to pass an exam. In daily life at Number Two High and other schools, teachers bear the responsibility of making sure that their students know the content of these texts and are able to reproduce them rather than debate them at the final exam. In classes, teachers often attempt to also make students apprehend, even appreciate, what they are reading. They use their own experiences, imagination, and knowledge of students' interests and ways of life in order to at least try to make the texts more directly relevant to them. However, in (mostly short) instances of such less structured forms of teaching and dialogues between teacher and students, uncertainties about how to transmit the official vision of a neosocialist innovative but dogmatic individual come to the front. Teachers are under great time pressure, and regardless of any attempts to appeal to students' interests and abilities to discuss different topics in the textbook, everyone—students as well as teachers—needs to stay focused on the ultimate goal: the final examination. Like one experienced female teacher in the subject of language and literature firmly concluded a longer conversation between us: "The students have their own thoughts about some of the things they read, but they think one thing and write down another for the examination. We teachers are no different. We have our own thoughts, but we teach according to the requirements for the final examination!"

Inevitably, in this process of teaching for the final examination, texts were interpreted for students, and interpretations were very rarely discussed. This was the case in classes regarding the ideal of the learned individual, as well as in the course Thought and Politics. These classes play an important role in transmitting officially sanctioned views on the individual as a citizen, consumer, and moral person.

THE INDIVIDUAL AS A MORAL CITIZEN AND CONSUMER

Much has been written about the subject of thought and politics and its equivalent at junior secondary school level, thought and values (*sixiang pinde*). The curricula have been of special interest to scholars studying the ways in which political authorities attempt to build a strong sense of patriotism among the coming generation, disseminate knowledge of what it implies to be a citizen of China, and foster an ideologically correct moral attitude among the young.[13] Thought and Politics and Thought and Values are the subjects most intimately associated with official ideological correctness, and as such they serve as benchmarks for the curriculum in other subjects such as history or language and literature (Vickers 2009a, 55). Changes in the moral political curriculum since the mid-1980s are reflective both of general ideological changes and new political priorities. However, the curriculum and the teaching of it has also been adapted to a changing student body made up by young people who are active consumers, users of new technology and means of communication, and participants in the intensified processes of individualization of Chinese society.

Students in Number Two High had only two classes of forty-five minutes a week in Thought and Politics. Students in humanities followed these courses for all three years of their high school studies (the third year was dedicated to repetition), while students in the natural sciences took Thoughts and Politics only during the first two years. Although this subject plays an indisputable political and ideological role in school curriculum, many students consider it to be boring and not very important. Number Two High's students were no different in this respect. They often used terms like "dull" (*dandiao*) or even "useless" (*meiyou yong*) when talking about this subject. However, "useless" here referred more to its status at the final examination than to its content. When asked very directly if they thought some of the contents of the course might be of potential use to them, for instance, when they would have to start working or take responsibility for their own private economy, some students answered positively and came up with a few concrete examples. However, although all students had to pass the course in order to fulfill the high school requirements, it was a subject in the national university entrance exam only for students in the humanities. Consequently, it was taken less seriously than most other subjects among the majority of students who were in the natural sciences and who comprised more than three times as many students as those in the humanities. In comparison to the limited number of classes assigned to the political course, students in grade 1 had nine weekly lessons in language and literature and eight lessons in history, and examination requirements in these subjects were heavy.

With a widespread lack of student engagement in thought and politics, teachers of this subject tended either to resign themselves and stick strictly to the textbooks and examination requirements or to actively stay updated on Chinese and global political and economic news, consciously trying to use this as a way to make the textbooks as relevant as possible to students' own experiences and lives. One teacher was especially proactive in this respect. She was able to engage students when talking about nationalism in connection with, for instance, strained relations between China and Japan, relating texts about general economic systems to the current economic crisis in Europe and the United States or, even better, the students' own economic situations and their consumption. In general, though, classes in thought and politics were remarkably similar to those I had witnessed in minority schools in Yunnan fifteen to eighteen years earlier, before the so-called quality reform. Teachers in the early 2000s, as well as in mid-1990s, tended to follow textbooks very closely, and mainly raised questions that were aimed at ensuring that students were able to answer precisely what was already written in the texts they studied. Questions were largely based on suggestions from the teacher's instruction book, and during classes students never took the initiative to raise questions regarding the content of the texts during classes.

Compared with rural minority schools in 1994–1995 (Hansen 1999), it was the form and content of textbooks rather than the teaching methods that had changed. The textbooks used in Yunnan during the mid-1990s contained only a handful of black-and-white drawings or color photos of poor quality, while the editions from 2007 that were studied in Number Two High were illustrated on each page with small drawings in the style of comic strips with dialogues between people, tables with statistics, or colorful photos of famous buildings or people that symbolized the technological development of New China or China's growing importance to other countries in the world. The form of the new books is clearly more appealing to students, and the content more directly approaching the individual student and his or her interests and obligations as a citizen, consumer, and member of society.

In the aftermath of the crushing of the student demonstrations in 1989, moral and political teaching material was adapted in order to more directly persuade students to resist what the political authorities perceived of as extreme individualism. A positive morality implied political obedience, and students were encouraged to put national and collective interests first, to adhere to collective decision making as defined by the political authorities (Cheung and Pan 2006, 45), while at the same time improving their personal morality through education (Bakken 2000). In society at large, and with a special appeal to the younger generation, the party-state simultaneously moved away from its earlier critical stance toward mass consumerism and promoted instead materialist consumption as an effective means to divert people's attention away from burning political issues and engagement (Yan 2012b). Twenty years later, mass consumerism as a practice and ideology has gained a strong foothold in society (Croll 2006; Griffiths 2012), something that was also clearly reflected in the 2007 curriculum taught in Number Two High. The textbooks approach the individual student through stories and examples explaining what a Chinese citizen (*guomin*) should be and do, and how the individual as a consumer (*xiaofeizhe*) should behave and think. Together, the texts and their stories merge into a vision of an individual as a "good citizen" who adheres to socialist laws and authorities and willingly contributes to the economic development of China through the creation of new things and by being a (model) consumer. This vision is not without its inherent dilemmas, as a few concrete examples from Number Two High illustrate.

Work and Consumption

One of the things that often struck me in conversations and interviews with grade 3 students in Number Two High was how promptly many responded with "I have no idea!" to questions of where they hoped to continue their studies, which subjects they would like to continue studying, or which kind of work they were hoping to qualify for later. In 2009, 2011, and again in 2012, I visited Number Two High in periods close to or just after the university entrance examination, and I talked at length to more than forty students, boys and girls, who were ready to graduate from high school about their plans and wishes for the future. Few of them had any idea of what they "wanted," and many were amused that I would ask such a question. They would "just wait and see" what kind of examination result they would get, and then, based on that, sign up for a college or university that was realistic to get into and for which their families could pay the tuition. The exceptions were students who specialized in arts or music and who were good enough to continue their studies without going through the ordinary university entrance exam. Students also several times referred to "a few students with very good marks," who they told me were more determined than themselves to pursue their studies in specific areas. However, no one was ever really able to introduce me to such students, and when I talked to two of those who had the best marks, they themselves denied that they had any such clear ideas about which studies they wanted to pursue. No students among the more than one hundred I talked to had given their future working careers much thought beyond the general idea that they should "study in a university" in order to find "a better job" than their relatives or friends who had no such education. Quite a few also referred to their parents as having told them that being a teacher was an attractive job, especially for a girl, because it was secure (*wending*), not too demanding, had a relatively high social status, and would allow a woman to spend time with the family rather than going to work in other places, a practice that was very common among women from rural areas of the province.

The dominant attitude among students was clearly that "choice" played hardly any important role at this stage of their lives when determining their future studies or work. Considering students' many discussions about their individual aspirations to find a certain type of boyfriend or girlfriend, their persistence in communicating electronically even when it was not allowed at the school, and their often clear opinions about where they wanted to live (rural v. urban being the most common distinction), their attitudes toward personal choice in work and studies seemed to reflect resignation, and to some extent cynicism based on the realities they experienced. Their own attitudes and experiences were in dire contrast to what they learned from their coursework in school regarding individual choice in socialist China. In the textbooks they read about the need to treat all professions with equal respect and to allow each individual to develop the skills he or she was best at in order to eventually qualify for, and find, the most appropriate job. The textbook titled *Economic Life* (*Jingji shenghuo*), for instance, explained that "the Party and government"[14] do everything they can to help securing a broadening labor market for its citizens while aiming at building an attitude of acceptance for individual choices of occupation (*shuli zizhuzeye guan*). Everyone should be able to choose his or her occupation based on interest, skills, and conditions (*tiaojian*), because "this helps to give full play to each individual's intelligence and wisdom, and it gives rise to each person's productive initiative [*shengchan jijixing*] and creativity [*chuangzaoxing*]." Furthermore, everyone should help build a spirit of competition in the labor market and acknowledge that all occupations are equally important (Ministry of Education Group 2008, 42–43).

Students memorized these ideals for the sake of the examination, but they had no idea about what they themselves were interested in studying or which occupation they would like to have, because they found it useless even to consider these issues before knowing the results of their final examination. The ideal might be of people making choices regarding studies and work based on their abilities and interests, but the reality for most students was completely different. One of the teachers found that the principles taught were very good, and that ideally students would indeed make such choices. The principles were not, however, of any direct relevance for her students, she explained, and consequently there was not much to discuss with students regarding this part of the curriculum.

Other teachers I talked to and observed during classes, or when they were discussing with colleagues how to improve their teaching, found it much easier to engage students in shorter exchanges of views if they focused on issues that they knew concerned the students and that were at the same time part of curriculum, for instance, the topic of consumerism and consumer behavior. As in the reading material for Language and Literature, the political course included short stories about consumer attitudes and mentalities among youth. These chapters were often comparatively popular among students, especially when they were about topics such as the purchase of electronic devices or fashion. In the words of one former student, "What to buy and how to spend your money was a very hot topic among us students." Through the textbooks' presentation of the morally correct behavior regarding consumption, students were taught that an individual should neither follow the crowds blindly nor attempt to stick his or her head out in an attempt to be "different." Under the headline "Every Aspect of Consumer Mentality" (*xiaofei xinli mianmian guan*), an introduction explains how students have recently started to buy expensive gifts for each other as New Year's presents. Parents complain that this puts pressure on the family, the text continues, but "since everybody does it," they believe that it would be bad for their own children not to join in (literally: the student would not be "able to keep his or her head up" (*taibuqitoulai*)). "What kind of mentality is this?" the textbook asks the student. "Have you also come under this kind of psychological influence?" and "How do you find this matter should be solved?" (Ministry of Education Group 2008, 20). The text does not leave the student in doubt about the correct answers that are clearly indicated after the questions. For instance, through an example of how "some students" always want the newest model of a mobile telephone, computer, mp3 player, or electronic game, or want brand names instead of just necessary clothing, the readers are told that this is a negative consumer mentality, when you just blindly follow the crowd. Clearly, this behavior is not desirable.

However, at the same time, the book goes on, it is not healthy to go to the other extreme, sticking your head out and trying too hard to be different from others. One example of such unwanted behavior also concerns the individual's choice of clothes and appearance. The book shows a drawing of a happy young man, self-confidently wearing a red jacket and what are supposed to be very fashionable trousers. He passes by a couple of giggling girls in plain dresses, and the accompanying text informs us that this boy, Xiao Lin, wears peculiar clothes (*fuzhuang guaiguaide*), with a big pocket on the right leg of the trousers and a small one on the left, both with iron hoops attached to them that clatter when he walks. "Don't look down on this guy's outfit, it is bound to be very expensive!" the text ironically remarks, and continues to ask "What do you think prompted Xiao Lin to buy this kind of clothes?" The answer is readily provided: It is an expression of consumption based on a mentality in which one strives for distinction (*qiuyi xinli*), and it is risky to exaggerate this kind of attitude in order just to stand out from the crowd: "Some people like to pursue something that is different from most other people and is unconventional [*biaoxinliyi*]. This kind of consumption may promote the emergence of new crafts and products, but when you display individuality [*zhanshi gexing*] you also need to consider if society will approve of it, and what the cost is. To exaggerate one's search for something unconventional in order just to be different from the crowd should not be encouraged" (Ministry of Education Group 2008, 20).

The ideal individual consumes in a rational way (*lizhi de xiaofei*) and does not follow the unhealthy (*bu jiankang de*) practices of comparing himself to others—a mentality of "making invidious comparison" (*panbi xinli*)—or of blindly following others. However, the ideal neosocialist consumer and individual also does not consciously try to make himself or herself stand out from others through, for instance, exceptional consumption or extraordinary outfits.

A person has the freedom (*ziyou*) to choose what to buy and how to consume, as a teacher in Number Two High formulated it, "so the textbooks try to explain to students what the advantages and disadvantages of certain kinds of consumption are, and how their own individual mentality is shaped by what other people say and do." This notion of "freedom" often turned up in conversations on very different topics, both with and among teachers and students: "We do not have freedom in the school"; "As teachers we have no freedom to decide what and how to teach"; "On weekends we have much more freedom to do what we want to"; "What we high school students lack is freedom"; "The leadership [at this school] allows us quite a lot of freedom where to spend our time when not teaching in class," to mention just a few examples.[15] It was a popularly employed notion that was mainly used to express perceptions regarding choice or possibility of behavior in relation not only to consumption, as mentioned here, but also to parents, teachers, school administrators, or other authorities. The concept of freedom was mostly applied in contexts in which people were talking about freedom *from* something. However, it was only to a very limited degree a concept that was used or explained in textbooks, although the vision of the ideal citizen transmitted to students did entail a more official explanation of what freedom was supposed to imply for the individual, as discussed following.

The Model Citizen and Individual Freedom

One-fourth of the curriculum in Thought and Politics is dedicated to "political life" (*zhengzhi shenghuo*). Apart from deepening the information from junior secondary school on, for instance, the basic political system of China and relations with other countries in the world, the textbook seeks to convince students that they are all active participants in political life. It goes on to explain what their role is and should be, including what kind of freedom they have as citizens.[16] The course manual instructs teachers to give ample time for students to discuss key issues in the book, and even to create a "democratic classroom atmosphere" (*minzhu ketang qifen*) (Curricula Research Institute 2007, 30). In practice, teachers in Number Two High found little time and few means to put this recommendation into practice, and they largely followed textbooks and the teachers manuals' instructions on how to interpret texts and address difficult issues. Therefore, the following examples are largely based on the curriculum and the interpretations teachers were instructed to use (and did use) through the *Teachers Teaching Manual* (Curricula Research Institute 2007). Manuals such as this one are generally comprehensive; in this case it was a book with more than 340 pages and two accompanying VCDs for just one of the four text books, the one on political life.

This curriculum is keen on transmitting to students the idea that the individual in contemporary China is fully capable of taking personal initiative in the economic market, engaging in political life (*canyu zhengzhi shenghuo*) while at the same time staying loyal to the Communist Party and the system of "people's democratic dictatorship" (*renmin minzhu zhuanzheng*)—all this on the firm basis of a collectively shared identity of Chinese patriotism. In addition to the examples of how students as consumers should handle the choices that modern society offers them, the specific part of the curriculum that focuses on "political life" provides an official version of what *ziyou*—used in the senses of "freedom" and "liberal"—implies for the individual as a citizen. The teachers are provided with a detailed analysis in order to give the correct interpretations and answers to students' possible questions regarding what kinds of freedom a citizen in the People's Republic of China (PRC) has.

The main problem, according to the text, is that Chinese society remains too much under the influence of an outdated understanding of freedom, stemming from the old Chinese society (*Zhongguo gudai shehui*) in which both peasants and the ruling classes, according to the book, simply understood freedom as the ability to "do what you do wanted to do" (*xiang gan shenme jiu gan shenme*), and do it the way that you wanted to (*xiang zenme gan jiu zenme gan*) (Curricula Research Institute 2007, 35). However, during the Enlightenment period in Europe, philosophers and political thinkers made clear that this was not the way to perceive individual freedom. Freedom was to be inseparably connected to the practice of law, the text explains, and likewise in China today it is the law that defines the kind and scope of freedom that students and other citizens are entitled to. "Freedom is man being free to do what he ought to do, and not being forced to do things that he should not do," the text quotes the political thinker Montesquieu (1689–1755). It is the law that will define the limits to this freedom, thereby also providing it to everyone on an equal basis (35). The law is to the citizen what water is to the fish: without the constraints of the water the fish has no freedom because it dies (42).

More concretely, teachers are instructed to explain to students that citizens have political rights and freedom (*zhengzhi quanli he ziyou*) within the limits of the law, and that absolute freedom (*juedui de ziyou*) beyond these constraints does not exist (Curricula Research Institute 2007, 37). The examples used to illustrate this are from the Declaration of Human Rights to which China has committed (40). The citizens of China have equal right to "freedom of speech," students learn, but this does not mean that an individual is free to express whatever he or she wants (*xiang shuo shenme jiu shuo shenme*). There are two restrictions. First, the freedom of speech is limited by law, which means that it cannot be used to instigate or incite any kinds of actions that endanger the security of the country, the political stability, the unity of the different Chinese ethnic groups (*minzu tuanjie*), or disturb the order of society. Second, a citizen may not use the freedom of speech to slander other citizens (37).

In other examples of citizens' freedoms (such as freedom of the press, freedom to form associations, freedom of assembly, and freedom to move)

(Curricula Research Institute 2007, 37), it is made clear that these are to be exercised within the constraints of Chinese law, and that freedom is also always limited to actions that do not disturb political or societal stability. The individual citizen of China has political rights as defined within the law and will at the same time perform the proper duties of a citizen, for instance, the duty of not disclosing state secrets (42). To help teachers give more specific examples of national secrets and how ordinary people have broken the regulations, the manual mentions a famous law case from 1981 in which a maid had disclosed secret information to a foreign newspaper about the political leader Deng Xiaoping's whereabouts and work and about training of the military. Another example is that the Internet is increasingly being illegally used to disclose secrets regarding state construction projects (42–43). There are also examples of the political rights that citizens enjoy, such as the right to receive an education, participate in national economic, political, and cultural activities, discuss issues of concern to the population on the Internet, and take part in elections (38–39).

However, within the socialist legal framework, nearly forty years after the death of Mao Zedong, students still learn that full citizen rights only apply to those who belong to the Maoist definition of "the people" (renmin) and not to those who belong to "the enemy of the people" (diren). Although an "enemy of the people" may certainly also be a Chinese citizen, he or she does not have the same full rights as other citizens, and he or she can consequently not be expected to perform the same duties (Curricula Research Institute 2007, 38). Although the Maoist distinction between "the people" and "the enemies of the people" is not explicitly articulated in Chinese law, and is indeed outdated from a legal perspective, it remains alive in public discourse and has some practical implications, for instance, because people who are convicted for political crimes may lose their political rights as citizens, such as their electoral rights, rights to assemble, freedom of speech, right to hold public office, and so on, for a period of time.[17] This was, for instance, what happened to the Nobel Peace Prize-winner Liu Xiaobo when he was convicted for inciting subversion of state power in 2009 and was sentenced not only to eleven years in prison but also to two years deprivation of political rights.

In brief, students learn—by repetition rather than discussion—that their role as citizens is to follow the laws and adhere to the overruling principle that any action or speech that can be interpreted as an incitement to endangering national security or political and societal stability is against the law. Thus, the consumer and economic individual takes initiative and is innovative, while the citizen follows the law and the authority of the party-government. How, then, does the ideal individual, who is an economically responsible, innovative, and law-abiding citizen with loyal sentiments toward the Communist Party, act as a moral person? To exemplify this we turn to a well-known figure, the heroic soldier of the people, Lei Feng.

When Lei Feng Went to Africa

The story of the heroic soldier Lei Feng (1940–1962) remains an important part of moral curriculum, and schools often have their own activities to promote the study of morality through the ideal of Lei Feng (Nie 2008, 72). Lei Feng was a soldier and model communist, and since the 1960s he has served as an example of an ideal youth. His image has changed since the time of the Cultural Revolution, and today, because the ideal youth is also an eager student, it is not surprising that statues of Lei Feng are still found in schools around the country. When I was doing fieldwork in rural areas of Fujian in 2005–2006, immigrant factory workers from poor villages in Sichuan, who often had fewer than nine years of schooling, would take me to the Lei Feng statue in the middle school so we could have our pictures taken together in front of it. It was the perfect place for this purpose, the sixteen- to eighteen-year-old workers explained, because we had both the modern school buildings and the impressive statue of this famous hero as our background, and, no less important, it was fun to get away from the dull and depressing factory and walk around in the schoolyard as if we belonged there. This place symbolized the status of learning that these workers had been deprived of, the heroic deeds of an ordinary soldier who could have been one of them, and the prospect of economic progress in rural areas like the poorer ones they had left.

It would probably be hard to find anyone above the age of eight, or maybe even younger, in China who does not know the name of Lei Feng who is no less than a celebrity (Edwards 2010). Ever since his death as a twenty-one-year-old soldier in 1962, Lei Feng has undergone several makeovers, as authorities have tried to keep him alive as a model by making his image keep pace with society. During the Cultural Revolution, as the cult of Mao gained ground, Lei Feng was "perfectly altruistic, without the slightest self-interested calculations or self-doubts, righteousness incarnate. But even more importantly, he personified total gratitude, unflinching loyalty and unswerving, unquestioning belief [in Mao]" (Chan 1985, 61). However, by the early 1980s, the model of Lei Feng was criticized by liberal reformers for having lost his individuality and for having been turned into a simple tool to make people docile (Bakken 2000, 189). Therefore, up through the 1980s and '90s values of modernization, including those related to consumption, were launched as part of the new Lei Feng image—alas, for the party, without the desired result of making him more credible or inspirational to the young generation. In the 1990s, Lei Feng even appeared "ridiculous to young people; a symbol of a dubious character" (Bakken 2000, 189). Also Hongping Annie Nie mentioned, in her fieldwork in the late 1990s, that students expressed a highly cynical attitude toward Lei Feng, one of the country's most celebrated models of "the people" (Nie 2008).[18]

Oblivious to students' eventual cynicism in the face of recurring national Lei Feng campaigns, educational authorities of the 2010s have by no means abandoned him, and the trust in his transformative powers seems intact in schools and also at the level of national official discourse. Year after year, weeks of March are dedicated to moralistic Lei Feng campaigns in schools all over the country. The trend to modernize Lei Feng has intensified, and by 2012 he had gone through an intensive period of individualization. Lei Feng is still performing as a model youth, citizen, member of the people, and consumer, but he has also been equipped with a more individual face: a face and an appearance that political authorities hope that students (and other young people) might identify with, and consequently learn from. The contemporary Lei Feng, as shown on TV and represented by teachers in Number Two High, is a more human, though no less perfect, model than the communist hero Lei Feng of earlier periods of the People's Republic of China. In official discourse found in moral teaching and campaigning in schools, Lei Feng remains the ultimate individual communist role model *from* "the people" and *for* "the people."[19]

In Number Two high, the face of Lei Feng decorated many classroom blackboards during the months of March and April 2012, and students were proudly pointing out to me the painters and the designers of the texts that accompanied impressive chalk drawings. Although I was not surprised that Lei Feng campaigns were still going strong in high schools such as Number Two High, I was somewhat puzzled about students' reactions to them. Like other researchers, I had talked to many students, especially in the late 1990s and in the period around the new millennium, who ridiculed the Lei Feng campaigns and found them superficial and completely out of tune with real life. However, in Number Two High, the students seemed genuinely interested in showing me the pictures they had painted of Lei Feng and in explaining the kind of person and hero he was. Lei Feng as a person was regarded very positively, and even the campaigns to study him were welcomed by many as a chance to do something other than studying the usual curriculum. "Lei Feng was a good person; there was nothing wrong with him," a teacher said, and many students talked about Lei Feng in the same way, as an old friend or acquaintance. But whether or not the campaigns about him had any capacity to change society, influence the upcoming generation that was faced both with difficult choices that Lei Feng himself had never had to make and rampant corruption among cadres who were themselves supposed to be living role models, was strongly doubted by teachers who were willing to discuss this topic.

Lei Feng as a person and model in contemporary moral campaigns was partly constructed through official media representations that some teachers in Number Two High turned to for inspiration when trying to teach "the life of Lei Feng" in a convincing way. Such campaigns were among the relatively few extracurricular activities offered to students in Number Two High, and they were welcomed as a break from the daily routines. In a CCTV (Central China TV) production from March 2012, called *This Is Lei Feng*, an individualized Lei Feng was created and presented through pictures and stories from people who had been his friends and comrades, including the person who indirectly caused his death. Contemporary younger soldiers and people working in the propaganda section or in administrative jobs in the Army were shown to be actively dedicating a considerable amount of time to creating "a true" image of *the person* Lei Feng (Xinwen diaocha: Ta shi Lei Feng 2012). One official who was interviewed in the program explained that because society was now characterized by heterogeneous values (*jiazhi duoyuan*), it was only to be expected that some would criticize the campaigns to study Lei Feng, question his true motives, and even abuse his name: "Before everybody followed one voice . . . but now we cannot force anybody to like Lei Feng; however, we can tell them about him" (Xinwen diaocha: Ta shi Lei Feng 2012).

People who had set up blogs to discuss Lei Feng were sometimes ridiculed or criticized, enthusiastic Lei Feng fans and proponents explained, and some companies had even taken the liberty of exploiting the name of Lei Feng in commercials for condoms. Just the fact that such information was given and discussed in the program suggests that national TV was determined to create an image of the contemporary Lei Feng campaign as an open forum for debate—something aimed at convincing contemporary youth that there is still something to be learned from him. Lei Feng, in the individualized version, remains a good communist and citizen, and just like in the 1990s he is a consumer who is very fond of his motorbike. In addition, he has become a young man who was humorous and charming, who possessed a certain degree of vanity as expressed through his love of posing for the camera (there are more than 250 pictures of him, which was a considerable number of photos of an ordinary soldier at the time), and who enjoyed dressing up in fancy leather shoes, jacket, and an (at that time for a soldier) expensive watch. Lei Feng was well-off compared to his fellow soldiers because he had no family to support. All these things together explain why some people do not believe that the stories of his deeds were true and claim that the image of him is fake, the program argued.

The moral message conveys that being rich and vain by no means prevents a young man from simultaneously displaying moral virtue and from being "lovable" (keai). Thus, the image of Lei Feng was recreated so that it may speak more directly to the young people of today, who are assumed to be hedonistic and vain. Lei Feng of the 2010s has even become a man of the world, and as such he is supposed to impress the youth of today. By means of Chinese members of the UN peace-keeping forces in Libya, the TV program also showed how Lei Feng was taken to the African continent as a symbol of the Chinese authorities' aspirations to rise to prominence not only as a global economic power but as a cultural and political inspiration. One aim of the program was to make Chinese people proud when they saw African children in Libya enthusiastically learning about Lei Feng as a window into Chinese culture. They would see an example of how Chinese peace-keeping forces were helping to promote a global moral vision based on neosocialist values embodied in the new Lei Feng. Lei Feng was no longer meant only for a local Chinese audience of youth. He has gone global, and he has become part of Chinese soft power and aid to Africa. He is an inspiration to the world beyond China, the program argued. One of the Chinese organizers of a Lei Feng speech competition among students in Libya were almost moved to tears when a young Libyan girl was asked if she liked Lei Feng: "No," she responded, "I do not like Lei Feng, I *love* him!" Lei Feng has moved beyond China and become a model for us all; and all those people who ridicule Lei Feng and his proponents come out of the TV program as pitiful cynics with no ability to see and learn from humanity's inherent good.

Appealing to students' emotions through the individualization of role models and their experiences—by, for instance, presenting Lei Feng as a lovable but also vain and slightly naive person in his ever-smiling attitude to life and people around him—was common in other moral campaigns in Number Two High. Role models would function as such, many teachers found, only if they were able to move students emotionally, and to do so, students needed to some extent to be able to identify with them. Several homeroom teachers were therefore particularly content when a show of the popular yearly organized TV program *Moving China* (Gandong Zhongguo) had caused a group of girls to start crying out of pity and sympathy for participants who had sacrificed health or money for a good cause. Both Lei Feng, as the ultimate example of a youth hero of the people, and the models promoted in various TV programs shown in classes for special occasions seemed to have an immediate effect on at least some students, although obviously the depth and meaning of this impact beyond the immediate outbursts of emotions are impossible to measure.

Official high school curriculum may be approached from a variety of angles, with our emphasis here on examples of how an official discourse on the individual is promoted through the integrated curriculum and school campaigns and how teachers inevitably participate in its interpretation. Educational authorities are trying to adapt school curriculum to some of the realities and social changes that students are facing, ensuring that it is in line with dominant political guidelines of the time. Therefore, current state curriculum, as compared to that of fifteen years ago, is using more examples from the everyday life that show how individuals—being both consumers and citizens—have to make difficult choices and decisions while at the same time making sure that the politically and morally correct answers are provided. This approach builds on a continuation of the methodology of employing exemplary models (Bakken 2000) for socializing and teaching proper behavior.

However, the battle about the role of the individual in the contemporary state school is not fought over the contents of textbooks. Textbooks and their contents are chosen by higher authorities; they are studied or memorized by students, but they are rarely analyzed or discussed. They provide us with an entrance to understanding the kind of individuals the political authorities in principle would like to make of the coming generation of adult citizens, and therefore also which flaws the authorities find—and attempt to correct—in the current population. Citizen training through teaching of the interpretations of law and the individual's obligations and rights in relation to it constitutes an important part of this. The individual whom the authorities envision to come out of the school has knowledge about the status of law in China as something that is in principle equal for everyone, regardless of position. The law sets the limits for the individual and thereby grants him or her the freedom that exists within these limits. Remnants of Maoist distinctions between "the people" and "the enemy" are simultaneously employed to explain to students why not all Chinese citizens at any given time will be able to uphold their full citizen rights, and to conclude that it is the political authorities, ultimately the party, who maintain the right to define the law and to interpret it. The emphasis on the citizen's simultaneous obligation not to instigate any kind of action that might challenge political or societal stability suggests that the authorities fear precisely this. Although teachers' manuals encourage discussions among students, textbooks always carefully provide the correct answers to broader political or ethical questions involving the individual. By explicitly providing these answers, the content of the curriculum inherently supports the practice of having students learning the principles regarding a citizen's rights and obligations by heart, as given facts and rules beyond interpretation.

It is very difficult to know to what extent there are parts of official curriculum regarding the role of the moral, consuming, law-abiding individual that hit a nerve with students and trigger their interest beyond the need for learning to pass an exam. According to several teachers, it was the parts about consumption and personal economy that were most convenient to choose as topics for discussions about individual mentality and proper behavior, and the Lei Feng and moral campaigns were put forward as examples of teaching activities in which more students tended to demonstrate at least some level of personal engagement. Consumption, especially of electronics and fashion, was a most timely topic for students, and moral campaigns connected, for instance, to Lei Feng spoke to their emotions while allowing some distraction from the usual classroom teaching. In comparison, topics such as the political status of citizens and the ideal of the learning individual (as exemplified in Hesse's text) were either too sensitive to debate in classes or too removed from students' everyday experiences to interest them.

From the perspective of official high school curriculum and the way it is taught as containing indisputable facts, the ideal Chinese individual is more multifaceted than in earlier periods of the PRC, and much is expected from him or her, such as a very high degree of self-control and self-discipline: the neosocialist individual is knowledgeable of his or her own rights and obligations as set within the limits of the law but respects the fact that the party-government provides the true interpretation of it. Each individual contributes to the economic development of China and her growing status in the world through controlled consumption and innovation in the fields of economy and technology, but he or she refrains from extending this innovative creativity to any fields that may challenge the party-state's definition of laws and limits. The ideal individual also fights the negative side effects of a rapidly individualizing society in which the ideology of consumption and urge to be different have replaced moral responsibility and benevolence.

Textbooks acknowledge (though sometimes only implicitly) that although Chinese society is benefiting from rapid economic development and increasing global influence, it is also experiencing hedonism, widespread corruption, lack of respect for the law, and challenges to stability. Few, if any, analytic insights are provided to students as to why these phenomena emerge, and the main solution to the problems is seemingly to "simply" teach the individual to behave correctly. Self-discipline and self-control are major virtues of the neosocialist individual as promoted through official discourse and curriculum in the contemporary state school.

CHAPTER 3

HIERARCHY AND DEMOCRACY

Controlled Rise of the Individual

Some of the most exciting periods of my fieldwork in Number Two High took place in autumn 2009 and spring 2010, when the students and teachers let me join their experiments with elections for the student association. The enthusiasm of the involved students and teachers was contagious, and those involved in the elections appreciated them as a most welcome break from daily routines.[1] Such developments of organizational practices within schools in contemporary China constitute an important technique in training students to become neosocialist citizens, willing to adhere to Leninist authoritarian rule, while at the same time, capable of succeeding in a fierce market economy that requires individual initiative. Organizations such as the Communist Party Youth League (*Gongqingtuan*), the system of student cadres (*xuesheng ganbu*), and the student association (*xueshenghui*) are different and complementary means of training students how to govern each other and themselves. Young teachers struggle to identify the best individual student leaders through experiments with democratic elections while simultaneously ensuring that discipline is adhered to and hierarchies accepted. Students have their own ulterior motives for joining so-called democratic elections or becoming temporary cadres, and they experience intense pressure from fellow students and teachers when they are in student leadership positions. In the increasingly individualized Chinese society, organizational practices in schools have in effect become arenas for negotiations of the role of the individual, its rise, and its options for promoting collective interests.

THE HIERARCHICAL STUDENT CADRE SYSTEM
AND THE DISCOURSE ON SELFISHNESS

All high schools (along with colleges and universities) practice an established system of appointing or electing student cadres. In the Chinese political system the term "cadre" (*ganbu*) refers to a person holding a responsible or managerial position in the public administration or government. Not all cadres are members of the Chinese Communist Party (CCP), but those holding sensitive or higher-level positions in the party or government are almost certainly party members. Like political cadres, student cadres occupy different positions of responsibility and management within a clearly demarcated hierarchy, and most but not all of them are members of the Communist Party's youth branch, the Youth League. They are called "cadres" to signify the role they play as leaders among peers. Student cadres are expected to set an example of commitment and good behavior through their participation in, and organizing of, student activities related to cleaning campaigns, sporting events, charity, and so forth; and they are assigned the task of keeping fellow students informed about school policies and activities in connection with national holidays and helping maintain general harmony among peers. They serve as connecting links between students and school authorities and are expected to participate in the disciplining of their fellow students.

To some extent, this way of organizing students is a simple emulation of the political system that all citizens, regardless of position, are expected to embrace; the organizational practices in high school, combined with the textbook studies regarding political life, in principle prepare students to become such citizens. The student cadre system is a continuation of a system that was established in the beginning of the PRC, most comprehensively in universities and high schools, but also, like today, in a form adapted to younger children in primary and junior secondary schools. The cadre system remains one of the most significant tools for training students to govern themselves and their peers and adapt to and internalize hierarchical structures. It is a political tool and a technology of discipline in the Foucauldian sense.

More as a result of societal processes of individualization than of any politically planned transformation or master plan, the internal dynamics of the student cadre system are undergoing profound changes. The boom in recent years in the number of training courses and multiple forms of instruction and discussion on how to become, or develop others into becoming, ideal student cadres are indicative of profound uncertainties among educational authorities on how to influence a young generation whose ideals, moralities, goals, and ambitions are sometimes incomprehensible to people who have grown up in earlier periods of the PRC. Therefore, the student cadres of today, as compared to the earlier periods of communist rule (see, for instance, Shirk 1982; Chan 1985), are at the same time more thoroughly and less explicitly supervised. The methods are modern means of governmentality with a strong emphasis on the need to promote students cadres who are capable of governing themselves as well as others. This was, for instance, emphasized in a speech during a training course for student cadres in one of China's elite universities: "Student cadres constitute a key factor for realizing students' self-education [*ziwo jiaoyu*], self-administration [*ziwo guanli*], and self-service [*ziwo fuwu*]" (Long 2008). Such debates, and the dominant concepts used to emphasize an ideal of self-governing, reach into rural schools such as Number Two High, and they help to form perceptions of, and indeed ways of talking about, youth and student cadres among its teachers.

The Chinese debates on individual responsibilities and duties of student cadres, in addition to their rights and privileges, tend to be highly normative, with a strong focus on what is perceived as an inherent conflict between self-interests (negative) and collective goals (positive) as defined by the Communist Party. In 2011, Chen Wei, a professor in political science, launched on his blog an unusually harsh critique against current student cadres connected to the CCP Youth League and the schools' student associations.[2] He compared contemporary student cadres unfavorably to his own experiences of being a student cadre in the early decades of the Maoist period. Chen's arguments, which were widely publicized in Chinese media sources, held that there was much more room for critical reflection and real representation of student interests when he was a student cadre in the 1950s as compared to now. He criticized contemporary student cadres in universities for their lack of sound skepticism toward leadership and for being too easily corrupted into power abuse and selfish behavior. Although this critique was unusual in pointing out how students failed to challenge corrupt practices among people with political authority, it echoed widespread views of student cadres as selfish and lacking a true collective spirit. Many examples of such a dominant discourse on "the contemporary selfish student cadre" are found in training course material from universities as well as high schools, on university web sites, and blogs and web sites discussing or presenting "current problems" and other aspects of students' lives. These materials tend to agree that the problem lies in corrupt individual morality rather than in systemic failure; and most authors therefore call for improved personal attitudes and behavior, though without specifying how this should be achieved in practice.

In general, these discussions are built upon normative ideals rather than on reflections on the cadre system itself. Regardless of whether such discursive material is produced by schools, officials, or students (for instance, in the form of blogs or web sites for student cadres), there seems to be an unspoken consensus about the advantages of maintaining the very system of student cadres. From the perspective of the authorities, the system remains a crucial tool for governing students and teaching them to govern each other; for students it still serves as a springboard to individual careers, providing at the same time options for engaging socially with fellow students in cadre positions and building networks that support collective interests. For teachers in Number Two High, it was simply a system that they were required to practice, a system they were accustomed to and that served the practical purpose of helping to maintain and develop discipline among students.

The content of teaching materials and training courses about student cadres suggest that educational authorities at all levels of the political system regard the crises, or at least the deficiencies, of the student cadre system as a result of individual students' lack of correct attitude and morality. This is regarded as a result of a generally negative trend of individualization that is taking place among the young generation and is even prevalent among those who are supposed to lead others by performing as models. Therefore, there is a plethora of material produced by educators all over the country explaining what the ideal student cadre should look like in China during the 2000s. Most of these materials refer to student cadres at college and university levels, but they clearly reflect the political and moral expectations that all student cadres should embrace, including those in Number Two High. The official discourse on student cadres as found, for instance, in documents from the Ministry of Education and the local education bureaus at provincial and county levels defines the political framework within which the school's leaders and its teachers have to interpret their own responsibilities and degree of autonomy in setting up and practicing the system of student cadres. It informs them about what local student hierarchies ought to look like and how individuals should ideally behave.

Official discourse and the many unofficial echoes of it emphasize that the ideal student cadre serves as a bridge between the broad masses of students and the school authorities, and he or she is in all respects a model for fellow students. This conforms to the image of China as an example-oriented society in which learning is to be built on the good example of role models (Bakken 2000). A web site specifically dedicated to the topic of student cadres describes the triple role of a model student cadre, who is at the same time a servant for the students, a "backbone" (*guguan*) in the party's work among them, and a tool or "right hand" of the school authorities:

> The student cadres form the tie and bridge of integration between a school and its vast body of students. They are the backbone of students, and the right hand of the school for developing its student work. The student cadres originate from the students, serve the students, and are models among the students. They set an example for other students with regard to their studies, work, and lives. Student cadres should firmly establish grass-root units, be of service to the development of fellow students' mentality, pay attention to their own attitude with regard to servicing, and their own style of working. They should make thorough investigations and promptly report on any kind of [critical] situation that arises among students. We cannot allow any student cadre to separate him/herself from the students, nor to set him/herself above the students. (Student Cadre Net 2011)[3]

The importance of having student cadres acting as role models was also emphasized by Feng Weiguang from Beijing Normal University in an article on the web page of the official *People's Daily*: "An outstanding student cadre is a model and a flag who sets an example for other students *that no other methods can possibly replace*" (my italics; Feng 2004).[4]

However, when looking more closely into the problems authorities and other proponents of the official discourse identify as typical for these irreplaceable student cadres, one of the most recurrent themes is their very *lack* of the characteristics that the model is supposed to embody: collective spirit and support to fellow students combined with unquestioned adherence to authorities at the school and the ability to bridge between these two demands. When student cadres fail to maintain this precarious balance, the reason is attributed to a dark side of an increasingly individually oriented society promoting consumerism and a "do-it-yourself" ideology, which the young especially seem to embrace. Seen from this perspective, the student cadre system is weakened because of students' exaggerated individualism and weak morality. One author on Student Cadre Net summarizes common views of problems that have emerged during the era of reform or "the new period" (*xin shiqi*):[5]

- Their [the student cadres] practical abilities are quite strong, but their theoretical level needs to be raised.
- The conflict between their studies and their work [as cadres] has not been solved.
- Their sense of organization is not strong, and they have a bureaucratic style of working. There are some student cadres who during work act on their own, and act arbitrarily. When something is the matter, they do not report to the teacher, and they may even make [personal] use of their own position
- Some cadres have a severe utilitarian way of thinking. They only value the personal benefits that come with being a student cadre, and ignore their job assignments.
- Their sense of responsibility is weak. They say one thing and do another, hence, they are not much of a model. (Tian 2010)

A somewhat more pointed but no less characteristic example of how student cadres (and to some extent students in general) have come under fierce criticism for being selfish and egoistic was expressed in a long normative list from a party secretary in Shandong University. Here student cadres were instructed to do away with "self-centeredness and utilitarianism," to not argue from a "selfish point of view" or for "individualistic heroism" (*geren yingxiongzhuyi*), and to "forsake the selfish promotion of individual interests" (Shandong University Law School 2011).

In articles and blogs debating the problems of individualistic and selfish student cadres, the solution is mostly to appeal to the sense of morality and consciousness of individual students or suggest training courses for them. However, typical of the many levels of authorities and individuals who participate in the debates about the crises of the student cadre system is their lack of concrete suggestions about how to solve the perceived problems in practice. They point to a general trend of individualism among students who are supposed to perform as models and see this as a weakness of society. It is largely left to teachers, for instance, in rural schools such as Number Two High, to improvise and experiment in order to foster better and less selfish student cadres—cadres who, it is hoped, will in turn be models for their fellow students and ultimately help create a better neosocialist China.

THE CADRE SYSTEM IN
PRACTICE: MOTIVES AND PRESSURES

In Number Two High, five to seven students were elected in every class as class cadres (*ban ganbu*). Among them were the class monitor (*banzhang*), the deputy class monitor (*fubanzhang*), and the secretary (*shuji*). The rest were responsible for five sections of discipline and security, health, propaganda, literature and art, and sports. Although students in principle elected their own class cadres and class monitors through secret ballot, the homeroom teacher had considerable influence both on the nomination of candidates and on the results of the election. The homeroom teacher organized class elections each semester but was free to call for re-elections any time if he or she found that some of the class cadres, and especially the class monitors, did not perform well enough. Sometimes teachers would let several students have a trial period as cadres before deciding who the monitor would be. The homeroom teacher had the power to either recommend or block the election of a given student. When asked about the criteria for choosing students as class monitors, homeroom teachers pointed out that they needed to find class monitors who were not only good models for fellow students but also enjoyed enough respect and prestige among the students to be able to execute authority. A student with high marks and a diligent attitude toward studying was not necessarily the best choice for a class monitor, although a student with low marks and poor study habits would definitely not be considered eligible. As one student exclaimed, to become a class monitor you need both "good academic results and good connections!" (*xuexi hao, guanxi hao*). In this regard, the student cadres of the 2010s are not very much different from the student leaders and activists of the 1970s. One of the informants from a study from that period remarked that "an ideal activist should be a leader, a model, be able to influence his fellow students, and be able to unite them for collective action" (Shirk 1982, 85).

Although students in Number Two High normally elected their class monitors and deputy monitors by direct vote once a year, the rest of the cadre positions were divided among students who had simply been generally elected as "student cadres." The possible division of positions was first negotiated among elected student cadres and their homeroom teachers, and the teacher would then assign the different positions to elected cadres. These student cadres all became part of a larger network of students holding equivalent positions in the other classes within the school. In this way, the system aimed at ensuring that every student who was, for instance, connected to the propaganda team knew exactly which messages to write on the blackboards in their respective classes, and the school could make sure the same campaigns, for instance, on morality and Lei Feng, were run in all classes at the same time and in the same fashion. This system requires that select students take responsibility for organizing practical tasks such as cleaning up, writing on the blackboard, doing practical work in connection with sporting activities, collecting homework, and relaying messages from teachers, to mention a few. It teaches students that the privileged position of a cadre requires unconditional acceptance of assignments coming from higher authorities, whether the homeroom teacher, the school's political office (*zhengjiaochu*), or the chairman and leaders of the student association. It also teaches students who are not in cadre positions to take instructions from their peers, to respect their peers' cadre positions, and to accept the fact that regardless of friendship, their class monitors are obliged to report to higher authorities any misbehavior or breaches of rules among students.

This aspect of disciplining and surveillance is at the heart of the organizational structure of a school's student cadre system. It is a very useful, in truth necessary, disciplinary tool for teachers and school administrators who find it increasingly difficult to supervise students' social activities and maintain discipline merely by means of the carrot of a successful examination or the stick of regulations or failure at the exam. More specifically, the class monitor plays an important role as the direct link between teachers and students. Most homeroom teachers meet with their class monitors briefly once a day to discuss how things are going and how students have been behaving not only during classes, but also in dormitories, in the dining hall, and during breaks. The class monitors are personally responsible for directly reporting to the teacher about everything concerning fellow students' daily lives, and especially about problems or conflicts among them: "The class monitor is definitely the most important student for me," a newly arrived young female teacher explained. "She is my only real entrance to the lives of my students, and I depend on her to know what is going on among them."

Teachers in Number Two High who had been assigned as homeroom teachers very openly acknowledged how deeply they depended on cultivating good relationships with their class monitors. The balance of power between homeroom teachers and class monitors was more precarious than their unequal status would suggest, because homeroom teachers found it increasingly difficult to monitor students. "In reality we are serving as nannies" (*baomu*), a young male teacher sighed after having returned from yet another evening check to see if the lights were off and his students quiet in the dormitory. Students used mobile telephones as means of communicating relatively freely among each other and with friends outside the school; they engaged in social activities (including romantic relationships or visiting Internet cafés) that were prohibited by the school; and they had expectations about their individual lives and rights that were often at odds with the demands of the education system. Many homeroom teachers therefore pointed out that it was really only through good and informative class monitors that they were able to at least partly fulfill the rather heavy duties as homeroom teachers. And even then, they often had no other choice than to turn a blind eye to student activities. To maintain discipline, homeroom teachers, at a minimum, needed to get access to reliable information regarding conflicts and breaches of regulations among students and to gain a basic understanding of their social and emotional lives. As homeroom teachers, they were responsible far beyond the mere academic education of their students. They were expected to solve social or personal behavioral problems, and, in the most extreme cases, to consult with parents. With most parents working outside the township, and with the continuing expansion of students' social activities, homeroom teachers had increasingly come to rely on successful cooperation with specially selected students rather than on direct authoritarian disciplinary methods. Therefore, homeroom teachers found it extremely important to play key roles in the selection of the class monitors especially, but also of the other student cadres. Teachers were searching not simply for the best academic students, or those most likely to be ideal role models, but just as much for those who were socially popular among their peers and seemed most likely to be able to influence the social behavior of other students, including their attitudes toward teachers and other authorities.

Despite of the heavy personal burden that these demands on class monitors entailed, the leadership position was popular among students. In my interpretation, this was both because of rational choices of students looking for specific benefits, such as improved résumés and direct access to their homeroom teachers, and because of many students' continual search for opportunities to involve themselves in more social activities with their peers. Students from Number Two High, just like other students in China, were no longer awarded extra points for having held the position as class monitor when applying for higher education. However, everybody knew that it was recorded in one's personal file, and that it might be useful later, when seeking a job, especially in the public sector, or when applying for a scholarship. It requires only a quick look at the résumés of college and university graduates from all over China today to get an idea of how common it is for students to emphasize their experience and training as cadres, especially an award as "outstanding student cadre" (*youxiu xuesheng ganbu*). Just the fact that one had been found eligible for the position as class monitor in high school might help a student to advance to cadre positions in college or university.

Students in Number Two High were correct in assuming that having been a student cadre might possibly help their personal careers. Yet, for the individual, the position as class monitor was pervaded with dilemmas and conflicts arising from the dual demands of surveying and reporting on fellow students, on the one hand, and representing fellow students' interests, on the other. Students in the class monitor position were themselves highly aware of the dilemmas and potential conflicts of interest inherent to the position. Several of them, girls and boys, explained to me how they experienced the dual pressures from teachers and fellow students: "Sometimes I really regret that I took on this position. I am embarrassed [*bu hao yisi*] to report on other students, but if I don't, I let the teacher down [*duibuqi laoshi*]," one eighteen-year-old male class monitor explained. Another more experienced monitor analyzed his own experiences of difficulties in several longer discussions that included his best friend, a girl who herself occupied the secretary position. He described some of the complexities of being a class monitor who was expected to solve very diverse kinds of problems involving one's peers and friends:

> Last year many students in our class were quite naughty, and our homeroom teacher insisted I found a solution to improve behavior. There is a lot of pressure on you when you are a class monitor. I really did not like to be in charge of my fellow students [*guan tongxuemen*]. It is difficult reporting on other students at the risk of their anger. It is quite hard to be a class monitor.... The biggest problem is discipline. Many students tend to arrive five or ten minutes late to classes, and I don't think it is easy to do anything about it. Many eat snacks during classes, which is not allowed, but that is really their own business. I'm not interested in taking charge of what they eat, or when they eat it! I'd say a degree of leniency is required [*bu hui guan tai duo le*]. It is sometimes easy to rule according to regulations, but then there are all the other difficult issues. For instance, the girls have some kind of conflict and they won't tell you what it is. So, I have to talk to them, try to figure out what it is, tell the teacher about it, but anyway.... I often end up saying that they should just ignore each other, or forget about the whole thing....

When I once again asked *why* this monitor position remained so popular when the potential advantages with regard to personal careers were limited and the personal problems of monitors seemed quite heavy, the female secretary who took part in the conversation took the word and responded in a very affirmative way: "Oh, they [the fellow students] are all concerned with face [*kandao biaomian*], but they do not know how it really is!" The male monitor interrupted her: "Because of all this trouble, I actually wanted to resign ... however, when students wrote my name on the ballots and the teacher wanted me to continue ... well, I guess it is a kind of a sense of responsibility...." It is understandable that students experiencing this kind of explicit support from their friends and fellow students, and even their teachers, would be tempted to take on this position of responsibility. It is obviously difficult, maybe impossible, to distinguish between explicit motives for becoming cadres and "inner" motivations that students were either not conscious of or did not intend to express openly. Most students, when asked directly, would refer to a personal sense of responsibility toward their classes or teachers, or they would emphasize that it was a learning process for them, a chance to practice leadership that would also improve their résumés at a later stage in their careers. A few would refer to their parents, who had told them that it was beneficial to take on a cadre position.

However, the fact that the position as class monitor was by and large the most popular of all cadre positions, regardless of all the hassles and dilemmas that came with it, suggested that an important motivation might also come from the implicit power that necessarily comes with a position that provides a formalized bond between an individual student and the class's homeroom teacher. It was the only position that provided a student with almost unlimited access to the homeroom teacher, the most influential of all teachers when evaluating students socially and academically in a range of different contexts. When students were dissatisfied with a teacher or with a certain regulation, they would sometimes talk to the class monitor and expect him or her to represent them and help solve the issue. The assumption was that because the class monitor and the homeroom teacher convened on a daily basis, there would be ample opportunity to take up issues that the students found relevant to raise. To what extent this happened in Number Two High almost entirely depended on the personal relationship between the class monitor and the homeroom teacher, and on the homeroom teacher's personality and interest in engaging with such issues that were sometimes far beyond what was expected of him or her. All homeroom teachers were burdened with heavy responsibilities, but quite a few of them nevertheless saw it as their duty to engage personally with student cadres in order, for instance, to help prevent individual students from dropping out of class or to resolve conflicts that may negatively affect individual students and their studies, discipline, or psychological well-being.

Although the class monitor was squeezed between fellow students and school authorities and teachers, many of them did enjoy a great deal of respect and sympathy from fellow students, often because they had been popular and well connected before being elected, but also because the new position gave them an air of importance as a direct link to the home-room teacher and to larger networks of cadres in other classes. For the class monitor himself or herself, the position provided an opportunity to practice organizational skills, and to many it was seen as a springboard to the next important step upward in the internal student hierarchy: To become a so-called high-level cadre (*gaoji ganbu*), as students jokingly, or sometimes mockingly, called the cadres of the student association. Most class cadres aspired to gain positions in this relatively new form of orga-nization within Number Two High, an organization that provided more options for student cadres to test and develop their abilities as organizers, to socialize with students from other classes, and to promote themselves individually in what was to them an entirely new experience of running for personal elections.

EXPERIMENTING WITH
DEMOCRACY: THE STUDENT ASSOCIATION

Experiments with student associations in high schools (and schools at other levels as well)[6] are part of a national policy to modernize the edu-cational system in the spirit of neosocialism and train young people to become citizens who actively take part in community work that is sanc-tioned by the authorities. Together with the Communist Party Youth League, which sometimes (though very rarely in the case of Number Two High) has its own activities for student members, it constitutes the only real possibility for full-time high school students to participate in any organizational collective activities with fellow students. Schools may allow other organizational activities, especially connected to charity or community work; however, such initiatives would normally be part of, or a subdivision of, the student association or the Youth League. All schools have at least one person who is charge of the Youth League members and activities connected to its students, and school authorities are obliged to also set up a student association. However, there is a very big difference between scope and content of activities in different schools, even within small townships such as Gaoshan.

One of the common features of the association is the principle (not necessarily practice) of recruitment through elections. The promotion of elections is based on the expectation that the association may work as a grassroots-level channel for spotting leadership talents and young people willing to put in extra efforts in the spirit of the common good. More important, though, controlled election procedures constitute a way of conducting top-down training of students to make them individually more assertive while remaining loyal to regulations and norms established by authorities, and it provides to students an image of democratic participation in decision-making processes. When carried out in practice, teachers inevitably bring in to the organizational practices their own experiences from an individualizing society, with rapid changes of family structures and increased demands on (and possibilities for) the individual in the labor market. The student association and its elections become in effect an arena for negotiations about which role the individual should and can play in school and in society.

Just like discourses on student cadres, scholarly and educational debates about the student association are colored by normative approaches emphasizing the association's intention to, and potential capacity for, building communal spirit among the young generation, which is commonly assumed to have become overly selfish.[7] "One of the fine goals of the student association in Number Two High is to counter widespread selfishness [*zisi*] among today's youth," Teacher Li, one of the administrators in charge of both the student association and the local Youth League, explained. The association should build a communal moral spirit and create an atmosphere in which students willingly work together with teachers to make the school a cleaner place and to organize sporting and cultural events. It also supplemented the student cadre system in its aim to work actively to build and maintain discipline among students, and although obviously the Youth League was in place in Number Two High, most of its work was channeled through the student association.[8] Teacher Li, himself a teacher in his early thirties who had graduated from a provincial university and advanced from full-time teaching to employment at the political bureau of the school, was made responsible for revitalizing Number Two High's student association in 2008. Up until then, the association had not yet held elections. Now, Teacher Li and four of his colleagues explained that it was finally time to teach rural students how to run an association. For that purpose, they needed to start experimenting with what they called "democratic elections." They insisted that as a rural school, Number Two High's students were naturally not used to presenting themselves in front of others; they were less confident, less advanced, less modernized than urban students; in other words, they were of a "lower quality" (*suzhi*), Teacher Li explained.[9]

By organizing elections, the teachers hoped to develop students' skills of self-presentation but also to identify and promote to higher cadre positions current student cadres who had the personal qualities needed to fill positions of trust in this formal association. The criteria for being eligible were largely similar to those used by homeroom teachers trying to identify potential class monitors. Teacher Li and his colleagues had the ambition to make the association more democratic (*minzhude*), to involve students more directly in its work, and to make sure that its members, and especially its leaders and those in cadre positions, would serve as role models. In line with official discourse, they repeatedly emphasized the moral obligations of students in the association to demonstrate collective spirit. At the same time, both the work of the association and the election processes were vivid examples of how views of the individual were negotiated and tested as much by the teachers in charge of the association and its elections as by students who had to present themselves to an audience in ways that were entirely new for them.

Organization and Practical Work

At the time of my fieldwork, the number of members in the student association in Number Two High was subject to certain changes, but there were usually approximately twenty-five members at any given time. Together, they represented the entire student body, though members were recruited only in grades 1 and 2, because third-year students were supposed to concentrate all their time and energy preparing for the university entrance exam. Of the twenty-five members, there were seventeen with the title of "student association cadre." Among them was the chairman (*zhuxi*), who was always a second-year student, the secretary, and the "heads of sections" (*buzhang*). About two-thirds of the cadres were male students, as was the chairman, though a bit more than half of all the students in the schools were girls. The cadres were elected every year, and after their election and the appointment of the chairman and secretary, the association went on to elect between eight and ten ordinary members (*chengyuan*). These members were commonly described as "assistants" (*ganshi*), because they assisted the heads of sections in their work. They were also sometimes called "reserve cadres" (*houbei ganbu*), and they would step into positions as cadres in case there was such a need. Consequently, the school trained, at an early stage, potential cadres for the coming year. Although there were formal elections, many of the assistants were in practice recruited by the chairman and the heads of sections long before elections. The cadres would find willing helpers for their sections among friends and classmates, and those who wanted a formal position as member of the student association would afterward try to get permission to run for election. This practice created quite a bit of uncertainty among students who had worked hard for the association as volunteers but feared they would fail at the ultimate test, namely, the election. Nonetheless, it concurrently strengthened the association as a venue for developing social connections and networks among students across the various classes.

I frequently talked to the heads of sections (there were several heads for each section in addition to a few helpers), and in the early days of my fieldwork they kindly organized, on their own initiative, a meeting especially for me. This was in order, they said, to get a chance to present and describe their work "as it really was." During this meeting, the presentations and following discussions took place in a mundane, rundown classroom with more than twenty student cadres and members of the association present. None of the teachers was present, but they had formally given their permission to hold this meeting. The student cadres had prepared their presentations, which were all characterized by what I thought was a remarkably strong emphasis on the disciplinary and governing aspects of their own work. This was a bit surprising for me, because the teachers responsible for the association were always attempting to play down the disciplinary aspects of the association's work in their talks with me. They would argue that it was much more important to focus on cooperation, student activities, sporting events, and other social activities than on the disciplinary aspects of the association's work. I had therefore expected the student cadres to repeat the same in a formally organized meeting with me.

It was the section for discipline and security (*jibaobu*) that was most explicit in its presentation of the disciplinary work it was supposed to carry out among fellow students. The head of the section, a very serious seventeen-year-old young man, explained:

We really have to help students control their own appearance. According to our regulations, boys may not grow long hair and girls may not perm or die their hair, nor may they wear earrings. Even after class, nobody is allowed to wear simple plastic sandals. Nobody may smoke, gamble or fight. We normally first warn students, and then, if they do not listen, we report to the teachers. The discipline section has one head of section, one vice-head, and two helpers, so we all need to assist each other in this work. At the same time, the student association has a circulating system of responsibility, so every week two new classes are responsible for helping us in our supervision work.

Members of the disciplinary section were busy and had multiple tasks to carry out. Therefore they were also assisted by all other members of the association in issuing warnings to students and maintaining discipline. Notwithstanding, the other sections of the association also strongly emphasized how their primary task was to assist in maintaining discipline among their fellow students. The head of the health section (*weishengbu*), for instance, explained that "our work is first and foremost to supervise (*jiandu*) the other students and make sure they maintain a neat and tidy appearance. We inspect the school areas, and organize cleaning shifts." Sporting activities were extremely popular, especially among the boys, and the physical education section (*tiyubu*) was centered on maintaining discipline in all aspects related to the students' compulsory physical activities:

Every morning when students get up, we have two members of the student association supervising each of the four buildings. The class currently in charge of discipline then ensures that all fellow students get out of bed. For the [obligatory] "morning runs," the student association also organizes the supervision. We also supervise and make students get started for the evening's "eye exercises" [*yanbao jiancao*]. At meal times, the student association supervises students to ensure no one goes elsewhere other than the cafeteria, or spends money buying snacks instead. If the school

organizes sporting events, as in basketball, or volleyball, then we assist in
maintaining discipline during the games.

Similarly, all section cadres had important functions in organizing fellow students. As "high-level cadres," they were responsible for organizing the (sub)ordinary class cadres to work together, for instance, to arrange cultural events in connection with festivals and national holidays (organized by the cadres in the "cultural entertainment section," *wenyubu*) or to decide on messages to be written on blackboards in the classes about patriotic campaigns or campaigns to plant trees (organized by the "propaganda section," *xuanchuanbu*).

Having completed their brief presentations about each section, the members of the student association raised questions directly to me and my Chinese research assistant. Students were especially eager to hear her views on the student association. She had herself been a high school teacher in China, but she had lived abroad for several years and was therefore to some extent able to compare Europe and China, something that students in general were very interested in. A few of the male students directly expressed a wish to use the platform of the student association for doing things other than simply supervising fellow students, and they explained that their impression from the Internet and popular TV series was that students "in the West" were "free" (*ziyou*). They extrapolated that Western students would have more options to decide what to do in a student association than they themselves had. They went on to ask if this was true, and they subsequently wondered if it *were* indeed true, how "foreign" (*waiguo*) schools were at all able to maintain discipline among their students. Despite both my Chinese assistant's and my own attempts to draw what we hoped was a nuanced picture of the difficulties of the responsibilities and duties facing student association members in democratic Western countries, most of the cadres in Number Two High were quick to conclude that in the West, students had much more freedom than they did. This, however, did not prevent them from finding that as members of the student association, their own disciplinary responsibilities toward fellow students had necessarily to be the most important part of their work. Some strongly defended the importance of their function as assistants to teachers in the disciplining of students, others expressed an almost fatalist view of simply having to obey and carry out whatever was expected of them; and others again were remarkably reflective regarding the precarious balance they experienced between top-down demands for performance and individual aspirations for representing students and making a difference. Some students expressed a keen interest in the potential implications of the student association being an association *for* students and run *by* students. Such expectations created uncertainties among teachers in charge, and the conflicts that evolved because of them were indicative of the tensions evolving around interpretations of just how much room for individual and collective student agency it was necessary, and desirable, to allow for in a rural school educating modern Chinese citizens.

In the first two years of my encounters with the cadres of the student association and its responsible teachers, there was an atmosphere of optimism and engagement in this new experiment. Gradually, though, the enthusiasm seemed to wane as the association's work in practice proved to be largely limited to keeping order. In the third year of my fieldwork, students in the association were kept busy with daily updates on a new large blackboard, placed in one of the corridors where practically all the more than one thousand students would pass by sometime during the day, listing by name students who had been too late for the morning runs, worn plastic sandals, talked in the dorm after lights were turned off, or broken other school rules. Because of the continuous pressure to act as student police, and the lack of real opportunities to do otherwise, the work in the association became fraught with dilemmas and difficulties for its members.

Maybe it was also for those reasons that one activity more than any other remained a highlight for all members and potential members, even for the teachers in charge of the association: namely the democratic elections. These elections stirred much more enthusiasm, excitement, and debates among students and teachers in charge of the association than I ever experienced in the daily work of the association members. In my interpretation, the reason for this was that the election processes constituted one of the few arenas in which both students and teachers were able to experiment with the form and genre of self-presentation and negotiate the role of the individual; what the individual should and could be, and how much room he or she had for raising issues of collective interest, not only within the formally acknowledged student association but in the general context of Chinese society.

Negotiating the Individual through Elections

From 2008 onward, elections for the student association in Number Two High became yearly activities that took quite some preparation and ran over several weeks for two subsequent periods, with one election for the student cadres and another for the student assistants. It was a long and complicated process, with several large meetings and discussions among students, and it was one of the few activities that did not imply any disciplinary work among fellow students for the cadres. For most who took part in it, it was clearly viewed as a welcome opportunity to observe friends and fellow students trying out the entirely new genre of self-presentation or to simply test one's own level of popularity. The process of election tended to take on a life of its own. Elections created excitement, engagement, and entertainment, all of which were rare commodities in the daily lives of the boarding school students. Teachers added importance to the elections by their serious involvement in the processes, which they presented to me as their own new experiment with grassroots democracy among a group of inexperienced and poorly educated rural students.

Teachers were almost as nervous as students about the outcome of the first elections, not because they worried about who would be elected (after all, their own influence in this regard was decisive), but because they were unsure about how students would respond to their calls for self-presentations and how they would manage to guide students properly thorough the process. I was warmly welcomed to follow the whole process, but admittedly my presence did probably nothing to diminish teachers' initial anxiety nor the students' excitement. However, because many students knew me quite well already, I made the same observation that I had when I first started sitting in on classes: after the brief initial thrill of having a foreigner present in the room, students and teachers became used to it. Unlike in the classes I normally followed, no one seemed to be bored during the elections, and therefore even those who did not know me from before very quickly became so engaged in the running of the elections they took no interest in me at all.

The young teachers in charge of organizing the first elections with individual self-presentations were stunned by the overwhelming interest among their students. Practically all of the 150 class cadres and current members of the student association had signed up in hope of being allowed to run for the election. This was far too large a number to handle for the few teachers in charge. Therefore, all homeroom teachers were asked to look carefully through the files of each student and give their own assessment regarding who would be proper candidates. Students' grades and study habits, records on their behavior, moral attitudes, and personal qualities were used as the basic criteria for the final selection of twenty-nine class cadre candidates representing all the first- and second-grade classes. Although voters were supposed to put their marks next to twenty-five of these names, a total of only between sixteen and twenty students would eventually be elected. The office for political education (*zhengjiaochu*), in consultation with the current chairman and secretary, would make the final decision about who would become cadres in the association. Depending on candidates' qualities, the political office, together with the chairman and secretary, would then decide how many students to choose. Thus, election results alone were never meant to decide the final outcome—something that again confirmed that for the school authorities, it was the very *process* of practicing organizing elections and negotiating self-presentations with students that was important. It was considered too risky to let the student vote alone decide the final outcome so votes were guiding, not decisive.

The young teachers in charge of the student association did not have a carefully prepared master plan for how things were to be done and worked out, except that they knew candidates had to be carefully screened before being allowed to run for election. They experimented with state-sanctioned grassroots organizational training, although they themselves had not received any specific training or clear political directives on how to do this. They largely had to base their practices on their own intuitions, values, and choices. Consequently, one of the most striking features of the two experimental election processes I observed was the ways in which students and teachers alike struggled to define the role of an individual association member. Like a student leader and activist of earlier times of Communist China (Shirk 1982, 155), successful candidates to the student association in the 2010s were told to put collective interests before individual ones. However, to a much larger extent than during the 1970s, student leadership candidates in the 2010s were not merely to be impersonalized models for others; they were compelled to demonstrate individual characteristics and self-initiative through self-presentations and a proved ability to create, on the spot, brief autobiographies. This did not imply that teachers or school authorities operated with an implicit notion of individual autonomy. It was imperative, at the same time, that candidates proved willing and able to adhere to authorities' rules and that they refrained from expressing what might be interpreted as individual political statements about the aims of the student association or students collective rights.

In the autumn evening of yet another round of elections, the cold and barren corridors were buzzing with voices of nervous candidates, running in and out of classrooms discussing and coordinating the evening's event with their equally excited supporters and audience. Five teachers, together with the student chairman, were preparing to take charge of the process. Arriving at the large classroom where elections were to take place, we were directed to our seats by members of the association. The teachers and I were, as usual, asked to sit in the front directly facing the speakers at a very close distance. The classroom was gradually filled with the students who were allowed to vote. Each class had been asked to select a certain number of class cadres who would represent their class by being allowed to vote, and in addition, all current members of the student association, the five teachers, and I were part of the electorate. We were given the list with the names of the twenty-nine students who had successfully passed the prescreening process, and we were instructed to vote for twenty-five of them after their self-presentations (after some discussion, though, I managed to avoid having to vote).

Students had prepared speeches on their own, and after a brief introduction by the chairman of the association, they were asked one by one to come up front and deliver their three-minute self-presentations (*ziwo jieshao*). Each time, when calling upon a new speaker, the chairman would ask the following speaker "to get prepared." The whole situation was a bit awkward, and the first candidates were literally shaking and showed other visible signs of being extremely nervous, as did the chairman who introduced them. All candidates had prepared short speeches, and they had learned them by heart so that they could recite them word for word. None of them brought any notes, but they depended completely on their memorized speeches. However, being exceptionally nervous, several of the first speakers froze in the middle of a sentence, completely unable to continue because they had forgotten one specific word of their prepared presentation. They were trying their best to emulate what they had been drilled to do during more than nine years in school: Learn a text by heart, recite it, and when asked a question, deliver an answer that is as close as possible to, and preferably exactly the same as, the original text.

But now, in this entirely new context of a student/teacher audience evaluating their performance in order to decide whether to put a vote next to their names, anxiety and excitement caused the speakers to forget the words they had so carefully prepared. One after the other, speeches were broken up with long pauses during which the audience seemed to hold their breaths, hoping for the friend or fellow student to quickly recover and continue. Some did manage to continue, while others had to give up entirely. We were anticipating no less than twenty-nine speakers, and time was quickly running out because of the prolonged breaks and returning moments of silence. Teacher Li could not let this go on, and in the fourth speech, frustrated, he jumped to his feet and interrupted, calling out to the whole audience:

> Now, wait a minute! Listen all of you, you shouldn't recite a prepared text, but simply *tell a bit about yourself*. Don't ask for other people to vote for you, and don't be so nervous [*jinzhang*]! You should just express yourself [*biaoxian ziji*]. And don't say that you want to be the leader of the association! We know that. Everybody wants that. Just *let us see who you are* [*jian ge mian*], and don't be so nervous. Don't simply recite something that you learned by heart! You are already cadres in your own classes, so we know you are good. You do not need to tell us this. What eventually counts is what you do in class, not so much what you say here. There will be more possibilities if you are not elected this time. Our school is not the best, we all know this, our marks are not the best, but our abilities are strong [*nengli bijiao qiang*]!

After this intervention, speeches continued, but now students were even more nervous, having just been told that they were not supposed to deliver their prepared speeches but had to improvise and focus more on themselves.

Up to this intervention, prepared speeches had largely echoed the politically correct discourse on the learned and morally responsible citizen taught, for instance, in the political courses, or the national calls for raising the quality especially of "rural students" such as themselves. This was not very surprising, considering the fact that all candidates were carefully selected class cadres. However, the intervention of the teachers, and the special circumstances the students found themselves in now—being explicitly told to "present themselves" and let the audience "get to know them"—not only encouraged but compelled them to redirect the focus of their presentations toward *themselves*. Therefore, rather than talking about how the quality of students in general should be raised, as they were used to hearing from teachers or during meetings, nearly all of them now started to emphasize how, if elected, the student association would help *themselves personally* to raise their *own* quality (*tigao ziji de suzhi*). They would list the qualities they saw in themselves by using adjectives such as "responsible," "hard-working," "reliable," "extroverted" (*xingge waixiang*), or "humorous." Speakers would furthermore draw attention to additional qualities they found important to develop, or improve, in themselves through work in the association, such as courage, self-improvement (*tigao ziji*), self-training (*duanlian ziji*), trust in myself (*xiangxin ziji*), making fellow students trust me (*rang tongxuemen xiangxin*), or learning how to be a good friend.

Nearly all speeches emphasized how the things they would do for others and for the association (parents or the nation were rarely mentioned) would indeed be good for themselves and their own self-development. In this way, student formulations resonated with the state's modernization discourse on how the improvement of the nation and its people depends on *each individual* citizen's quality and self-development (e.g., Tyl 2002), but they downplayed the collective responsibility toward the nation that textbooks and official discourse on moral education so strongly emphasized (e.g., Nie 2008; Vickers 2009a). It was striking to witness the extent to which a confident self and the ability to conduct self-evaluations were qualities that were emphasized by both teachers and students, while state and nation were virtually ignored in the vast majority of speeches. Students were much less concerned with paraphrasing the modernization discourse on quality in general than with finding ways to express and evaluate their own personal qualities and potential for self-development.

There were no obvious gender differences in the choices of expressions and wording, but there were other markers of gender stereotypes:

Female students tended to be much more interested in running for positions related to culture, and there were several instances when their male peers in the audience demanded that a female candidate sing a song in addition to her prepared speech. Young men never received such requests, and in their speeches they were more likely than girls to point out that they were good at "managing" (*guanli*) fellow students, interested in the sporting activities of the association, especially in the highest levels of leadership.

In combination, the content of the speeches, their deliveries, the perception of them, and not the least, the teacher interventions could be interpreted as expressions of a tension between the implicit call for greater emphasis on self-promotion and belief in the individual's ability to be self-made and authorities' demand to keep such expressions under firm control and promote feelings of collective spirit and responsibility. Students had explicitly been asked to present themselves and their reasons for running for election; nevertheless, whenever one of them began to suggest how the association might be improved or change its work in new directions of common interest to students, he or she was firmly interrupted and encouraged to stay focused on the self-presentation. This was exemplified by one of the interventions, which followed an odd period of ten to fifteen minutes during which candidates were presenting themselves while at the same time three of the teachers on the front bench were talking more and more intensely, and rather loudly, among themselves. The teachers' body language strongly suggested that they were debating something that had to do with the student presentations, and, suddenly, in the middle of a speech, one of them jumped up and called out in a loud voice, "Now your speeches are really getting too long, and the topics too big [*tai da le*]! You should not talk about what the student association is, or what it should become! Just stick to your self-presentation. Say something about *what is special about you* [*ziji you shenme tedian*], and the shorter the better!"

The candidates were then encouraged to demonstrate that they were "self-secure" and able "to present themselves." Again and again, through the election processes, teachers (sometimes supplemented by the male student chairman of the association) interrupted speeches to explain that a candidate should not talk about the association as such, nor about how to improve it, or why he or she wanted to be the chairman. Candidates should simply make "presentations of themselves," stay focused on how to "improve themselves," and show that they "believed in themselves." A common appeal from teachers and the chairman rang, "Don't be so nervous, just trust that you are the best!" (*xiangxin ni ziji zui bang de*). After more than four hours of speeches and interventions, everyone put their marks on the list with names, and teachers together with the current student leaders of the association went to the office to count the votes and discuss how it had all gone. At this point, teachers explained to me that there was really no need to base the final decision on how students voted, because they would by all means simply vote for their best friends and those who were most popular. Students who took part in the counting were firmly instructed to keep the voting results secret and under no circumstances reveal the result to their peers. This would only stir discussions, misery, and eventually jealousy, teachers explained. If no one knew the result, teachers, in agreement with the current student leaders, would be free to choose those who were the most competent for the job.

There was also general agreement among teachers in charge that some immediate changes to the process were needed. It was decided that despite what had earlier been announced, the chairman would now be appointed among all selected cadres only after some weeks of practice in the association, wherein teachers would have a chance to better observe how each student worked. It was also clear that in the next round of elections, students should not simply vote for the students they liked most and thought gave the best performance, but should rather give points from one to ten to each speaking candidate. And finally, teachers agreed, they needed to explain more clearly to future candidates what kind of speeches they were supposed to make.

Although it would in fact have been easy for teachers to simply let the students do what they were accustomed to, namely learn a written text by heart and deliver a set of politically correct statements about how they wanted to serve the collective, teachers chose a more difficult way. They nurtured the idea of building what they perceived as a properly "modern" and "democratizing" student association. Such an association, they found, needed elections based on self-presentations delivered in an unconstrained way. In subsequent rounds of elections that I was able to follow, teachers were careful to start out by introducing to the candidates the desired format of speeches: "Do not learn a text by heart, but speak more freely [*bu yao bei, yao ziran yidianr*]; do not stop if you suddenly do not remember what you planned to say, but just keep talking about your-self; do not argue about how you want to improve the work of the student association; you should tell us something about yourself, and let us get to know who you are." In other words, there was a continuous focus on the individual as a subject who should develop the qualities of being capable of self-presentation, having self-initiative, and taking personal responsi-bility, but without crossing the line at which authority was challenged and the individual started to require collective rights.

What is it like to be a student with this kind of responsibility? Prob-ably no one experienced these dilemmas more urgently than the few who managed to get into the desired position as chairman of the student asso-ciation. In this respect, the various chairmen of Number Two High's stu-dent association shared experiences with chairmen from higher levels of education, including China's most respected elite universities. In a Cen-tral China TV (CCTV) talk show from May 2012, the popular celebrity host Sa Beining took up the topic of personal and professional challenges for chairmen of student associations.[10] He had invited former and current chairmen of different generations, and one of the questions raised in the show was whether a chairman is—and should first of all be—student or cadre. A survey had shown that many students suspect their chairman of being corrupt and abusing his or her position, implying that the chair-man is regarded by other students as a cadre. Consequently, the personal challenges, sometimes even agonies, that chairmen experienced were considerable compared to student representatives. This dilemma of being both a student representative and a student cadre with leadership respon-sibilities also became very clear during longer conversations I had with one former chairman after his graduation from Number Two High. I had already talked several times with this student, but it was especially after graduation that he really started to reflect on his own role as chairman and the challenges for students and their leaders as he had experienced them.

The Insights of a Chairman

Huiliang was a mild and friendly boy, seventeen years old, with parents and an older sister working in a factory in Shanghai. With his parents working far away, Huiliang, like so many of his peers, came home to an empty house every weekend, but he frequently visited and dined with uncles and aunts in the township. Huiliang was ambitious, and at first he had been very disappointed that his marks from the high school entrance exam had only allowed him to get into Number Two High: "My uncle had already warned me there was no hope [*mei you xiwang*], because my marks from junior secondary school were not so good, but I nevertheless thought that I would do better on the final exam," he said. Nonetheless, Number Two High had proved to be a school of his liking, first because of the good possibilities for making friends and building social networks, second because many of the teachers were quite nice and supportive, he explained. With his outgoing and friendly personality, Huiliang quickly became popular among peers and teachers alike, and he was elected as class monitor in his first year. In his second year, he was then selected as chairman of the student association. When he graduated from Number Two High, Huiliang was experienced and had become more mature, and he clearly felt much freer than during earlier years to speak openly about his experiences and views.

When I met Huiliang shortly after the results of the university entrance exam were announced, he had still not recovered from this second educational disappointment. He was no different from the majority of graduates from Number Two High who scored below 350 points, but unlike many of his friends he was thoroughly disappointed that he got only 330 when at least 600 points were needed to get into a top university in the humanities stream that he had followed. In fact, no students from Number Two High even came close to that score in 2010 or 2011. Huiliang had not aimed at a national key university (none of the students I talked to at Number Two High had any such ambitions or hopes), but he was disappointed that he would now qualify only for what was considered to be a low-level college. Although his parents were willing to pay for an extra year in a private school (*fudu xuexiao*) to give him a chance to do better in the next year's national exam, Huiliang was not motivated to do this. He would prefer to apply for whatever school he could get in to with his 330 points. His plan was to subsequently try to use his experiences as cadre and chairman in some kind of charity or voluntary work that his older sister who was working in the provincial capital had told him about. In this way, he explained, "at least something good would come out of the tough experiences I had as a chairman and class monitor!"

What did he mean by tough experiences? Huiliang accounted for this in a quiet and serious way, without boasting of his own role or being condescending toward other students. He showed how conscientious students in the student association's leadership positions almost inevitably ran into considerable social and personal problems, because of the inescapable dual expectation to serve the school authorities in their work to maintain discipline and to work in the interests of fellow students:

> The main problem [of the student association] is that it is so unclear what the real purpose of it is. I had a lot of energy in the beginning when I was elected, and I really wanted to do something. But things just became worse and worse. The teachers we were supposed to work together with largely decided everything, and they found that the main purpose of the association was for us to help them control and administer fellow students. But discipline [*jilü*] is really quite bad at Number Two High, because so many students don't really want to study; and therefore they are also difficult to control.

He went on to tell how this situation gradually made the student leaders of the association increasingly unpopular among fellow students. These student cadres, who had been selected as leaders partly *because* they were socially well liked and had good student networks, now lost their popularity because of the top-down demands on them to control and rule fellow students and friends. His friend, the female secretary, ran into big personal problems because of this pressure when some boys who were not members of the association started to treat her badly. She eventually quit the association, as did several other cadres during the year when Huiliang was the chairman: "The pressure was too big [*yali tai da*], and it was just too much hardship [*tai xinku le*]." Nevertheless, Huiliang and the other cadres did not inform their teachers about how bad the situation had become for them because they were afraid that this would just make it worse. Huiliang himself lost a great number of friends and was never able to repair those relationships, but at least he kept six or seven friends who continued to support him. During his year in grade 3, he explained, things got a bit better again because by then everyone was absorbed in studying for the national exam.

When first running for elections, students like the female secretary and

Huiliang had shared a wish to work for student interests in closer cooperation with teachers (never imagining otherwise) and other students.
Based on my prolonged conversations with many of these student cadres,
I see no reason to assume that this was not true, or that they would have
joined the association merely for "selfish" or "self-promotional" reasons,
as they are so often criticized for. However, students were not given room
for working collectively in the interest of fellow students and they became
disillusioned, as Huiliang mused:

> Many students thought that the cadres in the student association decided
> much more than we actually did. Therefore, they contacted us because
> they wanted us to do a lot of different things. They wanted us to promote
> their interests, and help them when they had all kinds of problems. How
> could we do that? In reality, the student association has no possibility at all
> to do anything about these things. Our suggestions were not followed up
> on by the political office. Some said that our work should focus on the stu-
> dents themselves [*yi xuesheng wei zhu*], but that was just impossible. . . .
> We had huge conflicts [*maodun hen da*], and everybody had their own
> points of view [*mei ge ren you mei ge ren de xiangfa*]. The student associa-
> tion should change. There has to be real cooperation between teachers and
> students, and the student association should not be asked to administer
> and control fellow students.

Having mounted this explicit criticism toward the student association's
first and foremost function as a disciplinary institution, requiring student cadres to govern their fellow students' conduct, Huiliang brought
up another topic that had created heated debates in the school and that
echoed the dominant discourse in contemporary China on the educational
failures of students who attend vocational rather than regular schools.
Huiliang referred to the incident described in chapter 1, when a group of
parents demanded that vocational students be physically separated from
their own children in regular classes, and he again demonstrated his interest in building student collectives and "unity" rather than merely working
for individual self-interest:

> Many in this school think that it was due to the vocational classes that
> many students were naughty [*tiaopi*]. They enrolled with lower marks

than us; they had a smaller curriculum; and they were more relaxed in their attitude towards studying. Some of them were indeed naughty. Many family heads [*jiazhang*] did not even want us to socialize with the students from the vocational classes. I think the student association is going to change, now that we will no longer have vocational classes and there will be even greater focus on studies. But I think the vocational students were much more united [*tuanjie*] than we were in the regular classes. You could see this especially during sporting events when they really supported each other and united. This was because the vocational students were more relaxed in their studies, and therefore avoided many of the conflicts that we had. They also united as a group because they knew that everybody else had a tendency to look down on them just because they were vocational students.

In accordance with these views, Huiliang and some other students had in several contexts expressed their interest in using the association as a forum for working collectively and in support of general student interests. However, because teachers feared that student activities may turn out to be "unhealthy" (*bu jiankang de*)—a synonym for almost anything that went against the decisions of a given authority—student leaders, and the association as such, were kept on a very short leash. This probably helps explain why it was the teachers themselves who during the election processes strongly promoted a focus on the individual and called for purely personalized self-presentations. Huiliang, with his experience as chairman, argued instead for the need for breaking down stereotypes of "bad students" being collectively categorized as "bad *people*", and for "uniting" students in the same way as those who were stigmatized did on their own initiative. This complicates the widespread images of the student cadre being an ambitious, power-seeking, and self-absorbed individual, willing and able to first of all serve and support existing hierarchies. But it also raises interesting questions regarding the larger outcome of organizational training of neosocialist citizens in the Chinese state school under the profound influence of authoritarian individualization processes in Chinese society.

The student cadre system, the student association, and the Communist Party's Youth League are forms of organization that are integrated into the educational activities of hundreds of thousands of schools all over China, yet they have rarely been studied from within. Taken together, they may be seen to reflect the sociopolitical hierarchy of the broader Chinese administrative system (the student cadre system), the dominance of the Communist Party (the Youth League), and the contemporary societal experiments with grassroots influence through elections (the student association). By means of these forms of organization, the coming generation of Chinese citizens are trained to both contribute to and adapt to the development of a neosocialist China. Students are subjected to a kind of citizen training through practice, and ideally they learn to rule themselves and others under the guidance of their teachers.

The organization of students in student associations and as cadres may be perceived as part of the government's long-term strategy of building a form of "consultative authoritarianism" whereby societal actors and groups of particular importance to the maintenance of political stability are included in political processes and consulted, for instance, through experiments with local elections or public fora for input on infrastructure projects (He and Thøgersen 2010). Through the practices of the student association especially, both school authorities and the school branch of the Communist Party Youth League are supposed to gain more insight into the lives and views of students, who ideally are (admittedly on a very small scale) to be consulted in matters of relevance to the leadership of school and party. Thus, the organizational forms open up for some degree of consultancy, although the ultimate aim is to use this form of "democratization" to secure the authority of the party (and school) leadership.

There is no detailed political or educational master plan dictating how teachers should carry out their part of this work. Therefore, interestingly, the young teachers in charge of the student association in Number Two High intuitively resorted to a language of controlled individualism, adopting an ideology of the self-made and self-reliant individual through their continual pressure on students to create autobiographies and focus on themselves through election processes. At the same time, they were deeply afraid of the possibility that students might use this self-assertiveness to argue for collective interests through the student association and eventually challenge the authority of the teachers in charge of the association and the youth league, and more generally the school leadership's authority. Students represented a wide range of motivations about being student cadres in class and in the student association, from individualistic hopes for improving their careers to ambitions of promoting collective interests. Such motives are by no means necessarily exclusive; and given more room for action it is not unlikely that students who are continually taught to rely on themselves (whether through the examination system, training during elections, pep rallies, or the lack of a comprehensive social security system) would use this self-assertion in specific situations not merely to work on the basis of selfish interests, which is so commonly assumed, but to channel their expectations into more collective actions aimed at broader student interests.

CHAPTER 4

MOTIVATION AND EXAMINATION

The Making and Breaking of the Individual

A prominent emphasis on individual achievement in the contemporary Chinese state school is manifested in motivational activities, including the examination system. It is expressed in a complex web of pressures (*yali*), goals (*mudi*), responsibilities (*zeren*), and dreams (*meng*). Although an extreme focus on the individual's own abilities, achievements, and self-improvement may seem to contradict the political authorities' attempts to build a common collective morality through campaigns and textbooks, this is in fact a logical outcome of the Chinese path of authoritarian individualization and, at least in the short run, a convenient one for the party-government.

In China's reform era the most important institutional changes have been designed to "encourage, push, or even force the individual to be more self-reliant and proactive" (Yan 2012b, 9). Individual agency has never been more cherished, and the meaning of personal achievement has shifted from the collective—whether family, local community, or the state—to the individual. The state school is constructed as a collective in which groups of people, such as administrators, teachers, students, and parents, ideally strive together toward the common goal of producing learned, competent, moral, and nationalist citizens (see Yan 2012b on the Chinese "striving individual"). Within this collective endeavor, contemporary practices of education also demonstrate a fixation on personal achievement. This is, at the same time, an expression of teachers' subjective search for solutions to counter waning motivation among students, and a convenient—possibly even desired—outcome of the government's attempt to build neosocialist citizens in an era of rapid individualization.

An emphasis on individual achievement has for a long time been integral to the Chinese education system, through its persistent focus on individual examination and examination results and the general lack of teamwork and collective problem solving as a method of teaching. Today, however, the final examinations are not in themselves enough to ensure the desired individual spirit of consistent effort and striving to be successful. With growing expectations for educational success from parents, teachers, and leadership, schools need to experiment with new motivational activities. This is when teachers experience (as they did in the classroom teaching situations discussed in chapter 2) that it often works best to appeal to students' personal interests and emotions.

THE BLESSING AND CURSE
OF THE EXAMINATION SYSTEM

The test-driven nature of Chinese schools has been one of the most debated and criticized aspects of the education system, and there are continually suggestions within China to reconsider the consequences of the high school and university entrance examinations, as well as calls to reform their content and form.[1] When I asked teachers at Number Two High what they would change about their school and the education system if they had the power to do so, most of them pointed to the examination system, as did this male biology teacher in his late twenties:

The examination system! It is really difficult to be a good teacher because we always have to think about the results [chengji] rather than the process [guocheng]. Everything we do is aimed at the results. It is also the only thing parents care about, and what the education bureau is concerned about. They put a lot of pressure on the school. Many students have different kinds of personal interests, but they are prevented from pursuing them in high school, and slowly but surely, they lose interest. Everybody talks about quality education [suzhi jiaoyu], but as long as we have the national entrance examination as it is now, we cannot put quality into practice.

Similarly, most of the teachers I talked to found that examinations determined nearly every activity at school, limiting their own possibilities of teaching for any other purpose than exams that are based on the exact content of textbooks. At the same time, they would quickly point out to me that with China's large population, and the consequential immense pressure on the education system, there was not really any alternative to the final testing of students on a national examination based almost exclusively on textbook content. Despite local variations, the entrance examination gave, at least in principle, a degree of equal opportunity to youth across the country. Many teachers, as well as school administrators, nurtured and expressed strong opinions on this issue, revealing a most ambivalent relationship toward the examination system.

This, of course, is nothing new. The practice of examination has a long historical trajectory as a technology of governing in China (e.g., Kipnis 2011, 7), and although it was heavily criticized among teachers at Number Two High, there is little doubt that it enjoys a high degree of educational and political legitimacy in China. There has been widespread public critique of the unfortunate side effects of the Chinese examination system, but nevertheless, "its basic legitimacy seems to be intact" (Thøgersen 2002, 210). To both adult examiners and young examinees, "examination-based forms of performance audit, or forms of audit that are scored like exams" still seem reasonable (Kipnis 2011, 169). Likewise, it appears that a majority of Chinese education researchers are in favor of maintaining the system of national entrance exams, and one of its (critical) defenders argues, for instance, that "what we need is not to vehemently criticize the entrance exam at every turn, but rather from an in-depth, calm and objective perspective to rationally appraise, understand, and reform it" (Zheng 2010, 11).

Within Number Two High, students complained a great deal about the continuous pressure of examinations, which mainly tested their individual abilities to memorize large parts of the curriculum. At the same time, students had been accustomed to this practice since primary school, and they did not envision any realistic or even clearly desirable alternative to it. They found it to be relatively fair (*gongping*), although they often pointed to the unfair realities they were facing as rural students who had fewer chances of enrolling in the better urban schools because of their household registrations and social backgrounds. To some extent their perceptions have been supported by research findings. Confirming research from the early 1980s (Kwong 1983), a recent study by Hannum, Park, and Cheng (2011) of two thousand poor, rural children in Gansu showed that inequalities in education are shaped long before students reach the final and determining examinations. Educational inequalities are created by the same kind of socioeconomic disparities that influence education patterns in other parts of the world, and the high-stakes Chinese examination system is concurrently both a barrier to and an opportunity for social mobility of disadvantaged rural students (Hannum et al. 2011).

There is no reason to expect that eventual (and indeed likely) future reforms to downplay requirements for memorization in favor of more analytic skills will serve to improve equal opportunities for children of different social and economic backgrounds (Y. Wang and Ross 2010; Hannum et al. 2011). To the contrary, it seems to be in the interest of rural parents and their children to maintain a system of examination that is based on memorization and testing of textbook knowledge because these forms of learning require less assistance from parents (Kipnis 2001). Regardless of what objectively may be in the interests of rural parents and their children, it was a common view among both students and teachers at Number Two High that, with all its faults and built-in problems, a national examination based on quantifiable test results of each individual was the fairest system for selecting and grouping students into colleges and universities. It was also, in their view, the only realistic one to implement in contemporary China.

In conclusion, the examination system is a historically tested tool for governing students and making them disciplined subjects who also practice a high degree of self-discipline; it is a globally employed technique that is gaining rather than losing importance; and it is supported by many parents, teachers, educational authorities, even students themselves, as a familiar and comparatively fair practice. It is a system that is likely to remain in existence for quite some time, and that in addition to determining mobility and access to higher studies serves to emphasize the responsibility of the individual and push for the recognition of individual achievement. As such, it remains a basic motivating force in the Chinese high school.

Hardly a day passed at Number Two High without somebody mentioning the national entrance examination, the final high school examinations (*huikao*), or one of the numerous smaller tests that directed students' studies throughout the year. A lot was at stake for students and their parents—and for teachers whose salaries and promotions partly depended on their students' examination results—during the most intense examination periods. Yet, the pressure on students at Number Two High was not comparable to what has frequently been reported from urban and more elitist schools in other parts of the country. There was, for instance, a long way from Number Two High to the urban crying mothers and rich fathers desperately promising expensive cars as presents to teachers if their children would pass the exam successfully (Lafraniere 2009); or the celebrations of students in Beijing who score well above 600 points for the national key universities and whose mothers would call other mothers to competitively compare their children's results (Rabkin 2011). I also never heard of schools in Gaoshan that went to the extremes of a high school in Xiaogan municipality in Hubei that not only permitted but actively helped to organize intravenous amino acid injections in order to supply students with energy while they were studying for the final exam;[2] the realities of Number Two High and other schools in Gaoshan municipality were certainly very different from a poor rural county in Gansu that earned the name of "*Gaokao* county" after its repeated success in the national university entrance exam (Y. Wang and Ross 2010).

Like other students in China, third-year students at Number Two High would choose whether to take the examination aimed at the four-year *benke* studies in the top universities (*yi ben*), bachelor *benke* in one of the other universities (*er ben*), or the normally three-year *zhuanke* course of study (*san ben*). In 2011, the maximum possible score for the top universities was 810, for *er ben* 750, and for *san ben* or the *zhuanke* studies it was 550. In the same year in Zhejiang, a total of 338 students passed the threshold for one of the prestigious *yi ben* universities, but none of them came from Number Two High, where the highest score was 516. To pass for a *benke* study in an *er ben* university, a student normally needed at least 400 points, and in 2011, there were about forty Number Two High students, out of the total number of three hundred graduates, who qualified for this kind of study, in general the best Number Two High students and their parents could hope for. The Number Two High student with the highest score at the examination for *er ben* universities had 483 points, which on a national level was not considered to be especially high.

Both in 2009 and 2011, when I was at Number Two High during the period when results of the university entrance exam were announced, students and teachers expected the school's total results to turn out more or less like they did. Many students were disappointed, but fewer surprised, about their own results. As students at a regular rural high school, most of them had expected to score relatively low as compared to their peers in the local or provincial key point high schools, and most of their parents (according to students themselves) were prepared for this. Therefore, compared to some of the more widely known extreme examples of pressure and excitement related to the examinations, students at Number Two High experienced a more moderate degree of study pressure at home and at school. Apart from third-year students who were approaching the final half-year before their exams, few students seemed to spend all their waking hours studying.

Nevertheless, there was no doubt that many experienced and felt what they themselves regarded as a high level of psychological pressure to perform and succeed. This was primarily a result of feeling that they ought to live up to parents' expectations and were continually told how important this final exam was for determining their own lives and therefore also the future livelihoods of their families. They all knew that they were unlikely to make it to one of the prestigious universities in China, and many were not even convinced that they would get into relatively good provincial schools. They were very uncertain about what their examination results would bring and what their later job possibilities would be. They were pushed to work hard for the examination, but they often lacked the personal motivation for doing so.

This was acknowledged as a problem by teachers and school administrators alike. They were therefore struggling with how to develop students' motivation beyond the mere carrot-and-stick of the final examination. In lieu of better alternatives within the education system itself, they set their hopes on more unorthodox solutions provided by the emerging capitalist market in the larger Chinese society. The young staff responsible for the school's political education (including the activities and elections for the student association) were encouraged by the school leadership to find new ways to motivate students to perform better. From colleagues at other schools and from advertisements, they had heard about the "inspirational lectures" that Wang Guoquan's company was offering to schools all over the country. The company's credentials were backed by the fact that other schools had positive experiences with them and the announcements on their web site that other educational bureaus and student associations openly recommended them. The staff in the political section believed that this kind of inspirational lecture would serve as a welcome alternative to ordinary classes or the staff's own means of encouraging students to study harder. Consequently, teachers got approval from the school leadership to hire a lecturer from Wang's company in 2008. All classes and their home-room teachers were invited to the lectures, which exact content no one I talked to beforehand was aware of or familiar with.

PEP RALLIES: OLD MESSAGE IN NEW WRAPPING?

Students at Number Two High were accustomed to continual reminders that they needed to "study hard" (haohao xuexi) and to strive for academic success, which would presumably get them more secure jobs and better incomes, lives, and social status than their parents had. In this atmosphere of modernist belief in continual progress and collective improvement of lives through individual efforts, students were expected to feel motivated by their luck at having made it to a regular, rather than a vocational, high school. This would provide them with the privilege of participating in a final competition—the examination—that could potentially bring them to even higher levels of progress if only they would work hard enough for it. Students had, from the onset in primary school, listened to their teachers heralding this message, and all had taken part in numerous school meetings in which school authorities, teachers and administrators did their very best to convince them to strive harder. It was therefore hardly surprising that students at Number Two High were displaying little enthusiasm when in autumn 2008 they were told to gather in the school's lecture hall for yet another meeting aimed at encouraging them to study harder.

The first meeting was for all the third-year students, who by that time were studying six days a week at school for the final exam, with only Sundays to visit their relatives. In the lecture hall they were greeted by a large red banner informing them that this was to be a "Large-Scale Lecture to Fulfill Aspirations" and help them "Use the Spirit of the Olympics to Challenge Your Limits During the 2009 National Higher Education Exam." Students I conversed with while we were looking for our seats in the lecture hall dreaded yet another boring meeting with long moralistic lectures about the importance of studying hard for the exam.

The meeting started as everyone had expected: Two men from the school's political section solemnly introduced the aim of the lecture, and explained, to the sound of widespread sighing, yawning, and mumbling, that today an invited guest would help the students to improve self-discipline and provide them with tools that would enable them to study harder. Students were far from enthusiastic. The atmosphere quickly changed, though, when to everybody's surprise a young charismatic man walked on stage, immediately starting to tell jokes at an incredible speed and in a loud and engaging voice. To student audience's spontaneous reactions of "Wow" and "Ooh, so young," Mr. Zhang introduced himself as a student of philosophy, psychology, and religion, and someone who had spent "a lot of time abroad" (though to what extent, or to where were not specified). He continued warming up students by evoking laughter from jokes with sexual connotations and telling funny stories about his own and other students' personal mistakes and failures. He made the audience cheer, shout, and clap their hands; and when he had about five hundred students and teachers eating out the palm of his hand, he started to introduce a range of emotional appeals. Before returning to the form and content of these, let us first take a closer look at the kind of private company Number Two High had hired and the potential impact of this kind of private motivational meeting in the broader context of Chinese education.

The web page "Chinese Net for Inspirational Lectures" (*Zhongguo lizhi yanjiang wang*) presents the lectures and ideas of Mr. Wang Guoquan.[3] According to Wang himself, in 2004 he was the first in China to offer "inspirational lectures on the entrance examination" (*gaokao lizhi yanjiang*). Thanks to his entrepreneurship, oratory skills, and flair for identifying topics that appealed to students' emotions and concerns, he managed during the following nine years to build a successful company that offered lectures and courses to students and teachers all over the country on how to improve self-discipline or learn to speak (and speak well) in public. Wang also trained a number of young people to carry out speeches as he did, and it was one of his trainees, the twenty-four-year-old Mr. Zhang, who came to Number Two High in the autumn of 2008 to deliver two motivational speeches for students and afterward sell small self-help booklets produced by Wang.[4] On these occasions, students and teachers at Number Two High experienced a similar kind of motivational pep rally that millions of other students and teachers around the country have attended at some stage during their studies.

According to the web page, Mr. Wang and his staff have given lectures, speeches, and courses at thousands of schools in rural and urban areas, not the least in Zhejiang, where Mr. Wang's business originally started. Wang himself has organized summer camps teaching rhetorical skills; he has lectured at government offices and participated in shows on China Central TV stations. Additionally, he has been a teacher for staff in the Communist Party Youth League at provincial levels, and a number of educational bureaus and student associations now promote his lectures on their web sites. By 2008, Wang's company had lectured for more than three million people (Wang 2008, back cover), and in 2011 alone, Wang's company gave forty-eight lectures around the country, each time entertaining an audience of between 400 and 2,200 people (most with 1,300 to 1,500 students attending). In summer 2012, Wang announced on his website that because of "constraints of time and energy" he was organizing his final summer camp. At this time, he had become something of a celebrity in his field. His intense and emotional appeals regarding self-improvement and the building of self-discipline had already reached a very broad Chinese audience, especially of young people, through his own lectures or those of his protégés.

Wang's business success was partly based on his ability to identify a popular demand for new motivational activities that could push each student to study harder for the high-stakes university entrance exam; this remained a key topic of a majority of his and his trainees' lectures. The two motivational lectures I attended at Number Two High in 2008 were indeed an old message in new wrappings. At a general level, the message to students was to study hard and keep focused on the one major goal within reasonable sight: the exam. This message was delivered in a populist form of what is probably best described as a pep rally, or a mass suggestive meeting consciously appealing to the audience's emotions and actively stirring their enthusiasm in support of the messages delivered by the lecturer. Additionally, the message about the need to study hard was wrapped into—and at times overshadowed by—a range of advice, suggestions, and entertaining stunts aimed at promoting self-improvement, self-discipline, and ultimately individual success.

TACKLING PRESSURE BY
IDENTIFYING GOALS AND CREATING DREAMS

The stark contrast between the entertaining form of the short pep rallies and the monotonous daily life at school was striking, and this probably helps to explain why it took Mr. Zhang only a few minutes to get the students shouting and screaming, willingly taking part in all his stunts and repeating his self-building mantras. I was also, quite reluctantly, directly drawn into the show when Mr. Zhang in the rally for the first- and second-year students ordered one of the students to run through the audience and pick a teacher to come on stage. The lecture hall filled with noise of cheering and clapping when a student ran through the entire hall down to the back seats in order to pick me to join him. On stage, we were told to perform a small ritual. The boy had to show me respect by bowing toward me, and I, performing as the teacher I was not, was instructed to give him some encouraging advice: tell him to study hard and do his best to be successful. The most surprising part of this few-minutes-long stunt was probably that we were then asked to give each other a hug as a confirmation of our "deal" that the student would indeed do his best, while I would continue to encourage him. I had hardly ever seen this kind of physical expression of emotion or relationship displayed in public in Gaoshan, except on the popular dating programs or soap operas on TV, and it created a huge roar and laughter from the audience. It was clearly a powerful device of the lecturer to ensure the students' interest, demonstrating to them that this meeting was something out of the ordinary, and therefore worth listening to.

"What is your dream, what is your goal?" Mr. Zhang shouted in the lecture for the third-year students, asking the chairman of the student association to come on stage. Standing on a table, she explained that her dream was to get into Fudan University. Although several students in the audience jeered and sneered at such an ambitious and mostly likely unattainable goal, Mr. Zhang instead asked how many points she needed to pursue that aim. She responded that to the best of her knowledge she would need at least 533 points, which was far beyond her own prognosis of somewhere around 430 points in the best-case scenario. Mr. Zhang encouraged her to keep trying nevertheless, commending her for having an ambitious dream and asking her to conclude by shaking hands with as many students in the audience as possible, telling each of them to study hard. "Be aware of your goal and pursue it relentlessly" was Mr. Zhang's repeated advice.

Although giving his audience the impression that he was talking freely and spontaneously introducing his topics and stunts, the rhythm of Mr. Zhang's lecture was clearly carefully designed to first build up students' interest and remove whatever initial skepticism they might have to yet another meeting encouraging them to study. Subsequently, and only when he had made sure that students were fully engaged and attentively listening did Mr. Zhang start adding more seriously expressed advice and suggestions on how they should proceed with their studies. Although the contents of the messages delivered throughout the lecture were often long-winded, verbatim citations from the booklet sold to students afterward, they were delivered in a way that succeeded in momentarily engaging students actively through entertainment and high-pitched emotional appeals.

The lecture directly targeted issues that were known to be of general concern among students but were rarely discussed in classes or with teachers, such as emotional pressures, relating to the opposite sex, personal insecurity, and fears of not living up to expectations. By doing so, Mr. Zhang first demonstrated to his audience that he understood them, then offered, in various forms, a seemingly simple solution to all their problems: "Make your own dream, focus on your own goal, acknowledge that you yourself are the main obstacle to improvement." On the recurring topic of pressure, Mr. Zhang literally shouted, "It is very simple, pressure is a prerequisite to an animal's existence; every person experiences pressure. You have the pressure of the entrance examination, but what about your parents, your teacher, don't they also experience pressure?! We all experience pressure, and when we do so, we should calmly accept it!"

In the lecture, as well as in the booklet that the majority of nearly fifteen hundred students bought for ¥30 after the two lectures,[5] the students were told to abandon any idea they might have that their experiences of pressure, and their difficulties dealing with it, were in any way sufficient to create "psychological problems" (*xinli wenti*). Similarly, they were told to abandon the idea that psychological problems were preventing them from performing and doing their utmost in preparation for the examination. The idea behind the lecture, and the self-help book accompanying it, was that obstacles and difficulties in your studies and life are what you make of them. Therefore, you can overcome them simply by accepting them, ignoring them, and continuing to strive toward your own ultimate goal:

> Close to the time of the examination, a lot of students say that they have all kinds of psychological problems. What kind of psychological problems do you have? "Teacher Wang, recently my attention has started to wander . . . ," "Teacher Wang, I have developed paranoia . . . ," "Teacher Wang, I have such low self-confidence . . . ," "Teacher Wang, before examinations I experience high-altitude pressure reactions [*gaoyuan fanying*] . . . ," "Teacher Wang, I am deprived of sleep . . . ," "Teacher Wang, I am extremely nervous before the exam . . . ," "Teacher Wang, I have developed obsessive compulsive disorder [*qiangpozheng*] . . ." (Wang 2008, 15)

All these problems are created by students themselves, the booklet goes on to explain. People make problems out of objectively existing facts instead of just accepting them at face value and adapting to them. In the lecture hall, Mr. Zhang made his point crystal-clear by having students, individually and in the whole group, repeating "a few habits" (*jige xiguan*) they should now develop. They should make a habit of having confidence and trust in others and themselves; maintaining a positive attitude and mentality; and taking immediate action rather than postponing things. But most of all, the key to success at school and in life was "trust," Zhang shouted, trust in others, but first of all trust in yourself. "You are unique!" Zhang claimed, and he made individual students come up on stage and recite into the microphone the statement about their uniqueness that is quoted at the opening of this chapter.

Having recited this several times, Zhang shouted to the audience, "Who is the biggest miracle of nature?" and hundreds of students cheerfully replied, "ME!" At this point, I watched two of the homeroom teachers standing up, looking at each other slightly worried, clearly surprised, and not entirely certain about how to react to this extraordinary expression of collective enthusiasm among their normally not-so-engaged students. It was impossible not to sense the immediate massive response of support of the students to this lecturer's message, and Mr. Zhang himself was encouraged to repeat this "Q&A" a few times, warming up the students before telling them again that if they found it hard to study, or suffered under pressure to perform, the reason was lying in their own mentality, and the solution was to correct their personal attitudes. They should be strong, he explained, because only weak people let problems overcome them. A girl, volunteering by raising her hand, was called on stage and asked to repeat after Zhang: "The weak allow their thoughts to dominate their actions. The strong allow their actions to dominate their thoughts. When depressed, I will burst into singing; when sad, I will laugh to my heart's content; when feeling pain, I redouble my effort; when scared, I bravely advance."

So what should you do to make studying easier and eventually be successful? "Smile to the world!" Mr. Zhang answered his own rhetorical question, and made students repeat in a chorus: "I will smile to world. Smiling helps me to absorb. Smiling helps me to ease the pressure. Smiling is the secret to success in the national exam. From today onward, I smile to the world. From today onward, I smile to the world!" And students did indeed smile, at least throughout the two hours each of the lectures lasted. It was the only time at Number Two High that I heard and saw so many students at the same time having so much fun and enjoying themselves so extensively. They were more than willing to participate in this show, and I observed no objections to or reservations about the lecturer's strong emphasis on the responsibility of the individual simply to overcome any kind of obstacle toward the goal of the final examination and fulfilling the dream of a better life. To the contrary, during a short moment, it seemed as if everybody agreed to Mr. Zhang's dictum that it was now time to start a new life. Everybody joined in the shouting: "From today I start a new life; from today I start a new life!" (*wo jintian kaishi xin de shenghuo*). One of the first steps in this new life would be to stop blaming teachers, family background, parents, or anything or anyone else for whatever problems students might encounter. Blame yourself, if you have to, but, just move on and recognize your own responsibilities to yourself and your family. This was a key message of the pep rally.

INDIVIDUAL, FAMILY, AND
THE NATION THAT DISAPPEARED

The pep rally strongly emphasized the individual's responsibility for failure or success and completely evaded any suggestion that solutions to crippling experiences of intense pressure or lack of motivation may lie outside of the individual's mental and decision-making ability. It told students to teach themselves to renounce (*fangqi*) anything, such as boyfriends, reading for pleasure, or gaming on the Internet, that might obstruct their march toward the ultimate goal. It also encouraged them to stop blaming a "generational gap" or "parents' lack of understanding" for their own difficulties. The lecture tried instead to appeal to students' feelings of *personal* moral responsibility toward their parents by adding to the focus on self-improvement an obligation to perform acts of filial piety (*xiao*).

Filial piety has been described as "perhaps the single most important concept in traditional Chinese culture, encapsulating in a single continuum the moral structure of families in this world and relations with the dead in the next" (Goossaert and Palmer 2012, 226). Although during the twentieth century, the practices of filial piety became less centered on the aspect of caring for the dead, it has remained a strong moral value in Chinese society. By the late 1990s, it was "invoked in popular discourse about the relations among the living members of families, in which parents and grandparents had lost their traditional authority and, through the ownership of land and property, material control over their children" (Goossaert and Palmer 2012, 237). From their early years in the Chinese educational system, students are imbued with a notion of filial piety that requires them to study hard in order to pay back their parents' sacrifices and bring honor and material security to them in old age. The very meaning of educational filial dedication has also undergone more recent transformation. Rather than studying out of gratefulness to parents, and with the objective of looking after them in their old age, students now attempt to perform well in their education in order to live up to the desires that their parents project on them (Kipnis 2011, 145).

In the pep rally at Number Two High in 2008, rural students were presented with a commercialized version of filial piety that emphasized the individual's responsiblity to live up to parental expectations while adding to it an element of entertainment and performance. In one of the pep rallies' more spectacular stunts, Mr. Zhang asked individual students to come on stage, instructing them one after the other to stand on a table so all of us could see their facial reactions and then make surprise telephone calls to their parents. With the loudspeaker on, and with an audience of hundreds of cheering fellow students, a male student standing on the table first had to tell his baffled parent, whom he had not seen for about half a year, and who was oblivious of what was going on, that he loved him: "Daddy, I love you" (*Baba, wo ai ni*), which Zhang instructed the student to say. A gasp of surprise went through the audience, who were not used to this kind of performance nor to this kind of direct verbal expression of love toward parents. Mr. Zhang took over the phone call, quickly explaining to the father that he was part of a show to encourage his son to study harder, and that five hundred students were listening to them as they spoke. Two other students were asked to perform a similar stunt, each of them making the required solemn promise to their parents of always doing their best in school, surpassing their own personal limits in order to produce the best possible examination results. The performances delivered a message regarding individual responsibility toward parents that was recognizable within the cultural framework of filial piety while simultaneously emphasizing the importance of the individual's ability and willingness to stick out from the crowd and promote himself or herself before an audience. Filial piety was reduced to an emotional device used to push students to verbally express their individual moral responsibility for success or failure to their closest relatives. Additionally, it lacked the kind of subtleness that was otherwise characteristic of the way filial piety was talked about and acted out among students and parents in daily life.

Here, I return to notion of the striving individual. Yan writes that the rise in mental and physical problems among the Chinese population may be a result of "aggregated competitive pressures" that drive nearly everyone in society, regardless of gender or age, to strive ever harder for success (Yan 2012b, 9). In the pep rally and self-help booklet, the ideal of the striving individual explicitly includes references to the individual's needs (almost obligations) to control feelings and emotions (*kongzhi qingxu*) in the course of working toward a goal. The ideal striving individual takes full personal responsibility for any aspect of his or her current life and future in order to keep working toward a predefined goal (in this case the exam) that will in turn make the predefined dream of an ever-improving life and livelihood possible. The ideal transmitted to students was that everyone should keep striving on an individual basis toward an individual goal, recognizing in this process the special responsibility toward parents and the need to abstain from relying or counting on their support. In fact, the self-help booklet explains, too much support from parents, for instance, in the form of promises that they (the parents) will help the student go abroad if he or she fails the exam, may spoil the student while indirectly putting even more pressure on him or her. The solution is, again according to the booklet, not to let oneself get disturbed by this: Feel confident and happy, acknowledge that you are lucky to have parents who love you enough to do this for you, and keep studying (Wang 2008, 10–11).

This version of the striving individual has few gender-specific characteristics. However, on a rare note regarding gender, the self-help booklet explains that a girl in today's society should avoid relying on a future husband as a provider for herself and her future family. This is already a practice of the past, Wang writes, telling the male readers of the book to "close their ears" while he urges the girls to study as hard as any of the boys, learning from the example of a successful female Chinese executive who managed to work up from the bottom of a company, defying all odds on her way, and eventually writing a book about her experiences (Wang 2008, 9–10). This reference to gender, although very brief, was yet another example of how the pep rally and self-help book attempted to build on experienced realities among students in order to strengthen their appeal to them. Reports have long shown the tendency in China of a closing gender gap in education, although gender inequalities remain pronounced at the two ends of the education spectrum, with more female illiteracy and a male dominance at the highest levels of education (World Bank 2009).[6] My findings from Number Two High suggested that girls experienced at least as much pressure from parents to study hard as did the boys, especially because many parents I talked to in Gaoshan hoped for their daughters to get stable (*wending*) jobs in the state sector by means of education. Parents would therefore be likely to applaud this message delivered by the booklet to the female students.

However, with the pep rally's emphasis on male and female students' equal obligations to study hard for their own sake and that of their parents, one obvious question remains: What about the individual's obligation to study for the sake of strengthening the nation and developing the country—obligations that are still emphasized in the state school curriculum and in other official discourses on development and education in China? I was somewhat surprised to find that this issue was not highlighted in either the pep rallies I attended or the booklet accompanying them. In fact it was close to being a non-issue. The closest the booklet ever comes to any reference to the Communist Party is in a brief note on Mao Zedong's famous essay on contradictions (*maodun*), which is used simply to tell students that, as Mao once explained, they should spend time only on "the important" contradictions. The booklet does not mention any of the social or class contradictions that Mao was thinking of, but uses the reference to conclude that, for students today, there is no point in trying to deal with less important "contradictions" found in interpersonal relationships with parents, teachers, or friends. As long as one is "honest" (*zhencheng*), everyone will eventually understand you, this section concludes (Wang 2008, 8).

We can only try to guess the reasons why the pep rallies were cleansed of political references, including issues of nationalism and obligations to study out of devotion to the nation and the country's future development. First of all, the pep rallies were offered by a private company that makes its money by offering something completely different from what the schools themselves are able to provide. Most educational leaders, and many teachers at Number Two High, would have been fully able to deliver a more traditional motivational lecture to students, but as state school employees, and because of their training as state school teachers, they would to a much larger extent have been bound to conventions of both content and form of such a meeting. They would most likely have relied on the dominant official educational discourse expressed, for instance, through the notion of quality (*suzhi*), emphasizing the simultaneous need for moral self-acculturation and nation building (e.g., Tomba 2009). Consequently, the content and genre would most likely be familiar and unexciting to students who were accustomed to textbooks and classes emphasizing the obligation to study for the sake of the nation and its development; and teachers would probably urge students to adhere to stereotypical models that in their textbook versions provide well-meant advice.

The strength of the pep rally was precisely its shock effect on students. This was produced by its fast pace, the jokes that students were certainly not used to hearing from teachers or lecturers, the entertaining elements of students' own active participation, and the unequivocal focus on the individual. The pep rallies offered something out of the ordinary for the students, and Wang Guoqiang and his lecturers clearly had a good grasp on which topics were capable of securing students' interest. Considering the general national appeal of the 2008 Olympics in Beijing—a time during which the government created what has been coined as a campaign of mass distraction from pressing social issues, such as rampant corruption, inflation and unemployment (Brady 2009)—one might indeed have expected a strong emotional focus on nationalism as a motivating force. The pep rallies I attended took place shortly after the Olympics, and according to their title they were carried out in the "spirit" of the Olympics as a means to motivate students. There were some sporadic and anecdotal references to sports heroes in the talks; but they were not connected to any broader nationalist propaganda or encouragement to motivate students to study for the sake of the nation, state, or Communist Party. The topic of nationalism, had it been invoked, might have aroused enthusiasm among quite a number of students who demonstrated great pride in China's many Olympic medals and the government's ability to organize such an important, globally appraised sporting event, something that has also been suggested in other studies of nationalism and Chinese youth (e.g., Liu 2012; Rosen 2009; Shan and Guo 2011).

The fact that the Chinese government before and up to the Olympics had shown ambivalence toward strong, explicit expressions of nationalism among youth, for instance, in connection with disputes with Japan or the Tibetan demonstrations, may have made this a risky topic for a pep rally that was consciously trying to appeal to students' emotions and making them shout and scream. In comparison, an exclusive focus on the individual and his or her obligation to conduct self-improvement and self-discipline for the sake of fulfilling goals that were in accordance with expectations from parents, school, and society was politically innocuous. It drew on a massive commercialized interest in the self and self-improvement, and its form, style, and choice of language had more in common with popular talk shows and dating programs on TV than with classroom teaching and formal lectures by teachers and school leaders trying to urge students to study harder. The pep rallies employed and emphasized some of the same references to the individual's need to formulate "dreams" and "goals" and means to achieving these as did some of the most popular talk shows, soap operas, and dating programs on TV. For instance, in the weekly dating program *If You Are the One* (*Feichang wurao*), which has drawn more than 50 million viewers, participants often talked about their "dreams" in their self-presentations; they asked potential partners about their dreams, or they got challenged by the host and the two participating "psychologists" to express and explain what their individual dreams or hopes consisted of, and why.

In another example from a talk show by the popular TV host, Sa Beining, the focus was on individual elderly people's relentless pursuit of said dreams that may set an example for young people as well. One elderly man, for instance, was writing a book and selling his apartment just to get it published, while another elderly couple had spent four years as backpackers, traveling the world and rediscovering their love for each other in the process.[7] Talk shows and dating programs were well known to both students and teachers at Number Two High. One of the reasons behind their popularity seemed to be precisely the ability of a new generation of hosts and participants to display and celebrate what was perceived, and presented, as individuality and creativity in an improvisational style—as demonstrated, for instance, in a 2011 award honoring a group of China's most talented TV hosts for displaying precisely these qualities.[8]

The pep rallies' cocktail of entertainment, high-pitched emotional appeals, and pseudo-psychological advice on how to successfully pursue one's goals echoed a form similar to some of these popular TV programs. As such, the pep rallies were warmly received by students, but they got more mixed reactions from teachers. After each of the two lectures I attended, hundreds of students lined up to shop for the ¥30 self-help booklet that Mr. Zhang announced would be of further help to them. While queuing up, some of the girls were rather emotional: "Teacher, I was so moved by this! Did you also almost have to cry?" one of the first-year female students I knew quite well asked me with tears in her eyes. Several of her female classmates in the queue agreed that it was indeed a very moving lecture, and they started to discuss among themselves how they would now really start studying harder. Some of the boys next to us seemed much less affected, but they were nevertheless all laughing and telling me that they had never experienced so much fun during an afternoon at school. When asked what they actually got out of the meeting, most of the students I talked to said that it encouraged them to study harder, and they paraphrased Mr. Zhang in saying that from now on they would try to have more "self-confidence" and "believe in themselves" in order to be successful. At least in the immediate aftermath of the meetings, the students I talked to all expressed in different ways that the main message from the meetings had been that it was up to them—and them alone—to work hard, pushing beyond their own boundaries, and become successful.

Teachers' views on the meeting, however, varied from pragmatic to highly incredulous. They knew that students, especially those in their third year, were exhausted from studying, and they thought the students deserved to "have a bit of fun," as one female teacher who was a mother of a girl in (a better) high school explained. None of them had any illusions that this one event would make any substantial change to what they saw as the combined problem of an old-fashioned examination regime and a cohort of not exceptionally qualified, talented, or motivated rural students. They did not regard the pep rally as an effective means to put pressure on the individual student to study harder, but rather as innocent entertainment with serious content that might, at least in the short run, serve as encouragement for the students. However, several teachers were much more critical of this kind of meeting and found that it was useless at best, and might even be harmful. One male teacher in his late forties was extremely negative about students being exposed to what he found to be a fully commercialized event with no important or scholarly based advice to students, simulating and legitimizing a contemporary entertainment culture that did nothing to improve students' attitudes or level of knowledge. He thought that meetings like this reflected a more general degeneration of the school system in particular and of morality and attitude in society in general.

The mass-suggestive ways of the pep rallies propagating an ideology of self-reliance, self-improvement, and self-discipline was to some extent a short-term and intensive emulation of self-help courses and coaching that have for a long time been offered in liberal Western countries among students and young people in general. One example, among an endless list of American and European self-help courses, was a 2012 Danish course in "Teenpower," specifically designed to strengthen teenagers' self-esteem (*selvværd*).[9] The Number Two High pep rallies and the

Danish Teenpower courses were in principle all aimed at building more self-confidence among young people, providing them with means to pursue their own interests, or, as the Danish course organizers explained, building young people's inner strength, courage, and ability to express themselves.[10] There were, however, major difference between the two types of courses. One of the differences in form between the Danish courses and the pep rallies at Number Two High was that the latter was a one-off, two-hour, high-speed event for a group of several hundreds of students at a time, while the Danish courses offered four days made up of four hours each (costing more than €300 per student), with smaller groups of youth working together with professional coaches.

More important, there were profound differences in the kind of individualism that students were encouraged to internalize. At a superficial level, the Teenpower courses and the pep rallies at Number Two High both represent a global trend of individualization in which the demand to create your own do-it-yourself autobiography is so broadly accepted that there is a private market for offering courses or lectures to youth even at Chinese state schools. The lecturers at the Chinese pep rallies would have been able to directly borrow some (but not all) of the slogans from the short film propagating the Danish course, such as "The best way to predict your future is to make it yourself" or "Say Yes to being yourself."[11] However, whereas Wang's lectures and book were centered on behavior and actions as a means to control one's thoughts and emotions and thereby achieve one's goals and dreams, the commercials for the Danish Teenpower course stressed the need to discover oneself, find a kind of true or real self, and build individuality: "Be yourself rather than a copy of somebody else" and "You are the best at being you" are examples from the promotional web site. The aim was to explicitly teach youth how to define and argue for their own individual wishes and at the same time set limits to what they did not want or found unacceptable: "[Having completed the Teenpower course] I now emphasize what I think is correct, rather than following everybody else," one seventeen-year-old Danish course participant explained in the film.[12] The Danish courses stressed values of individuality and autonomy—the individual should explore and express his or her own characteristics, and search for and pursue his or her own wishes and goals. In comparison, the private courses offered to Chinese state schools in the form of pep rallies emphasized neosocialist values of individual inner strength, self-reliance, and personal responsibility for failure or success, all in pursuit of a predefined and unquestioned dream of educational achievement.

There was nothing startling about the example of the Danish Teenpower course, and comparable courses have been held across Europe and the United States for many years as part of the neoliberalist trends and intensified individualization of these societies. Likewise, there are many examples from other parts of the world of courses organized to socialize youth and cultivate the individual, for instance, in Japan, where private companies have long been engaged in training employees to become more efficient and better socialized through spiritual courses that emphasize mental training and outward manifestations of individual strength (e.g., Rohlen 1973, 1557).[13] The comparison with the Danish case demonstrates how the pep rallies I attended at Number Two High were developed and adapted in a specific context of a Chinese path of authoritarian individualization, where motivational lectures were keen to emphasize the students' individual responsibility to perform and live up to their own and their parents' (by definition equivalent) expectations, while stressing the unquestioned ability of each individual to take control of success by managing emotions and letting his or her conscious actions be the guide.

However extraordinary the form and content of the commercial pep rallies may seem in the context of a mainstream Chinese state school, they are illustrative of the Chinese path of individualization. They are also acceptable—possibly even convenient—events for the political authorities who aim to cultivate a new generation of neosocialist citizens. Even though state school curriculum and organization remain largely centralized, teachers and administrators transmit to students their own interpretations of why and how they ought to study and what to emphasize. In their aim to live up to societal, parental, and indeed their own hopes and expectations for students' educational success, they are looking for ways to appeal not only to the consciousness and feelings of obligation of students, but to their personal interests and motivations. With a rapidly developing private education market, profiting from widespread educational desires, it was therefore not surprising that motivational lectures employing means of entertainment comparable to those of popular TV programs would find a market among schools that are looking for new ways to enhance their results in increasing competition with others.

The formal high school curriculum promotes a learning individual who simultaneously takes individual responsibilities as a citizen and moral being while not attempting to stick out from the crowd by, for instance, indulging in extravagant consumption or demeanor. This individual does his or her best to contribute to the economic, political, and moral development of the motherland while striving to live up to the models that are presented in classes and textbooks. The ideal promoted by the commercialized pep rallies performed within the state school is a more ego-centered individual who takes full personal responsibility for failures or successes while refraining from criticizing, blaming, or in any way analyzing the impact of anyone or anything but himself or herself. This individual is not only politically neutral, but completely devoid of any interest in understanding or placing him- or herself in the context of social structures or relations of power. This individual remains concentrated on his or her own abilities, efforts, and levels of success and cares little about authorities and relations of power beyond the required filial obligations. Political, educational, or parental authorities are not necessarily regarded as representing "the truth," but instead they are seen as an unquestionable "fate" to be accepted by the individual. The pep rallies do not exactly paraphrase the official curriculum's call for individuals who improve themselves in order to benefit the collective state and nation, but it represents a convenient and politically acceptable form of the promotion of the individual as a striving, innovative, filial, responsible person who leaves authorities and power relations unquestioned and refrains from analyzing him- or herself in a broader social context.

CHAPTER 5

DREAMS AND DEDICATIONS

Teachers' Views and the Construction of a Generation Gap

Many people working at all levels within the state schools I visited expressed to me the feeling that they did not have a choice or a voice in their professional positions, although this very same profession provided a desired sense of security and a certain degree of respect and status in society. Reading that a teacher claims that he and his colleagues have no kind of freedom, one could easily picture a school with strict discipline and formal means of communication, students in spotless uniforms, and teachers' offices with neat stacks of examination papers on orderly desks. Instead, I invite you to visualize ten teachers' offices, each of which accommodates anywhere from eight to twenty teachers, and each of which demonstrates how people live a large portion part of their lives there. At any time of the day between 7 A.M. and 9 P.M., one could encounter people in these offices, mostly teachers, but also often members of the administrative staff, sometimes children of staff members, spouses, students, parents, or just people from the neighborhood who wanted to talk to people at the school. In these offices, teachers prepared classes and corrected students' papers, chatted over a cup of tea, or watched popular dating programs or TV series on their laptops. Sometimes a teacher would chat on the instant messaging service, QQ, while others searched for information on the Internet, listened to downloaded music, or were busy scolding a group of students or discussing student behavior with a class monitor.

All the time, students could be observed on their way in or out of offices to fetch something, deliver books to the homeroom teachers, or complain about a headache, their peers' bad behavior, or the loss of a mobile telephone. There was an abundance of litter in the corners of offices, blackboards were covered with a mixture of messages and unstructured drawings, the water kettle was boiling on the floor, and teachers would send cookies or fruit across the tables, chatting or laughing about the latest news or yesterday's events. In other words, the offices at Number Two High were by no means a prisonlike space in which "inmates" were devoid of "any kinds of freedom" or room for agency. The school was private and public space integrated. Teachers' offices were places for socialization and free exchange of views on anything from student suicides to the political failure in "quality education," and at the same time, embodiments of the lack of power and freedom teachers experienced in their public lives.

In these offices, I spent a great deal of time talking with teachers, interviewing those who were especially willing to talk at length about their lives and views on education, students, and the role of the individual in contemporary China; or I simply listened to or took part in their conversations on all kinds of topics. Such interviews and prolonged conversations in the period between 2008 and 2012 with mainly thirty-six out of the school's 120 teachers and administrators (many of whom had previously worked as teachers or even continued to do so on a part-time basis) revealed how the younger teachers, born between 1976 and 1987, viewed their own lives as individuals and as teachers and how they interpreted societal processes of individualization in terms of heightened demands on rural students' individual performance and what they regarded as students' increased selfishness.

Teachers tended to be highly critical when referring to what they saw as a general trend of negative individualism (*ziwozhuyi*) among their students, and they expressed ambiguity about how to deal with the multiple life choices—real or imagined—that faced not only their students, but, just as much, their own children. They also had much in common with their students. None of them belonged to the generations who had lived their adult lives during the Cultural Revolution and who have been described as being fearful, watchful, and exhausted in the early aftermath of the Mao era (Kleinman 2011a, 267). In fact, most of the teachers in the relatively young Number Two High belonged to the much-discussed "post-1980 generation" (the so called *balinghou*), representing about 200 million people born between 1980 and 1989, who have experienced China only as a country of rapid growth and have no personal memories of the kind of political repression their parents' generation experienced (Rosen 2009, 369). Chinese quantitative surveys of how people born in the 1960s and 1970s view this post-1980 generation have shown that they characterize them as being addicted to the Internet and QQ (78.3 percent); highly concerned with their outer appearances (73.2 percent); always considering themselves the center of attention (61.4 percent); having a high assessment of their own abilities, and always feeling they are really great (64.2 percent); and lacking a strong sense of responsibility (61.4 percent) (referred by Rosen 2009, 363). In other words, the post-1980s generation to which these teachers belonged was characterized by, and criticized for, many of the very same things that teachers themselves projected on their students who were born only ten to fifteen years later in the early 1990s.

There was obviously a vertical power relation between teachers and their students regardless of the relatively few years of difference in age, but there was also a perception among young teachers that the rural society they knew best had changed so rapidly in the past ten to fifteen years that it had generated a compressed generation gap. Teachers emphasized generational differences between themselves and their students, while for the outside observer such as myself, they seemed to have much in common with their students who had grown up in the same period of rapid individualization, growth of materialism, and popularization of new means of electronic communication. In spite of teachers' widespread complaints about "selfish" attitudes and students' lack of concern for others, they also shared with their students a wider spectrum of perceptions of what "a good life" implied and how one might achieve it. More than 80 percent of teachers in Number Two High had grown up within the local area, nearly all had parents with a rural backgrounds as peasants, shop owners or workers or managers in smaller enterprises, or (much more rarely) as teachers or cadres locally. They had received their education within the province and had been assigned jobs in their own home area. Among the thirty-six teachers I interviewed several times and had close contact with over the whole period of fieldwork, only three had moved to Gaoshan from other provinces after having been hired by Number Two High.

Teachers born in the late 1970s and 1980s shared with their students the intuition to seek individual rather than collective explanations and solutions to larger societal challenges, and their concerns and aspirations for the future were not necessarily any more or any less "selfish" than those of their students. They did display a kind of "divided self" (Kleinman 2011a) that is not only internally experienced by many Chinese people today but is also used to govern China. Since the 1980s, the state has created much better life conditions for the vast majority of the Chinese population, and there are "numerous freedoms in everyday life"; but at the same time, "each individual is socialized indirectly by the state and directly by the family to understand the very real limits of those small freedoms as well as the responsibility to live a divided life with great alertness to the boundaries that one does not trespass, no matter what is at stake" (Kleinman 2011a, 286). These external boundaries of the political subject have been internalized by the self as self-division (Kleinman 2011a). How was this expressed and experienced by teachers who were professionally required to represent and promote official discourse on the moral obligations of the individual citizen in relation to the party-state but who were at the same time individuals with their own life aspirations and visions of the good life?

Teachers in a state school are perhaps among the individuals in China who most directly experience, in their daily professional lives, the requirement of promoting to the upcoming generation the intertwined ideals of individual decision making and collective political loyalty. As teachers they need not only to construct their own lives within the system of neosocialism but also to actively and professionally socialize their students into this contemporary Chinese form of governmentality—a form which, as noted by Lisa Hoffman (2010), exhibits many of the same kinds of governing technologies, norms, and modes of self-formation that are observed in many other parts of the modern world but also contains more distinctive socialist elements.

With the introduction of the ideal "new socialist man" (*shehuizhuyi xinren*) in the 1950s, teachers were expected to motivate children to actively take part in new forms of learning processes rather than practicing traditional rote learning and memorization, while at the same time they were required to teach children to be submissive to party authorities (Chan 1985). In the early twentieth century, when new ideas about the education and socialization of individuals and citizens flourished in China, John Dewey's promotion of new educational practices focusing on the individual child and processes of learning by doing had become highly influential among Chinese educators and intellectuals. Those Chinese educators who had studied under Dewey even regarded him as "the great apostle of philosophic liberalism and experimental methodology, the advocate of complete freedom of thought, and the man who, above all other teachers, equated education to the practical problems of civic cooperation and useful living" (Su 1995, 305). Dewey's writings and lectures were very popular among a much broader segment of the Chinese population than merely his students, but his ideas and their influence in China were also severely criticized, first by Confucianists and then by Marxists. Although the Communist Party educators in principle continued to agree with Dewey and his followers' doctrine of the self-motivated, purposive, and creative child, the other side of the "new socialist man" was consciously self-abnegated and submissive to the collective (Chan 1985, 12). The same Communist Party authorities who condemned physical abuse in schools and promoted the self-motivated student also "strongly believed that children had to start from an acceptance of authoritatively given 'right principles,' to which they had to learn to conform" (14).

Throughout the time of communist rule, teachers have been expected to handle this basic duality. However, during the time of reform and increased individualization of society, the inherent contradiction in this political ambition has deepened rather than diminished. How did these young rural teachers, born after the death of Mao and the introduction of political and economic reform, view these changes and the implications they have for themselves, both as individuals and as professional teachers?

STRIVING FOR A "SENSE OF SECURITY"

In an interview, a female teacher in Number Two High, born by peasant parents in a mountain village Gaoshan in 1978, told me:

> Studying was tough and we were kept busy; but it was nothing compared to today. I recall this very clearly. When I was in my first year of high school [in 1994 in the best school in Gaoshan] I would grab a copy of *Red Sorghum* and find a place to sit and read through the breaks. We had no

idea about which books we ought to have read, so I would choose anything I could get my hands on. No teachers would interfere. Later during the day, we would freely chat and have fun in our dormitories, or sit in a worn-out chair in the sun and read. Of course the teachers would tell us to study hard, but in reality, whatever you read, or even if you decided not to sleep in your own dormitory, nobody really cared. This was also quite free [*zhege ye hen ziyoude*].

Among the things that all interviewed teachers agreed on was that their own time in school had been more relaxed and less controlled than what students experienced now. This was not only a matter of a changing school but of a changing rural society in which parents, to a much larger extent than before, could afford to let their children study, and therefore also had much higher expectations of them. It was also a trend of a society in which people needed to be more efficient and run faster to achieve their goals. If you were busy and occupied, it showed that you were a good teacher or serious student; and it was in any case necessary to stay busy—or at least pretend to be busy—because as a student you were expected to work through a large mandatory curriculum, and as a teacher you were expected to move as many students as possible successfully through the system in order to improve your own chances for a pay rise and a promotion. Teachers at the more elite Number One High in Gaoshan shook their heads, laughed, and complained about the newest motto of their school, conveyed to them in solemn speeches by their leaders: "Get up early, don't rest at noon, be efficient in the evening!"

This drive for success in Chinese society has been described as a relatively new phenomenon, but one that has manifested itself as a core of what makes the moral Chinese person: "Driven by the urge for success, the individual strives by all possible means to make it out there, to deal with his anxieties, and to strike a balance in the torment between conflicting moral visions and values, resulting in a noticeable change in China's moral landscape, that is, as I will call it, the ethics of the striving individual" (Yan 2013). Among teachers and students in Number Two High, a number of practices related to studies, the profession of teaching, and students' and teachers' individual lives may to some extent be understood in this perspective of an ethics of the striving individual. In general, the teachers at Number Two High clearly worked hard to deal with anxieties and make sense of the world they lived in. However, as children of disadvantaged parents growing up in rural areas without a social security net, they were largely striving for goals associated with "first" rather than "second" or "reflexive" modernity, and this striving was not continuous; it tended to end when some quite specific goals were reached.

Moreover, the very concept of success was not used by teachers themselves in narratives about their lives and goals, and I doubt they would explicitly describe themselves with words such as *successful* if directly asked. Nevertheless, an individual urge for success in the sense of achieving certain rather concrete goals for oneself and one's family characterized many of the activities and attitudes within ordinary Number Two High, because in many respects such schools were trying to emulate elite schools. Students in Number Two High were urged to be successful graduates, and the teachers expected to successfully get their students through the examination. In principle, it was, of course, also expected that everyone would voluntarily participate in striving that was aimed at ultimately creating a more prosperous and continuously developing China, with the Communist Party in the indisputable leadership position. However, there were two aspects of this ethics of striving that I found particularly noticeable in the daily life of educational, social, and personal interactions within Number Two High.

First, I found an overwhelming emphasis on the goal of being successful for one's own, or one's family's sake rather than for the more abstract sake of country, nation, or Communist Party, as described in research on education in earlier periods of the People's Republic of China (PRC) (e.g., Shirk 1982; Chan 1985; Thøgersen 2002). In both their private lives and in practices of their profession, I found that rural teachers, similar to urban "patriotic professionals," had embraced the self-enterprising ethos while also emphasizing the importance of caring for their families (Hoffman 2010, 10). However, unlike urban middle-class, white-collar workers, the rural teachers rarely mentioned the nation or duties to the country when talking about these issues. They limited their discourse on the necessity of developing the self in order to fulfill one's duty to the nation and the prosperity of China to classes in which these topics were part of the curriculum. They lectured students in the politically appropriate way about national requirements of each individual to develop him- or herself in order to help strengthen the socialist nationally united China; but in private discussions and beyond the contexts of formal teaching they hardly ever brought this up, and they did not integrate lofty ambitions to help "developing the nation" into their narratives about individual career pursuits or ambitions for their children, or even students.

Second, for these rural teachers success was equivalent to reaching a certain level of social security and stability. *Success* referred to a clear goal of private and socioeconomic safety rather than implying an endless effort of striving. To be successful was effectively to have secured one's own (and thereby also one's family's) social, private, and economic assets. So when a teacher married before the age of thirty, had a child, and bought an apartment in the township or (even better) in the county capital, the striving for herself and for the older generation of the family was largely over. The urge for success was instead projected onto the child and his or her future prospects, something that, in the shorter perspective, implied a major concern with the child's education. The emphasis was on the choices parents would have to make on behalf of their child in order to pave the way for social security and preferably upward mobility, and the important long-term goal was to secure the livelihood, satisfactory lifestyle, and status of the child—again, state and nation were hardly ever mentioned in these conversations.

Teachers often pointed out to me that their rural background determined their relative modest measure of individual success, namely basic social security, and that students today were less conscious of this goal than they themselves had been when they were younger. One female teacher argued, in agreement with many other teachers, that students in Gaoshan today "do not care about their studies; they do not have a goal [*mubiao*], they are excessively concerned about having fun; and they are controlled by their mobile phones." However, she also acknowledged that when she was a student, she hardly had to make any difficult choices about her studies. She explained that she and her friends just went with the flow and simply did their best to focus on the upcoming examination and their results without questioning the relevance or whether or not it was "interesting" to them. Another male teacher compared his own experiences with that of his students in the following way: "The only thing we thought about was our grades, which would define which school we would advance to, and therefore also eventually which job we would get. I could go into the military, or become a local cadre, or a teacher, and I just knew that this depended on my marks, not on any kind of 'choice,' like you [referring to me as the interviewer] seem to think."

This was the road, they had been told by their parents, to a desired social and economic stability, and they believed it. If proven successful, this path would create the "sense of security" (*anquangan*) that was— and still is—longed for by many people in China today, not least people who have grown up in social contexts in which social security depends entirely on the whole family's level of income rather than on secure state income. In the discourse of many parents of teachers—as recalled by the teachers themselves—the most certain way to gain this sense of security was to get a stable job in the state sector. For many of those born in the latter part of the 1970s and 1980s, and who belonged to the above-average group of rural students in Gaoshan, this meant a job as a teacher. The better students among their peers had aimed at higher-degree studies in a university in the hope that it would lead to a more prestigious and well-paid job in the secure state sector.

Working to achieve this kind of desired social, economic, and personal security was regarded by the young teachers at Number Two High as something they were practically bound to do as "rural children" (*nong-cun de haizi*). It was created out of their inherent sense of responsibility (*zerengan*) and their concern for their closest family members, not only themselves. There was no state-sponsored or other kind of collective safety net ready to save them if they failed, and yet they did not complain about the lack of a welfare state in their descriptions of why they were so keen to find "security." For them, becoming a teacher was definitely not regarded as a "selfish choice" on the road toward an individual career and self-fulfillment. In fact, it was hardly regarded as a choice at all. Rather, it was seen as a lucky outcome of the efforts to do what was expected of one as a filial child and as the most obvious path toward social security. Compared to this, teachers regarded their not-so-much-younger students as being more selfish and more (economically) privileged, but also subjected to more social control and pressure to succeed.

Compared to the status teachers enjoyed pre-1990s (when rural students' options for college education were broadened considerably), the status of being a teacher had diminished by 2012, although it was still regarded as a secure and acceptable profession for a rural student with above-average grades. In the early 2000s and 2010s, when many students in urban areas would graduate from college also without any kind of job security, a position as a rural high school teacher was reemphasized as a secure choice, although it was less prestigious than before. A teaching position in a state school had maintained its reputation for being a good job, especially for women, providing the "iron rice bowl" to the individual and therefore also to the individual's closest family. However, teaching had lost the kind of respect and awe with which it had been viewed throughout China's history and up through the 1980s and early 1990s. One of the male teachers, born in the late 1970s, expressed this in a very explicit way. He argued strongly that teachers had become a "vulnerable group" (ruoshi qunti). They had secure jobs, but their income was low, not least compared to the many successful businesspeople with no education at all. In the period of my fieldwork from Zhejiang between 2008 and 2012, most teachers in Number Two High received salaries between ¥1,500 and ¥3,000 per month, and those who were homeroom teachers earned ¥100–¥200 extra. For most teachers, this was less than what a taxi driver would make. More important, several teachers emphasized, they lacked political influence and appropriate social respect as teachers. A male teacher in his thirties told me:

> What do I mean by this? I will explain. For instance, now look at us teachers, even regarding the topic of education we are not really in a position to say much [mei you duoda shuohua de diwei], right? But other people require a lot from us. They have very high expectations of us, and you cannot make any kind of mistake without getting a warning. Before everybody trusted the teachers, and parents respected the teachers. The status of the teachers was sacred [shensheng]. Now with this educational law . . . I am not sure if it is progress or regress. We cannot touch a hair on the students, we have to respect [zunzhong] the students. . . . We have raised the status of the students. The student is God [xuesheng shi shangdi]. . . . Nowadays, if we criticize a student, sometimes the parents . . . that is, parents of quite a low quality . . . will come and talk to us, even to the

headmaster. Before they would criticize their children, but now they do everything to criticize the teacher instead!

Even after this rather harsh outburst, the teacher continued on to praise the social environment for him and his colleagues at Number Two High, and like most teachers, he talked positively about his personal experience of being a teacher. The younger teachers at Number Two High presented themselves as having been "not-so-good-students" because they had "only" managed to get assigned jobs as teachers in a school like Number Two High; but at the same time they considered themselves to be relatively fortunate among their rural peers, and the majority of them expressed a remarkable degree of satisfaction with a very predictable life even at the age of thirty or younger. Almost without exception, teachers I interviewed (including the one just quoted) displayed reactions of surprise and sometimes even disbelief when I asked them if I would be able to find them at Number Two High as teachers in ten years' time. "Of course!" most would exclaim after pondering why I would even ask such an odd question. "The school has become my home," one teacher continued. "I have lived here for twelve years now, and when we manage to save enough money to buy our own flat, I will of course still be working here!" A couple of more pragmatic teachers explained that because it was only the very few with exceptionally good personal connections who could ever dream of transferring to a better school, they were certainly destined to stay at Number Two High forever. Very few complained about this prospect or saw it as something negative. Only five teachers answered positively to the question of whether or not they had consciously and actively made a decision to become teachers, and the vast majority stated that although they liked being teachers, they were at the same time very critical of the educational system. The profession was good, the structures bad.

Only a few young female teachers who were not happy about being teachers at all explained that they would still like to do other things in their professional lives, such as becoming a journalist who could travel around the country and "develop herself" (*fahui ziji*) or study to become an academic or an artist. One thirty-two-year-old female teacher, who was quite unhappy in her marriage, dreamed of making "a new life" for herself around the age of fifty when her child had settled down. She envied my ability to travel on my own, and she started to ponder about her own options in this regard: "What do you think? Maybe when I turn fifty and my daughter is grown-up I could start to live for the sake of just myself? Forget about the students and all their troubles. . . . I could go traveling, maybe looking for real love . . . just go for a kind of life that I really long for?!" But in accordance with the other teachers, this woman mentioned afterward that it was a completely unrealistic dream, and not even something worth actively working for. She ended one of our conversations by concluding that "especially in the first year of teaching I felt completely miserable, and the students treated me badly because I was not able to keep them under control. I wanted to stop being a teacher, but wouldn't that have been very selfish? I had a stable job, my parents had supported me, of course I would never abandon this job, and now things are anyway much better. . . ."

In regards to the teachers in Number Two High, it seemed that their individual struggles for success were accomplished, and largely complete, when they got permanent jobs in the school, got married, and had a child. As a result, although the school and the students kept them busy in their everyday lives at work, their main expectations and urges for success were now projected onto their children. For those who were still unmarried or without partners, the search for boyfriends or girlfriends was intensified as soon as they had permanent positions as teachers and realized that they would likely be staying in Gaoshan area and in Number Two High for the rest of their lives. Colleagues, local friends, and relatives would all help in the search for appropriate partners, and everyone was happy when a young unmarried teacher succeeded in this regard—for instance, if he or she entered into a relationship with another young, single teacher from Number Two High or from one of the other schools in the municipality.

Job searches, ambitions for children, or attempts to secure their private lives were not interpreted by the teachers as acts of selfishness that were in any way comparable to the "selfishness" they identified among their students. Nor were they, for teachers, matters of individual choice or professional preferences. Teachers presented them to me as the "normal way of life," something that grew out of established social structures and mentalities. Perhaps they could best be described through the notion of habitus—those social and individual practices that are immediately intelligible and foreseeable and hence taken for granted, an automatic and impersonal ordinary practice that lends itself to an understanding no less automatic and impersonal (Brubaker 1993, 224; Bourdieu 1977). For the teachers in Number Two High, living up to their responsibilities as relatively successful rural students used to mean following the path that opened in front of them rather than to make explicit choices based on their own self-interest. Living under the current conditions of intensified individualization and the idealization of individual choice, the teachers at Number Two High were conscious and explicit about the path toward higher education being their "fate." They had taken the path for granted at the time simply because it was possible for them to follow it, though not so much for granted that they were unable to account for it. They would read-ily talk at length precisely about the reasons *why* they took it for granted, thus using this "fate" in their professional and personal lives to create their own autobiographies. The acceptance of this given path or fate was something that, in their views, qualitatively divided their own lives and perceptions from those of their students, with whom they experienced what many teachers referred to as a "generation gap" (*daigou*), although they were not even old enough to be the students' parents.

THE IMAGINARIES OF A GENERATION GAP

The term *generation gap* was used by teachers in a loose and intuitive way to describe what they regarded as profound differences between their own and their students' attitudes, life conditions, and ways of behavior and reaction. In sum, it seemed to define a lack of mutual understanding that they interpreted as rooted in simple generational differences and rapid changes of society rather than in specific vertical power relations between themselves and their students. The vast majority of teachers and students came from within the same small rural region and spoke the same dialect. They had their family relations there; they regarded themselves as "rural" (*nongcunde*); and they had all grown up in the era of political and eco-nomic reform. The term *generation gap* was used to suggest that cultural and socioeconomic conditions had changed so rapidly over such a short period of time that teachers found it difficult, sometimes even impossible, to accept their students' moral behavior and expressions of views, even when they to some extent found it possible to explain the reasons behind them. They followed the growth and psychological development of their students between the ages of sixteen and nineteen, and they compared their students to themselves at the same age and following a largely similar form of education.

Attitude and Choice

Most teachers were critical of their students' attitudes toward studies, parents, teachers, and their own futures. In their discussions among themselves, teachers would often exchange concrete experiences or ask each other for advice on how to solve a certain acute problem regarding an individual student or groups of students who were falling behind or breaking school regulations. However, when talking specifically with me about such topics, they tended to choose a more analytical approach. They wanted me to understand that although they were indeed very critical of many of their students' ways of behaving and found serious flaws in their students' attitudes, they largely understood the reasons behind this behavior.

A male teacher who graduated from high school in 2003 explained:

> I understand why they act and behave the way they do, but there is really a big difference between them and us. They absolutely want to have fun [wanr]. We also had a lot of fun in high school. Everybody likes to have fun, right? But we knew there was a purpose with our studies. We felt that there was a contradiction between having fun and studying. We also knew what was most important. I know for sure that we used to put studies first and pleasure second. . . . Students today first want pleasure, and then only when they have had enough, will they start studying.

Many teachers also expressed, at the same time, a considerable degree of empathy for students who they feared would have to face huge difficulties in a society where successful education was seen as the most important road to upward mobility. They mostly identified structural reasons for what they regarded as ill behavior and negative attitudes among their students, and they expressed a profound lack of trust that the problems could be solved under the current system of education or with the limited resources of rural schools such as Number Two High. They resorted instead to solutions within each family, such as the need to raise the quality of parental care and improve students' individual morality and attitudes.

For example, on the issue of love relationships among students, teachers would talk about how profoundly different their own attitudes had been only yen to fifteen years earlier. There were several couples among students in each class at Number Two High, and although school regulations did not allow it, some of these students did not do much to conceal their relationships. Teachers regarded this as an inevitable trend in a society where it had become much more common than in previous generations to openly express emotions toward a boyfriend or girlfriend and for students to ignore regulations if they did not suit the students' purposes: "We would never have done like they do now [holding hands or kissing in public]. When I started here as a teacher, I was told that this kind of 'early love' [zao lian] was unacceptable, and I was expected to instruct students who were seen too much together that they should not exaggerate in this way. Now teachers just ignore it because there is really nothing we can do about it!" a thirty-two-year-old teacher explained.

Teachers regarded this as a major problem which was difficult for them to handle, especially if parents found out. They also believed it had a profoundly negative influence on students' performance—not merely that of the students involved in love relationships but of everyone around them who was influenced or intrigued by the possibility of engaging in such relationships. It was taken as—yet another—sign of students' lack of consideration for their own studies and thereby also for their teachers, peers, parents, and their own and their families' futures. The problem was also regarded with a mixture of surprise at the courage students displayed and a fear of spreading moral decay. One thirty-year-old female teacher who had herself been in a (secret) relationship during high school explained:

In this respect there is really a huge generation gap between the students and us. They are much more direct when it comes to dating [tan lianai]. They just ask . . . Really, where do they get this courage from?! . . . They just ask, "Do you want to become my girlfriend?" They really belong to a different generation from me. . . . We experienced a kind of innocent early love, but today they are under so much more influence from the Internet, TV series, Korean movies. I mean, the influence on their way of looking at romantic love is huge. Our notions of romantic love came from magazines and books, but our feelings were much more sincere [zhenzhi] than today. We were more pure and honest [chunjie].

Teachers' ways of analyzing unwanted behavior among their students at Number Two High suggested a widespread lack of trust in any chances of structurally changing the education system in directions that would improve their students' interests in serious studies or correct their "selfish" attitudes. To the teachers, it was a sign of selfishness when a girl chose to spend time with a boy instead of studying, when teachers' assignments were ignored in favor of chatting on QQ, or when boys who were summoned for a serious scolding would keep quiet or accuse other peers for their own misbehavior. Most teachers I talked to were fond of most of their students and expressed this in different ways, but it did not prevent them from repeating the dominant discourse on contemporary youth being representatives of a more selfish generation—a generation whose uncoordinated, small, and largely individual acts of defiance would force the school and its teachers to strengthen social control and discipline. The individualization of society generates ever-higher expectations that students will be able to create their own lives as professionals, family members, and individuals by expressing themselves, making choices, and pursuing their own interests. That said, the school is at the same time under severe pressure to adapt its technologies of governmentality to ensure students' self-discipline, encouraging them to strive for the specific goals and kind of success that parents have in mind for their children and that political authorities have in mind for their citizens.

Teachers emphasized the unquestioned improvement of students' economic conditions today as compared to just ten years ago, but they argued that the negative side effect of this material advance was that relatively well-off but distant parents tended to spoil their children materially while letting them down psychologically. This negative trend, they argued, was enforced by parents' peasant backgrounds and their inherent "low quality" and lack of education. According to many teachers, the combination of parents' lack of education and their urge to make money, even when it meant that they had to leave their children behind, made parents unable to raise their children to become properly responsible youth, practicing sufficient self-discipline in their studies while showing the desired level of respect toward teachers and parents. It also created an unprecedented pressure on teachers from parents who expected payoffs for their own sacrifices and investment in the form of good examination results for their children. Consequently, teachers in rural schools such as Number Two

High were compelled to strengthen discipline and develop new technologies of governmentality, emulating more elite schools to an ever-higher degree while recognizing that their students held lower status and more limited future prospects than did the much envied urban and better educated middle class students.

Students' inability to mobilize a degree of self-discipline and self-motivation sufficient to prevent a negative spiraling of external disciplinary practices was interpreted by quite a few teachers as a sign of general moral decay among rural youth. It was not so much that students were looking for love relationships among their peers; this was, after all, regarded as natural for people of this age in these times. What was really perceived as an expression of a serious moral flaw was the so-called selfishness that teachers identified in their students' behavior when "lack of self-discipline" resulted in poor grades. It was considered "selfish" when students allowed themselves to be distracted from their studies because of psychological or bodily needs or attractions; it was interpreted as a lack of consideration for parents' hopes and sacrifices, for teachers' daily efforts, and for peers' need for good role models. This "giving in to short-term individual interests" would, in the view of teachers, jeopardize most of their students' futures, because they were unlikely to reach the same kind of security in life that the teachers themselves had achieved.

There were, however, a few teachers who pointed to developments in students' perceptions of their own future working lives and society's examination craze that puzzled them but that they saw as being potentially positive: "We teachers are often surprised that students are less focused on the university entrance examination than we were. They are not like earlier students who became really depressed and gloomy if they failed to get into a good university. But this is in a way also a positive change. They are much more capable of, and also willing to, find work. As soon as they graduate they are willing to take on some work [*dagong*]. Students before . . . or when we were students . . . we would never have done that!" It was indeed not uncommon that students' older siblings had started to work immediately after graduation while waiting for responses from the schools they had applied to, or that they immediately started to look for alternatives to college education. This suggested a kind of counter-discourse—in fact counter-practice—to the dominant societal and parental discourse on the indisputable benefits of education and the loss of "hope for the future" if one did not have the desired success as a student.

Choice in the post-Mao state has become an important technique of governmentality—a means to create subjects who seemingly out of their own free will depend less on state assignments and allocations than people did during the earlier socialist periods (Hoffman 2010). Students in Number Two High were faced with choices that even teachers in their late twenties had not experienced to the same degree. There were choices to be made regarding the growing options within rural areas for college studies and repetition classes, the increasingly complex job market, and the possibilities of "testing" potential partners and engaging in several close relationships before marriage. At the same time, students were faced with new options for expanding their knowledge of society and global changes through cheap and easy access to the Internet and for increasing their possibilities of communication through the mobile phones that nearly everyone had. Young people were continually forced to make choices, teachers acknowledged, but in their view the students tended to make them selfishly, based on their own individual short-term interests and immediate needs rather than through a broader filial, or even long-term individual, perspective in mind. This, they thought, was especially critical for the students themselves, because they were "rural," "disadvantaged," "of low quality," and would therefore have an especially hard time climbing the social ladder unless they made the right choices at the right time.

Social Challenges, Individual Solutions

The intensified individualization processes that simultaneously allow and require of students that they make a large number of choices and create their own autobiographies was experienced by rural teachers as young as in their thirties or late twenties as both attractive and dangerous. They themselves had reached the immediate goals of their individual and families striving and were now largely projecting their worries onto their children. In their professional lives as teachers they were often conflicted about how to socialize their students to be obedient to authorities, including to themselves as teachers. They recognized the limits to the "little freedoms" of their own and their students' everyday lives (Kleinman 2011a). One of the male teachers who graduated from a normal college in 1996 pointed to the new electronic media as the most decisive factor in creating differences between the lives of youth in the late 1990s and in the early 2000s:

> We grew up in this area playing with sticks, stones and sand. Now they have TV, computers and mobile phones. They know a lot, but understand so little! They really do not have any self-discipline anymore. They do not respect their parents, but only think about themselves. We had so much more self-discipline than they do now. We knew what to do, and we did it. Now they are exposed to so much information from TV and the PC, but they do not understand it, and they do not know how to use it.

He agreed with many other teachers that neither the education system nor their own education as teachers were designed to help students *understand* more or make their choices more informed. As teachers, their main task was to get their students through the examinations in the specific disciplines they were teaching. In order to do so, they felt that they needed to at least try to prevent students from acting in "selfish" ways, thereby pursuing what both teachers and parents seemed to agree were short-term interests that disrupted the long-term goal of successful studies. "The students are very self-confident [*ziwo yishi hen qiang*], but it is not in a good way—it is in a selfish way [*ziside*]," one teacher explained, and she continued to blame the students' selfish behaviors on their insufficient education and the low quality of their parents.

On the one hand, many teachers perceived their students as simply belonging to another generation than themselves, and on the other, they emphasized the social difference between themselves and their students which was a result of their own successful upward movement from peasant backgrounds (like their students) to teaching positions in a state regular high school. They had successfully "jumped out of the agricultural door" (*tiaochu nongmen*), as one of older teachers, born in 1975, explained. In comparison, they regarded only a small minority of their current students as capable of ever achieving this kind of social mobility. Although the vast majority of students would at some point continue on to two- or three-year colleges, most would study vocational subjects and become skilled blue-collar workers or low-level white-collar employees in poorly paid jobs at businesses or in the service sector. This was a fate that teachers would do almost anything to prevent from happening to their own children. They believed that their own single children were in much better positions of gaining higher social status and secure levels of income than their students were, because they themselves were educated parents and teachers. There was, to my best knowledge, only one of the 120 teachers at Number Two High whose child was a student at the school, and other teachers openly admitted that they would regard it as a failure of their own parenthood if their children would make it "only" to a school like Number Two High. Teachers' hopes for their only children, regardless of gender, was that they would get good educations, stable incomes in relatively comfortable jobs, and eventually the sense of a secure life equivalent to, or preferably better than, what they as parents experienced. They hoped that their children would be more successful than themselves. However, they also nurtured a fear that problems of widespread "selfishness" among youth would be so deeply entrenched in the darker sides of economic development and uncontrolled access to information and influence from electronic media that their children would not be able to escape them.

Teachers who were parents of children below the age of their own high school students quite often wanted to talk to me about the advantages and dangers of their children watching the highly popular (and explicitly violent) Japanese and Chinese animated films on TV and playing computer games. Like so many other parents in China, they tried to enroll their children in special classes of art, music, English, math, or sports to give them "good educational alternatives," and because there were not many of these activities available in Gaoshan, some of the most ambitious parents would move to the county capital for the one purpose of improving their children's educational options. They strongly believed in individual solutions to the risks of falling behind in education and on the future job market, and they hoped that because their own "quality" (*suzhi*) was higher than that of most parents of their students, their children would stand much better chances of succeeding.

Just like the parents of their students, they regarded their own children's grandparents as unsuitable caretakers. Grandparents they found, were already too old to understand the requirements of contemporary society. They had not received good educations, and consequently they were regarded as incapable of socializing and educating their grandchildren to become successful at the first step toward a good life—namely, in their basic education. In other words, the expectations of teachers of their own children were really not that different from the expectations of their students' parents. They all wanted their children to get better educations than themselves and secure jobs. Teachers were certainly concerned for their students, but they would use whatever means they had to improve their own children's chances of having better and more secure futures than they saw possible for the students in their own school. Their first priority was to invest in their own children's possibilities of advancing to a better school than the one they were teaching in.

Post-Mao China's simultaneous display of premodern, modern, and postmodern conditions within the context of unchanging political authoritarianism (Yan 2011, 71–72) was reflected in the lives and experiences of the teachers in Number Two High. They recalled their own youth and the pursuit of professional careers as something that was in effect given and logical because of their relative success as students. It was a largely undisputed, reasonable, and desirable first modernity family strategy, aimed at ensuring long-term economic security and growing wealth. Becoming a teacher was not merely, or even primarily, beneficial for the individual but for the entire family. It was not a matter of individual choice or preference, and the teachers were only to a limited degree trying to fulfill a more abstract late-modernity wish for achievement of "individual desires" or quest for "developing oneself." Teachers explained their career path in terms of long trajectories of (premodern) ethics of filial piety and a resulting deep-rooted sense of responsibility toward their families' interests and obedience to family authority. It was a path made possible by the Communist Party's modernized mass education. By being successful students within a context of otherwise limited options for upward mobility, they had broken with their family's inherited status as peasants, rural workers, or small-scale businesspeople. They were active participants in the modern struggle for economic development, formal education, and marriage based on individual choice, and they had found the desired social and economic security for themselves. At the same time, they were under as much influence as were their students and children (and the rest of us, for that matter) from globalized media's postmodern celebrations of individuality, intimacy, and choice through the many series and talk shows they watched, the increasingly flexible job market that they worried would make life difficult for their children and students, and an increased sense of risk and danger related to environmental change and fragile economic structures (Beck 2008) that were a reality also in the local area they knew best.

However, in their professional lives as teachers in the state school they were required to promote the Chinese official views on the role of the individual in the socialist state and its responsibility in relation to the experienced results of an individualizing society. As teachers they had to socialize their students to recognize and internalize the individual's responsibility to remain loyal to political authorities and not misinterpret the increased requirements on people to make choices about their own lives as new options for challenging "basic truths," such as the exclusive right and ability of the Communist Party to rule. The teachers' task was to ensure that rural students would recognize the blurred boundaries between private and public, to distinguish a sphere that allowed for (even required) individual exploration, experimentation, and (e.g., professional) choice making from one that required unquestioned obedience, acceptance, or at least silence.

As teachers, they were on a daily basis obliged to accommodate to the realities of a society where the private sphere opened up ever-new possibilities for negotiations of self and self-interests, but where the public sphere remained under much tighter control of political authorities whom teachers should not—and largely did not—question. In political debates about how to create an educational system that was better adapted to the challenges facing their students and children, teachers felt they had no voice. There were no independent teachers' associations, or any kind of public forum in which they could discuss their working conditions or experiences as teachers, and they chose to discuss these issues only in the private sphere. They could also not risk letting their students freely organize in the student association, and they could not encourage them to otherwise use organizational means to support each other or promote their interests as a group. They did not translate their own criticism of a traditionalist education system or disappointing rural students into acts or ideas of resistance. Instead, their ways of dealing with a divided self that accepted and taught political obedience while celebrating individual choice and initiative was to promote individual solutions, individual responsibility, and individual morality as means to overcome most immediate social challenges.

CONCLUSION

Authoritarian Individualization

Since the 1980s, China has successfully expanded education at all levels. The country has implemented nine years of free compulsory schooling for nearly all children and opened up universities and colleges for an unprecedented number of students, including students from rural areas. By 2009, the world's largest education system had altogether 260 million students at all levels, nearly 14 million full-time teachers, and 552,000 schools (Ministry of Education of the People's Republic of China 2012). In rural areas of richer provinces like Zhejiang, a large majority of youth now graduate from high schools or vocational secondary schools. In the 1980s and early 1990s, a whole village would rejoice when a child made it into university but now only acceptance by a top university, or at least a bachelor *benke* study in a provincial capital, is regarded as worthy of larger celebrations. Since the late 1990s, the state no longer allocated jobs to university and college graduates, and with the huge growth in the number of youth with such degrees since the early 2000s, the competition for more attractive jobs has intensified. This is reflected in the enormous interest in the national civil service examinations,[1] which are a main entrance to positions in the state bureaucracy. These examinations often attract thousands of candidates for just a few positions, and people will sit several times for the exams in the hope of winning the lottery for a secure income and permanent job in the state sector.[2] Rather than seeking low-paid or low-status jobs, an increasing number of students and graduates choose to seek further education abroad; parents are investing heavily in children's formal education, which, despite reports about rising unemployment among university graduates, is still perceived as a key to more stable incomes, prestigious positions, secure lives for parents at old age, and "face" for the entire family.

Education in its different forms has enjoyed a continuous popularity in the history of China (e.g., Thøgersen 2002; Kipnis 2011). Yet, in the 2010s it has become the object of criticism from many groups and individuals for being outmoded in relation to the demands of the labor market and out of pace with international standards and developments in the field of education and research. This criticism is not so different from earlier periods of the post-Mao era, but it is intensifying. Although the Chinese authorities after Mao's death have been celebrated for their initiatives to revolutionize the country's economy, creating what in the context of world history is nothing less than extraordinary rapid improvements of living standards and state capacities, the very same authorities have repeatedly criticized the ability of their own education system to sufficiently adapt to international standards and live up to the global desire for ever more "outstanding talent" (*jiechu rencai*). Hefty investments in education, and several attempts at reform, have not satisfied the leaders' explicit aspiration to develop an educational system that focuses more on training young people to become "creative" and "innovative." One of the most prominent and explicit criticisms of the lack of emphasis on innovation and creativity in the education system has come from former prime minister Wen Jiabao,[3] who is joined by many teachers, intellectuals, students, educators, and parents from all over the country.

Taking the state school as a case, the research presented in this book helps us better understand not only why schooling of young people in China has changed much less than one would expect considering the dominant critical discourses regarding its shortcomings, but also how irreversible processes of individualization in China are reforming institutional practices from within as well as people's lives and perceptions.

CHOICE AS TECHNIQUE OF GOVERNING
AND AS EXPERIENCE OF PEOPLE

Theories of individualization have served here as a framework to explore how a prominent state institution—the school—attempts to develop learned individuals and citizens who willingly take responsibility for their own lives and livelihoods while contributing to the global neoliberal economy and the growth of China. Equally important are the perspectives on the individualization of Chinese society as seen by teachers and students: how they view their roles as individuals and perceive the choices and responsibilities they have toward themselves, their families, the school, and the nation. Individualization has been a strategy to pursue modernity in China, first formulated by intellectuals at the turn of the nineteenth century and later practiced at the societal level. A common thread in the political discourse and societal practice of the Chinese version of individualization has been, and still is, that the individual must take more responsibility for contributing to the modernization of China, that is, for generating wealth and power for the party-state (Yan 2010). This state-initiated rise of the individual has opened up new possibilities for people in many spheres of their lives. As scholars have shown since the 1980s through empirical studies of nongovernmental organizations (NGOs), women's organizations, consumption, careers, barefoot lawyers, and so forth, "the individual on the rise has gained more awareness of entitlement and rights, becoming more determined to pursue individual interests and to take proactive actions in the form of identity politics and a rights movement against the oppression of various collectivities" (Yan 2010, 509). Thus, up to a certain level it is in the common interest of both the party-state and the Chinese population to continuously recreate and expand the social space for individual initiative, creativity, and decision making.

Viewed in this way, choice, which has been a key tenet throughout this book, may be regarded both as a technique of governing in the neoliberal economy of China and as a specific form of experience. These two aspects are inseparable from each other, and choice as a condition is simultaneously a social practice, an ideal, a possibility, a requirement, and a burden. Taking choice as a technique of governing, it is possible to better grasp how neoliberalism with Chinese, or rather Chinese socialist characteristics, creates and shapes new subjects and selves. This perspective on choice as a technique of governing has been convincingly put forward, for instance, in studies of urban professionals, showing how "late-socialist neo-liberal governmentality has cultivated active and enterprising subjects who are able to make choices about appropriate employment that develop the individual, the city, and even the nation" (Hoffman 2010, 10). The ever-expanding demands for people to make what seem to be their own individual choices is by no means an outcome of the state retreating or ending its ambition of governance; rather, it is an actively employed technique.

In the ethnography presented in this book, there are many examples of the ways governmental techniques of choice are employed by Chinese school authorities and adopted, sometimes ideologically idealized, by teachers and students as a life condition. Experiments with student associations and elections of voluntary candidates from among the "most suitable" students are examples of how such governing techniques can be internalized and put into practice by teachers in the state school. Similarly, pep rallies intended to raise students' motivation demonstrate how personal choice and self-discipline are idealized and presented as a way—in fact the only way—"forward" for students, and for human beings in general. However, while choice is something that is expected of the individual, it also provides a genuine perception of being offered options that were not available to people of older generations. By carrying out the study of Number Two High from the perspective of the ways social processes of individualization were played out between people, and between the state and the individuals in the daily life of school, it became clearer how choice and other techniques of governing modern subjects in China today also create popular ideologies of individualism. Choice is a potentially dangerous condition of life, and it creates uncertainty, as shown especially in the interviews with teachers; however, at the same time, it is perceived and experienced by many teachers and students as a highly positive thing, often reformulated into an ideal of "freedom" (ziyou).

The subjective experience of choice in post-Mao neosocialist China is real, and it is almost impossible to imagine that people who have collectively experienced such immense changes regarding the scope of life choices—and, not least, imagined choices—over a time span of just thirty to forty years would accept a major pullback. Processes of individualization, as part of the broader Chinese modernization project, appear to be irreversible, partly because people rapidly embrace choice when it is provided and adopt ideologies of individualism. With China's complete integration into the global network of trade and politics, this trend of individualization is further enforced by people's increasing experiences of the failure of "experts in the management of risks" as reflected in a growing mistrust in the rationality and ability of science, politics, mass media, business, legal systems, and even the military to solve critical problems and prevent major risks related to, for instance, the environment or armed conflict (Beck 2008, 54). None of these institutions is in a position to sufficiently define or control risks in a rational way, and as a consequence many people mistrust their promises of rationality and feel forced to rely on themselves instead. To an increasing extent, this happens within China, where endless scandals of food poisoning, fake medicine, and environmental destruction have led to a widespread mistrust in officials' abilities and willingness to curb these and other risks (e.g., Yan 2012a; Jing 2000). At the same time, the mistrust appears in many respects to be mutual. Although political authorities, through their policies of structural and institutional change, encourage (and indeed compel) people to be self-reliant and take economic initiative, they also continue to take surveillance systems and censoring practices to new heights. They are continually developing new technologies to control the Internet, for instance, and huge numbers of increasingly advanced surveillance cameras have been installed in public areas, sometimes even in classrooms in institutions of higher education (Langfitt 2013). This reveals a growing mistrust on the part of the political authorities of the population's ability to govern itself and live up to the ideals and requirements of neosocialism.

The simultaneous liberation of the individual as a private and economic unit, combined with the strengthening of direct political control and development of ever-new technologies of governing, is reflected also in school practices. When teachers in schools such as Number Two High experiment with new means to encourage their students to study harder, and promote student "democracy" in order to involve students directly in disciplining their peers, it is a reflection of teachers' attempts to be skilled professionals helping young people to regulate their practices as individuals and citizens in a rapidly changing society. In the individualizing China, young people are increasingly required to take responsibility for their own futures and rely on themselves rather than on their families or the state's limited welfare structure. Teachers sometimes encourage high school students, for instance, when they are participating in elections to the student associations, to come forward as highly self-disciplined individuals who are willingly learning how to recognize the invisible borders between acceptable and unacceptable (politicized) behavior. However, a potential rise of the students through, for example, inclusive student associations would be difficult to control by a government that in the social sphere is demonstrating a growing distrust of its population. The result is a shaky balance between the emphasis on developing students' self-discipline and the enforcing and strengthening of schools' direct forms of disciplining students. This illustrates how the individualization of society, spurred by policies of institutional change, forces school administrators and teachers to continually invent and remake techniques of governmentality.

DISCIPLINE AND SELF-DISCIPLINE
IN AN INDIVIDUALIZING SOCIETY

The turn to the individual as the main unit responsible for failure or success in society, for welfare insurance, work, and private life, was reflected in teachers' educational practices and in some of their attempts to better prepare students for life after graduation by pushing them to study harder and motivating them by appealing to their responsibility toward self, family, and nation—in that order. The reason why the strengthening of the nation was not at the forefront in motivational activities was not a lack of patriotism or disregard of the requirements of official curriculum on the part of teachers. Rather, it was due to many teachers' intuitive feeling that speaking directly to students' self-interests, their consciences, and dreams for the future would be considerably more efficient than sticking to the official discourse of the ideal individual striving toward collective goals of the socialist state and the Chinese nation. For the very same reasons, the image of the famous communist hero Lei Feng, and the campaigns to use him as an example of self-sacrifice and socialist morality, were molded to revitalize his figure as a young man of flesh and blood with a higher degree of self-consciousness (bordering on vanity) than what was the case in earlier post-Mao campaigns.

Various local and national campaigns directed at students, such as patriotic speech competitions, visits to the elderly, cleaning-up campaigns in local communities, and so forth, were aimed at fostering in students stronger feelings of collective responsibility and compassion toward both the local and the broader national communities. Students and teachers willingly participated in these activities, though most of them displayed limited enthusiasm and engagement beyond the exact duration of the activity. Rarely did the official discourse on the good citizen and individual, as promoted through campaigns and textbooks, seem to hit a nerve with students—major exceptions being the very emotional media presentations in connection with the Olympic Games in Beijing in 2008 and the yearly TV celebrations of heroes among the people.

The version of socialist collective morality and ideals of the learning individual that is promoted in schools through standard curriculum may seem out of step with students' own experiences and the demands from society. The state promotes the vision of a self-reliant and responsible individual who willingly contributes to the neoliberal economy, but it requires at the same time unquestioned loyalty to a Chinese socialist ideal of a one-party state that is ruling individuals who are supposed to be forever connected to each other through bonds of lineage, history, and shared goals for the national future. In this vision, there is no room for alternative ideologies, and the only available formal structures for students to organize within are the Communist Party's youth organization or the internal student associations. In practice, the school strongly emphasizes that within a predefined and non-negotiable political authoritarian framework, students (and teachers) are individually responsible for success or failure. It promotes a version of individualism that contains a strong message of a do-it-yourself and pay-less-attention-to-the-rest ideology, but without the notion of the individual being autonomous with inherent rights as such.

Much is demanded from students who have to take responsibility for their studies, orient themselves in the market of education, make decisions regarding jobs and income, keep themselves up to date with developments in society and in the world, strengthen self-discipline, and secure their own futures. Many students at Number Two High have grown up with parents who work in other places, and they experience an unprecedented level of material wealth compared to the older generations in the area. Students feel quite free to embrace the opportunities they see to develop close friendships, begin love relationships, and communicate through the readily available electronic media, sometimes pushing the limits as to what the school and their parents can accept. Consequently, both schools and the teachers feel pressed, not least by parents, to continually recreate disciplinary techniques and enforce, rather than weaken, social control over students. When I started my research at Number Two High in 2008, I was expecting to find a less rigid system of education with more room for debating the content of the curriculum and allowing for student participation than I had seen during fieldwork in minority high schools in 1995–1996 (Hansen 1999). To the contrary, I experienced at Number Two High a school that to a much greater degree than the minority schools at that time was governed through techniques that ensured that students are kept busy in a controlled way throughout most days and evenings, hardly leaving any sanctioned public room for critical discussions of knowledge, content of education, form of schooling, or just the daily challenges of living one's life largely within school walls.

These are the direct causes for many complaints about the Chinese educational system from teachers and people engaged in China's possibility of rising not only as a world economic power but as a nation of an ever-increasing number of so-called outstanding talents. It is the reason why many teachers and educators may be heard arguing that despite the government's huge investments in human resources, Chinese education is out of pace with the requirements of a globalized society in which the demand for innovative and creative skills is growing. From another perspective, though, the data from Number Two High suggest that the school is much better adapted to the current political realities of China and to global trends in the field of education than its reputation suggests. Seen from a global perspective, the Chinese education system may in some respects be at a vanguard position of some major changes in that liberal states are also increasingly adopting strict regimes of testing, evaluation, and other forms of auditing—practices that enjoy a long and strong tradition in China (Kipnis 2011, 157). Most likely, nothing completely novel will occur on the Chinese educational scene in the near future because of the structural constraints that are generated by the population's high levels of "educational desire" (172). Education has become a value in and of itself— a strategy by which parents and their children can accumulate human capital, even in cases in which education as such neither provides the skills and training that it promises nor the attractive and secure positions within the labor market that constitute the dream for many students and parents (Woronov 2012a). Woronov's research of educational practices in urban vocational schools have shown that many students, instead of being engaged in developing specific job-related practical skills, are trained to endure years of boredom and meaningless tasks in a new kind of labor that mimics a school-like system. This kind of "training" may in fact be a better preparation for many of these young people's future employment than what they are taught in a formal curriculum (Woronov 2012a, 711).

This book suggests that the form and content of high school education may also be much better adapted to the political system of neosocialist China than many of its critics tend to acknowledge. The contemporary Chinese version of individualization mostly speaks the language of privatization and market economy and remains under the tight management of the party-state (Yan 2010, 494–495). It is a kind of authoritarian individualization that requires a state school that, in the face of risking uncontrollable outcomes of a rise of the individual, aims at building loyalty to political authorities and acceptance of the party's monopoly on truth. Despite the dominant neoliberal discourse on the demands for innovation and creativity, it seems unlikely that the Communist Party leadership will be willing to take a calculated risk and introduce into the broad base of the state education system significant elements of critical debate, student participation, training of intellectual, creative, and analytical skills, or experiment with substantially new forms of teaching and learning. It is likely that some elite schools, and possibly an increasing number of private schools, will be able to continue along this path, but it would most likely not include the vast majority of mainstream, non-elite schools all over the country. The neosocialist Chinese state experiments with a model that integrates capitalist market economy with an authoritarian socialist form of government; and "capitalizing on rapidly rising prosperity and continued economic growth, the party-state has reinvented itself, putting the rule of the CCP on an increasingly solid footing both materially and organizationally, and, increasingly, ideologically" (Pieke 2009, 4). In this ongoing project, the state school continues to play a key role, and its combination of a formal curriculum that emphasizes socialist ideals, on the one hand, and practices that emphasize the demands on the individual in a neoliberal economy, on the other, fits quite well with the political realities and the characteristics of the individualization processes of Chinese society.

AUTHORITARIAN INDIVIDUALIZATION
AND ROOM FOR RESISTANCE

Exemplary teaching methods and a lack of critical debates in schools do not necessarily produce compliant adolescent and adult subjects (Kipnis 2011, 162); nor does an individualized society with a rising of the individual necessarily create political resistance toward an authoritarian form of government or school organization. During times of combined global and local feelings of risk and insecurity, the neosocialist state constitutes a framework of safety and certainty for many people that should not be underestimated. On a smaller and more localized scale, the rural school, as part of a national Chinese education system, constitutes for many individuals and their families a familiar institution with long historical trajectories and a persistent reputation for providing options for upward social mobility. During my years of fieldwork on education, I have often been struck by the outspokenness and devastating critiques that so many teachers and students have voiced against an education system that, after all, continues to enjoy extremely high status and respect in Chinese society. A concern that this highly valued education system now runs the risk of impeding the very rise of China on the global scene of technological advance and economic growth—unless it is thoroughly reformed to provide room for creativity and innovation—seems to have intensified through the 2000s. During my fieldwork, teachers and students repeatedly and spontaneously brought forward their long lists of critique against current educational policies and practices; but at the same time, practically all the teachers and students would point out that radical changes were impossible because of the size of the Chinese population as compared to its resources, the need to have a nationally comparative examination system building on objective tests rather than subjective analysis, and the general low educational level especially in rural areas.

Teachers' and students' critiques of the public sphere—in this case the educational policies and practices—were mainly raised in the private sphere. There is ample room for this kind of criticism, which has no practical consequences and requires hardly any responsibility on the part of those who raise it. It is relatively easy to criticize the school system from within, because no one expects students or teachers to act on their criticism and engage collectively to promote real change. Consequently, criticism of the school's lack of space for developing creative skills, or failure to counter students' presumed selfishness, remains in and of itself an individual endeavor—a privatized act of resistance that echoes official discourse on the shortcomings of the school system and has no collective consequences. The most vocal critics of the education system whom I have encountered are those who know the school best from the inside, but this view does not prevent them from working very hard to make sure that their own children are successful in the very same system, to which there is no real alternative. The Chinese version of authoritarian individualization has created a social environment of both political and interhuman tolerance for this kind of criticism of the public sphere that is raised in the private sphere without any real consequences.

Practical consequences of privately raised criticism seem to emerge only when private interests are threatened to the extent that people see no other options than to collectively organize, for instance, through protests, demonstrations, in NGOs, and the like. However much it is criticized, the schooling of children in the Chinese educational system continues to serve the interest of people's private ambitions so well that few see any need for collective action to change it. Those who come out of the school have been taught to stay focused on their own interests and blame themselves for eventual failure or success in their lives. If they were to collectively organize to promote change, as some have argued often happens among people living in highly individualized societies that, unlike China, are based on cultural democracy, a welfare state, and a notion of the individual being autonomous (Beck and Beck-Gernsheim 2002; Beck and Grande 2010), they would most likely do so only if private interests were clearly and directly threatened. This could be in the familiar cases of confiscations of land, local corruption, polluted drinking water, or loss of work, as we already see happening in tens of thousands yearly (mainly rural) protests. Surveys of Chinese university graduates have suggested that the post-1980s generation have placed their public lives in service to their private ambitions (Rosen 2009). Compared to the urban educated university graduates of these surveys, students from Number Two High are likely to remain rural, and many of them will eventually have to find jobs as blue-collar workers in the service sector or in small-scale businesses. They may nurture ambitions to work toward lower-middle-class status, and it is very likely that they will hope for improved educations for their children as the main means toward this end, just like their own parents did. Some of them might eventually experience threats against private interests that will cause them to link up in protest with other discontented migrant workers, peasants, or rural people without jobs or social security, but they are likely to concentrate on their own social and economic investments in the private sphere for the sake of their own individual and closer families' interests—as the neosocialist school has in effect prepared them to do.

NOTES

INTRODUCTION

1   For example, Alpermann 2011; Griffiths 2012; Hansen and Svarverud 2010; Liu 2010; D. Wang 2010; Yan 2009, 2010, 2012a.

2   For a brief Chinese summary of the Shanghai results and some of their possible implications, see appendix B 35 in Yang D. and Chai 2011, 324–326.

3   See, for instance, the official web page of the Ministry of Education (www.moe.edu.cn/) for a number of official speeches regarding the need to reform the system and form of education, and, e.g., Chang et al. 2009 for summaries of educational reform debates in 2009.

4   See, for instance, a brief overview on parts of the debate in the United States in Fong and Altbach 2011.

5   Alpermann 2011; Hansen and Svarverud 2010; Yan 2009, 2010, 2011, 2012b; Griffiths 2012; Kleinman et al. 2011; Zhang, Kleinman, and Tu 2010.

6   For instance, Pepper 1996; Cleverley 1991; Rawski 1979; articles in Peterson et al. 2001; Paul Bailey 2007 on women's public education; and Benjamin Elman and Alexander Woodside's (1994) collection of articles, some of which take the reader back to premodern forms of education.

7   Unger 1982; Kwong 1988; Seeberg 2000; Shirk 1982.

8   For example, Hayhoe 1992; Hannum and Park 2007; Liu, Ross, and Kelly 2000; Postiglione 2006; Murphy and Johnson 2009; Kipnis 2011; Schoenhals 1993; and, e.g., Vickers 2009b; Vickers and Zeng 2012; Vickers 2009a; Murphy 2004; Kennedy, Fairbrother, and Zhao 2012; Jones 2012; Cheung and Pan 2006.

9   For example, Yu 2009; Postiglione 1999; Iredale, Bilik, and Su 2001; Hansen 1999; Y. Chen 2008; Tsung 2009.

10 During my fieldwork in minority areas of Yunnan in the 1990s, I found that vocational education was a preferred path for many poorer parents (including Han)

because at that time children graduating from vocational middle schools were guaranteed local jobs in the state sector, and it was a cheaper educational path than the regular one (Hansen 1999).

11 Thøgersen 1990; Guo and Lamb 2010; Zhang and Hao 1993; Shi 2008; Schulte 2013.

12 For instance, on the system of work units (*danwei*), (Bray 2005), one-child policy and biopolitics (Greenhalgh 2005, 2008), personal files (J. Yang 2011), sex and prostitution (Jeffreys 2004), citizenship (Culp 2006), the discourse of *suzhi* "quality" (e.g., Anagnost 2004; Kipnis 2006; Woronov 2009; Brownell 2009; Murphy 2004; Sun 2009), policing and punishment (Bakken 2005), training of urban professionals (Hoffman 2010) and, of course, the educational system.

Regarding Michel Foucault's theory of governmentality and its impact on education studies in general, see, for instance, Ball 2009; Besley and Peters 2007; Peters and Besley 2007.

13 Foucault's notion of *conduire des conduites* (often referred to as "the conduct of conduct") is used to express how power is exercised through the leading of others in order to make them act upon themselves. Foucault writes, "The exercise of power consists in guiding the possibility of conduct and putting in order the possible outcome," and to govern is "to structure the possible field of action of others" (Foucault 1982, 789–790). See also Dean 2009; Rose 1999.

14 See also Kipnis 2008.

15 Bauman 2000, 2001; Beck and Beck-Gernsheim 2002; Beck, Giddens, and Lash 1994; Beck and Grande 2010; Beck and Willms 2004; Giddens 1991. For a brief overview of the individualization thesis, or "cluster of individualization theses" see, for instance, Howard 2007a. See also other articles in Howard 2007b.

16 See Steven Lukes's classic study from 1973 (reprinted with new introduction) regarding the multiple interpretations and perceptions of individualism (Lukes 2006). See also William T. Greene's critique of the notion of individualism being one specific ideology (Greene 2008).

17 Calhoun 2010; Suzuki et al. 2010; Han and Shim 2010; Yan 2010; Kyung-Sup 2010; Kyung-Sup and Min-Young 2010.

18 Noted also in a comment by Craig Calhoun (2010).

19 The extremely popular TV show Super Girls was banned on several occasions, first in 2006 and then again in 2011, both times mainly because of its assumed bad moral influence on youth. The show was first known as *Super Voice Girls* (Chaoji nüsheng), and when it was relaunched in 2009 it was called *Happy Girls* (Kuaile nüsheng).

20 On expressions of self in Chinese media and pop culture, see for example, Latham 2007. On the discipline of psychology and the increasing interest in psychoanalysis and psychological counseling in China, see, for instance Osnos 2011; Hou and Zhang 2007; Kleinman et al. 2011; Scharff and Varvin 2014.

21 The section is partly built on Hansen 2012a.

22 For official regulations on education, news on policies, educational research, and so on, see the Chinese Education and Research Network (CERNET), which is managed by the Ministry of Education in cooperation with several universities (http://www.edu.cn/index.shtml).

23 See the lists of each province at the web page of the Ministry of Education http://www.moe.gov.cn/publicfiles/business/htmlfiles/moe/s5200/201103/116066.html (accessed October 15, 2011).

24 For example, Wellens 2010, 87–93.

25 Barabasch, Huang, and Lawson 2009; Guo and Lamb 2010; Shi 2008; Melinda Liu 2009; Xinhua 2011.

26 See also Nancy Abelmann's ethnographic study of Korean- American students in a US university (Abelmann 2009).

27 As in the case of the high school, names of the township, county, most people, and other local institutions studied have been anonymized throughout the book.

28 This information is from the official web site of the county, but in order to maintain anonymity I do not provide the link to the web page.

29 The reference to "parents" in this book does not necessarily refer to parents of students who were currently studying in Number Two High when the fieldwork was carried out. I knew and talked to a large number of people with children in Gaoshan and other places during fieldwork, and they have all contributed to my analysis of how parents' view their children's education, and how they choose to invest in it.

CHAPTER 1. DISCIPLINE AND AGENCY

1 The total number of students had decreased from approximately 1,500 students in 2008 to 1,179 in 2012 because of the elimination of vocational classes.

2 The survey was made of all the 1,123 students who were present during one day of school in 2012. Only two students did not respond to the questionnaire.

3 A number of families who originated from rural areas had achieved urban household registrations and yet managed to have two children. They either paid the fine imposed on them or accepted a longer period without a job and then eventually paid a fine to have the second child legally registered in the city. On a national level, there was (in early 2013) much discussion about the possibility of easing birth control further and allowing not only two singletons who marry to have two children, but also granting the same option to a singleton marrying a partner with siblings. This would help ease the future burden on children who were required according to law to take financial responsibility for their parents in old age, and in the long run it would help China secure a larger labor force. See also Greenhalgh 2010.

4 See also Hansen 2012c.

5 According to the National Population and Family Commission of China, the average sex ratio has in recent years been slowly decreasing, but it remains very high at 118.08 males per 100 females in 2012. (http://www.npfpc.gov.cn/en/activities/detail.aspx?articleid=110818165111159972) (accessed March 5, 2012). Moreover, the average figure does not reveal the significant differences across the country, with some rural areas having an even more unequal ratio and, for instance, some ethnic minority areas having a much less unequal ration (see articles on demography and population in Zhao and Guo 2007).

6 The phenomenon was, for instance, debated in the Central Chinese TV's *News Probe,* January 22, 2011.

7 Although I have talked to teachers and parents in Guangdong who had heard examples of similar practices, it seems to be far more widespread in rural areas of Zhejiang than in other places of China. See also Pang 2004 for a brief report about this phenomenon.

8   The reactions among older people to these quite profound changes in families lie beyond the scope of this book. In general, much less fieldwork has been done among older people than among the young in China, but see, for instance, Boermel 2009; Hansen 2008; Thøgersen and Ni 2010.

9   See also Fei 2011 regarding suicide in rural China.

10   See Strickland 2010 for a rare study of close male friendships among youth in China.

11   According to the *South China Morning Post*, the number of suicides among primary and middle school students was thirteen in 2011, up from eight in 2010 ("China Has More Than 70,000 Private Schools" 2012). For recent studies regarding psychological counseling in China, see, for instance, Hou and Zhang 2007; Scharff and Varvin 2013. See also Fei 2011 regarding suicides in China.

12   An example of negative influence of corrupt school leadership on a whole school's atmosphere and performance is discussed in D. Wang 2012.

13   A better translation here would probably be the Danish word *sammenhold*, which also expresses the social and psychological dimensions of this form of "companionship."

14   See also Trevor Grimshaw's study of students in universities, in which he argues that students display much more agency and resistance to disciplinary practices than commonly assumed (Grimshaw 2007).

15   For example, Duffell 2000; Gaztambide-Fernández 2009; Lomawaima 1994; Trafzer, Keller, and Sisquoc 2006.

16   This Confucian saying was also employed during the Cultural Revolution to support the ideology that intellectual knowledge was of no use in itself.

CHAPTER 2. TEXT AND TRUTH

1   Some parts of this chapter and chapter 4 have been published in Hansen 2013.

2   Dello-Iacovo 2009; Nie 2008; Zhan and Wujie 2004; W. O. Lee and Ho 2005; Vickers 2009b; Vickers 2009a; Tyl 2002; Jones 2005.

3   Ding et al. 2008a, 4.

4   Because I am interested in showing what students read and study, the translations of text extracts are from the Chinese textbook version rather than the original German version. In the last sentence, the textbook version used here is a shortened version of the Chinese translation in Ding et al. 2008, 40.

5   Ding et al. 2008a, 4.

6   Nienhauser 1985, 397–400.

7   See, e.g., De Bary et al. 2000, 582–583.

8   It poses a dilemma to the Chinese authorities that the Nobel Prize, on the one hand, has a very high status in China, and on the other hand, has been fiercely criticized in most of the few instances when Chinese citizens (or former citizens) have been awarded the price: For instance, Gao Xingjian (Chinese citizen until 1997), who received the Literature Prize in 2000; Liu Xiaobo, who received the controversial Peace Prize in 2010; the Dalai Lama, who fled China in 1959 and received the Peace Prize in 1989. In 2012, though, the authorities endorsed the decision by the Nobel Literature Committee to award the Literature Prize to the author Mo Yan.

9   The German term *Bildung* (not entirely covered by the English "education" or "learning," but equivalent to the Danish *dannelse*) is translated as *xiuyang* in the article in *Dushu* where part of the school text is derived from. However, in the schoolbook, it is translated as *jiaoyang*. For a collection of the original works of Herman Hesse, see Michels 2007.

10   *Dushu* no. 4, 1990, and no. 3, 1991.

11   In fact, it is not mentioned in *Dushu* that the translation is from *Magie des Buches*, but based on the original text by Hesse I assume that this must be the case.

12   Ding Fan and Yang Jiujun, *Yuwen* (*Language and Literature*), 41–42. The translation is based on the Chinese textbook version, not the original German, which is slightly different at some points.

13   For example, Nie 2008; Zhan and Wujie 2004; Cheung and Pan 2006; Vickers 2009b; Tyl 2002.

14   The textbooks consistently uses "Party and government" (*dang he zhengfu*) rather than the expression of "Party-government" (*dangzheng*) that has been commonly used in academic articles, but has been criticized and banned from publications in the early 2000s through censorship in publishing houses.

15   See also Hansen and Pang 2008 regarding the concept of "freedom" used among young migrant workers.

16   For a very good discussion of patriotism and a range of other aspects (not specifically related to perceptions of the individual) taught through the dual courses of Thought and Values and Thought and Politics, see especially Vickers 2009a.

17   I am grateful to Flora Sapio for informing and helping me clarify this issue.

18   Nie fails to mention in her book when her fieldwork was carried out, but based on the publications she uses and some other indicators, I assume it must have been in the late 1990s or maybe around the year 2000.

19   See also Bakken's discussion of various (largely failed) attempts to introduce other more credible role models to young people (Bakken 2000, 194–196).

CHAPTER 3. HIERARCHY AND DEMOCRACY

1   Parts of the chapter have previously been published in Hansen 2012b.

2   The debate was broadcast and referred to on a large number of web pages assembling news; for just one example, see http://big5.chinanews.com.cn:89/gate/big5/www.chinanews.com/edu/2011/10-04/3368641.shtml (accessed November 3, 2011).

3   This web page, Student Cadre Net (*Xuesheng ganbu wang*), dedicated to the topic of student cadres, was set up in 2010 in Shijiazhuang, the capital of Henan, and clearly many articles are from that area. However, it is unclear who is responsible for the web page. It has a dot-com address and seems not to be a government-sponsored page, but its numerous articles echo official discourse. It also includes individual accounts of life as a student cadre, speeches, and a chat room that was not frequently visited at the time of my research. Several attempts to contact the webmaster to clarify origin and leadership of the page failed, because the e-mail address of the webmaster was not in use. http://www.xsgbw.com/ (accessed April 4, 2011).

4   See also a range of articles on model students and student cadres in articles on the web site of the Ministry of Education.

5   The article refers specifically to student cadres in higher education, but the issues referred are equivalent to views I commonly heard raised regarding cadres in high schools, and they are found in many documents on the Internet and in various educational documents.

6   The documentary movie *Please Vote for Me* (W. Chen 2008) gives, for example, a very interesting account of the voting process and its many implications for children at the primary school level.

7   See, for instance, Li R. 2007; Yang 1997; Ma 2008; Zhang 2006.

8   This also explains why there is no detailed discussion in the book about the activities of the Youth League as such. For all practical purposes, the Youth League and the student association were merged in Number Two High.

9   Concerning *suzhi* see also "Introduction" in this book and especially Anagnost 2004; Kipnis 2006; Sun 2009; Woronov 2009; Murphy 2004.

10   http://news.cntv.cn/program/shouxiyehua/20120514/100037.shtml (accessed December 5, 2012).

CHAPTER 4. MOTIVATION AND EXAMINATION

1   Thomas and Peng 2011; Davey, De Lian, and Higgins 2007; Hannum, An, and Cherng 2011; Ross and Wang 2010a. See also the special issue of *Chinese Education and Society* on the national entrance examination system, edited by Ross and Wang 2010b.

2   Adopted from Sina Weibo and published May 7, 2012, on *China Smack* www.chinasmack.com/2012/pictures/chinese-students-get-iv-drips-while-studying-for-gaokao-exam.html (accessed April 7, 2014).

3   www.o6b.com/. See also Wang's blog: http://blog.sina.com.cn/wangguoquan (accessed June 4, 2012).

4   Wang 2008.

5   During the second of Mr. Zhang's lectures my research assistant joined me, and her transcripts of the lecture supplied my own notes, which were not complete because I was not able to understand all of the vocabulary and each sentence in the lecture, which was delivered at a very high speed. Comparing my assistant's notes and my own notes from the first lecture with the booklet sold to students after the show, we saw that apart from some personal stories and some of the stunts described later in this chapter, most of what Mr. Zhang said was based directly on text of the booklet. Therefore, in this and the following section of the chapter I sometimes refer to the text in the booklet, sometimes to the talk by Mr. Zhang.

6   According to a joint 2008 report by the Chinese Ministry of Foreign Affairs and the United Nations (based on Chinese official data), China is "likely" to reach the UN Millennium Development Goal of eliminating gender disparities at all levels of education by 2015, and the government provides "strong" support for this goal (Ministry of Foreign Affairs of the People's Republic of China and United Nation System in China 2010).

7   *Shouxi yehua* (officially translated by CCTV as "Night Talk in the Seat of Honour"): *Zhui meng de laoren* ("Old People in Pursuit of Their Dreams"). TV program broad-

cast May 20, 2012. http://news.cntv.cn/program/shouxiyehua/20120521/100270 .shtml (accessed June 18, 2012)

8   See, for instance, http://en.cnci.gov.cn/HtmlFiles/News/2011-6-7/14116.shtml (accessed June 18, 2012).

9   For example, www.hverdagenshelte.com/ (accessed June 19, 2012).

10 Ibid.

11 www.hverdagenshelte.com/teenpower-filmen.php (accessed June 19, 2012).

12 Ibid.

13 For Japanese discourses on the individual as expressed in school education, see especially Cave 2007.

CONCLUSION

1   www.gjgwy.org/ (accessed January 31 2013).

2   In 2012, a record number of 1.12 million people took part in the examinations for a total of 20,800 available positions around the country (Chen and Xu 2012).

3   See, for instance, a summary of former prime minister Wen Jiabao's discussion with university rectors in 2006 regarding how to "foster more outstanding talents" in Liu 2006.

GLOSSARY OF CHINESE NAMES AND TERMS

anquangan	安全感	sense of security
Baba, wo ai ni	爸爸我爱你	Daddy, I love you
balinghou	八零后	post-1980 generation
ban ganbu	班干部	class cadre
banzhang	班长	class monitor
banzhuren	班主任	homeroom teachers
baomu	保姆	nanny
benke	本科	bachelor's education
biaoxian ziji	表现自己	express yourself
biaoxinliyi	标新立异	unconventional
bu dong shi	不懂事	to not understand things
bu hao yisi	不好意思	embarrassed
bu hui guan tai duo le	不会管太多了	to not be able to control many things
bu jiankang de	不健康的	unhealthy
bu yao bei, yao ziran yi dair	不要背，要自然一点	don't recite, be natural
buzhang	部长	head of a section
canyu zhengzhi shenghuo	参与政治生活	to engage in political life

Chaoji Nüsheng	超级女声	*Super Voice Girls* (TV show)
chengji	成绩	results
chengren gaozhong	成人高中	adult high school
chengyuan	成员	ordinary member
chi ku	吃苦	to endure bitterness
chuangzaoxing	创造性	creativity
chunjie	纯洁	pure and honest
chuzhong	初中	junior secondary school
dagong	打工	to work, to conduct manual labor
daigou	代沟	generation gap
dang'an	档案	file
dang he zhengfu	党和政府	party and government
dangzheng	党政	party-government
dandiao	单调	dull
danwei	单位	work unit
danzi hen da	胆子很大	to have a lot of nerve
daxue	大学	university
difangxing daxue	地方性大学	local university
diren	敌人	enemies of the people
duanlian ziji	锻炼自己	self-training
duibuqi laoshi	对不起老师	to let down the teacher
dushu wuyong lun	读书无用论	view that studying is of no use
er ben	二本	second-rank university
fahui ziji	发挥自己	to develop oneself
fangzi	放弃	to renounce
Feichang wurao	非常无扰	*If You Are the One* (TV show)
fubanzhang	副班长	deputy class monitor
fudu xuexiao	复读学校	private school where a student can prepare to retake the university entrance examination

fuzhuang guaiguaide	服装怪怪的	peculiar clothes
gaige kaifang	改革开放	reform and opening-up policy
ganbu	干部	cadre
ganshi	干事	assistant
gaoji ganbu	高级干部	high-level cadre
gaokao	高考	university entrance exam
gaokao lizhi yanjiang	高考励志演讲	inspirational lectures on the entrance examination
gaoyuan fanying	高原反应	high-altitude pressure reactions
gaozhong	高中	high school/senior secondary school
geren yingxiongzhuyi	个人英雄主义	individualistic heroism
gongping	公平	fair
Gongqingtuan	共青团	Communist Party Youth League
guai	乖	well behaved
guan	管	to manage
guan tongxuemen	管同学们	to be in charge of fellow students
guanhai	惯坏	spoiled
guanli	管理	to manage
guanxi	关系	connections
guguan	股管	backbone
guocheng	过程	process
guomin	国民	citizen
Han Yu	韩愈	Han Yu
hangtian jingshen	航天精神	spaceship spirit
hao xuesheng	好学生	good students
haohao xuexi	好好学习	study hard
hexie shehui	和谐社会	harmonious society
houbei ganbu	后备干部	reserve cadre
huikao	会考	final high school examinations

huji	户籍	household registration
Huode jiaoyang de tujing	获得教养的途径	*The Way to Acquire Education*
jian ge mian	见个面	to show who you are
jiandu	监督	to supervise
jianfu	减负	to reduce the burden
jiaoyang	教养	education, learning
jiazhang	家长	head of the family
jiazhi duoyuan	价值多元	heterogeneous values
jibaobu	纪保部	section for discipline and security
jige xiguan	几个习惯	some habits
jilü	纪录	discipline
jiechu rencai	杰出人才	outstanding talent
jingji shenghuo	经济生活	economic life
jinzhang	紧张	nervous
juedui de ziyou	绝对的自由	absolute freedom
kai dian	开店	to run a shop
kai houmen	开后门	to open the back door
kandao biaomian	看到表面	to be concerned with face
kao daxue	考大学	to test into a university
keai	可爱	loveable, cute
kongzhi qingxu	控制情绪	to control feelings and emotions
Kuaile Nüsheng	快乐女声	*Happy Girls* (TV show)
la guanxi	拉关系	using connections
like	理科	natural sciences
lizhe de xiaofei	理智的消	rational consumption
Lunyu	论语	*The Analects*
luohun	裸婚	naked marriage
maodun	矛盾	contradiction
maodun hen da	矛盾很大	big conflicts
meng	梦	dream

Mengzi	孟子	Mencius
mei ge ren you mei ge ren de xianfa	每个人有每个人的想法	everybody has their own point of view
mei you duoda shuohua de diwei	没有多大说话的地位	to not be in a position to say much
mei you xiwang	没有希望	no hope
mei you yong	没有用	useless
mianzi	面子	face
minzhude	民主的	democratic
minzhu ketang qifen	民主课堂气氛	democratic classroom atmosphere
minzu jiaoyu	民族教育	minority education
minzu tuanjie	民族团结	unity of Chinese nationalities
mubiao	目标	goal
mudi	目的	goal
muxiao	母校	mother school
Nalaizhuyi	拿来主义	Grabism (essay by Lu Xun)
nengli bijiao qiang	能力比较强	to possess strong abilities
nongcun de haize	农村的孩子	rural children
nongcunde	农村的	rural
nuli	努力	hardworking
panbi xinli	攀比心理	mentality of making invidious comparison
pugao	普高	regular high school
putong	普通	regular
putong gaozhong	普通高中	regular high school
qiangpozheng	强迫症	obsessive compulsive disorder
quantuo bantuo	全拖半拖	full- or part-time boarding
quiyi xinli	求异心理	mentality of striving for distinction

rang tongxuemen xiangxin	让同学们相信	to gain the trust of fellow students
renmin	人民	people
renmin minzhu zhuanzheng	人民民主专政	people's democratic dictatorship
ruoshi qunti	弱势群体	vulnerable group
san ben	三本	third-rank university
Shangdi	上帝	God
shehuizhuyi xinren	社会主义新人	new socialist man
shengchan jijixing	生产积极性	productive initiative
shensheng	神圣	sacred
Shi shuo	师说	*Discourse on Teachers*
Shouxi yehua	首席夜话	*Night Talk in the Seat of Honour* (TV show)
shuji	书记	secretary
shuli zizhuzeye guan	树立自主择业观	attitude of acceptance of individual choice of occupation
sixiang pinde	思想品德	thought and values
sixiang zhengzhi	思想政治	thought and politics
songquzhuyi	送去主义	sendism (opposed to grabism)
suzhi	素质	"quality"/with education and good manners
suzhi di de xuesheng	素质低的学生	low-"quality" students
suzhi jiaoyu	素质教育	"quality" education
suzhi zhende hen cha	素质真的很	the "quality" is really poor
tai da le	太大了	too big
tai xinku le	太辛苦了	too much hardship
taibuqitoulai	抬不起头来	unable to keep his or her head up
taidu	态度	attitude
tan lianai	谈恋爱	dating
tiaochu nongment	跳出农门	to jump out of the agricultural door

tiaojian	条件	conditions
tiaopi	调皮	naughty
tigao ziji	提高自己	improve oneself
tigao ziji de suzhi	提高自己的素质	to raise one's own "quality"
tiyubu	体育部	physical education section
tuanjie	团结	unity/ to be united
waiguo	外国	foreign
wanr	玩儿	fun
weishengbu	卫生部	health section
wending	稳定	secure, stable
wenke	文科	humanities
wenyubu	文娱不	cultural entertainment section
wo jintian kaishi xin de shenghuo 我今天开始新的生活	today I start a new life	
xiandai	现代	modern
xiang gan shenme jiu gan shenme	想干什么就干什么	to do what you want to do
xiang shuo shenme jiu shuo shenme	想说什么就说什么	to say what you want
xiang zenme gan jiu zenme gan	想怎么干就怎么干	to do things the way you want to
xiangxin ni ziji zui bang de	相信你自己最棒的	believe you are the best
xiangxin ziji	相信自己	to believe in oneself
xiao	孝	filial piety
xiaofei xinli mianmian guan	消费心理面面观	every aspect of consumer mentality
xiaofeizhe	消费者	consumer
xiaoxue	小学	primary school
xin shiqi	新时期	new period
xingge waixiang	性格外向	extrovert
xinli wenti	心理问题	psychological problems
xiuyang	修养	education, learning

xuanchuanbu	宣传部	propaganda section
xuesheng ganbu	学生干部	student cadres
Xuesheng ganbu wang	学生干部网	Student Cadre Net
xuesheng libukai shouji	学生离不开手机	students are inseparable from their phones
xuesheng shi shangdi	学生是上帝	the student is God
xueshenghui	学生会	student association
xuexi hao, guanxi hao	学习好,关系好	good academic results and good connections
yali	压力	pressure
yali tai da	压力太大	too much pressure
yanbao jiancao	眼保健操	eye exercises
yi ben	一本	top university
yi xuesheng wei zhu	以学生为主	to focus on students
you jiaoyang de ren	有教养的人	educated person
youxiu xuesheng ganbu	优秀学生干部	outstanding student cadre
Yuwen	语文	*Language and Literature*
zao lian	早恋	early love
zeren	责任	responsibility
zerengan	责任感	sense of responsibility
zhanshi gexing	展示个性	to display individuality
zhege ye hen ziyoude	这个也很自由的	this was also quite free
zhen	镇	municipality
zhencheng	真诚	honest
zhengjiaochu	政教处	school political office
zhengzhi quanli he ziyou	政治权利和自由	political rights and freedoms
zhengzhi shenghuo	政治生活	political life
zhenqu	镇区	town area
zhenzheng de jiaoyang	真正的教养	genuine education
zhenzhi	真挚	sincere
zhigao	职高	vocational high school
zhiye jishu jiaoyu	职业技术教育	vocational education
Zhiye Jishu Xueyuan	职业技术学院	College of Professional Technology

zhongdeng zhiye xuexiao	中等职业学校	vocational high school
zhongdian xuexiao	重点学校	elite key school
Zhongguo gudai shehui	中国古代社会	old Chinese society
Zhongguo lizhi yanjian wang	中国励志演讲网	Chinese Net for Inspirational Lectures
zhuxi	主席	chairman
zhuanke	专科	specialized shorter university training
Zhui meng de laoren	追梦的老人	"Old People in Pursuit of Their Dreams" (TV episode)
ziji you shenme tedian	自己有什么特点	what is special about you
zisi	自私	selfish
ziside	自私的	selfishly
ziwo fuwu	自我服务	self-service
ziwo guanli	自我管理	self-administration
ziwo jiaoyu	自我教育	self-education
ziwo jieshao	自我介绍	self-presentation
ziwo wanshan	自我完善	to perfect oneself
ziwo yishi hen qiang	自我意识很强	to be very self-confident
ziwozhuyi	自我主义	individualism
ziyou	自由	freedom, free
zunzhong	尊重	to respect
zou houmen	走后门	to use the backdoor
zuo shengyi	做生意	to do business
zuowei ouxiang	作为偶像	being regarded as an idol

BIBLIOGRAPHY

Abelmann, Nancy. 2009. *The Intimate University: Korean American Students and the Problems of Segregation*. Durham, NC: Duke University Press.

Ako, Tomoko. 2003. "Strategic Ambiguity of Chinese Public Space and Private Space: Ethnographic Study of Three Shanghai's Middle Schools under the Socialist Market Economy." PhD diss., Hong Kong: Hong Kong University.

Alpermann, Björn. 2011. "Class, Citizenship and Individualization in China's Modernization." *ProtoSociology* 28: 7–25.

Anagnost, Ann. 2004. "The Corporeal Politics of Quality (*Suzhi*)." *Public Culture* 16 (2): 189–208.

Associated Press. 2013. "China Figures Show Wide Income Gap." *New York Times*, January 18, sec. Business Day / Global Business. www.nytimes.com/2013/01/19/business/global/china-figures-show-wide-income-gap.html (accessed January 21, 2013).

Atkinson, Paul. 2005. "Qualitative Research—Unity and Diversity." *Forum: Qualitative Social Research*. Special Issue: *The State of the Art of Qualitative Research in Europe* 6 (3): 1–11.

Atkinson, Paul, and David Silverman. 1997. "Kundera's Immortality: The Interview Society and the Invention of the Self." *Qualitative Inquiry* 3 (3): 304–325.

Bailey, Paul John. 2007. *Gender and Education in China: Gender Discourses and Women's Schooling in the Early Twentieth Century*. London: Taylor & Francis.

Bakken, Børge. 2000. *The Exemplary Society: Human Improvement, Social Control and the Dangers of Modernity in China*. Oxford: Oxford University Press.

———, ed. 2005. *Crime, Punishment, and Policing in China*. Lanham, MD: Rowman & Littlefield.

Ball, Stephen J. 2009. *Foucault and Education*. London: Routledge.

Barabasch, Antje, Sui Huang, and Robert Lawson. 2009. "Planned Policy Transfer: The Impact of the German Model on Chinese Vocational Education." *Compare: A Journal of Comparative and International Education* 38: 5–20.

Bauman, Zygmunt. 2000. *Liquid Modernity*. Cambridge: Polity Press.

———. 2001. *The Individualized Society*. Cambridge: Polity Press.

Beck, Ulrich. 1992. *Risk Society: Towards a New Modernity*. Thousand Oaks, CA: Sage.

———. 2007. "Beyond Class and Nation: Reframing Social Inequalities in a Globalizing World." *British Journal of Sociology* 58: 679–705.

———. 2008. *World at Risk*. Cambridge: Polity Press.

Beck, Ulrich, and Elisabeth Beck-Gernsheim. 2002. *Individualization: Institutionalized Individualism and Its Social and Political Consequences*. Thousand Oaks, CA: Sage.

Beck, Ulrich, Anthony Giddens, and Scott Lash, eds. 1994. *Reflexive Modernization: Politics, Tradition and Aesthetics in the Modern Social Order*. Cambridge: Polity Press.

Beck, Ulrich, and Edgar Grande. 2010. "Varieties of Second Modernity: The Cosmopolitan Turn in Social and Political Theory and Research." *British Journal of Sociology* 61 (3): 409–443.

Beck, Ulrich, and Johannes Willms. 2004. *Conversations with Ulrich Beck*. Cambridge: Polity Press.

Besley, Tina, and Michael Peters, eds. 2007. *Subjectivity and Truth: Foucault, Education, and the Culture of Self*. New York: Peter Lang.

Boermel, Anna. 2009. "Beyond the Red Sunset: An Anthropological Study of Old Age in Urban China." PhD diss., Oxford University.

Bourdieu, Pierre. 1977. *Outline of a Theory of Practice*. Cambridge: Cambridge University Press.

Brady, Anne-Marie. 2009. "The Beijing Olympics as a Campaign of Mass Distraction." *China Quarterly* 197: 1–24.

Bray, David. 2005. *Social Space and Governance in Urban China: The Danwei System from Origins to Reform*. Stanford, CA: Stanford University Press.

Brock, Andy. 2009. "Moving Mountains Stone by Stone: Reforming Rural Education in China." *International Journal of Educational Development* 29 (5): 454–462.

Brownell, Susan. 2009. "Beijing's Olympic Education Programme: Re-Thinking *Suzhi* Education, Re-Imagining an International China." *China Quarterly* 197: 44–63.

Brubaker, Rogers. 1993. "Social Theory as Habitus." In *Bourdieu: Critical Perspectives*, edited by Edward Lipuma, Moishe Postone, and Craig J. Calhoun, 212–234. Chicago: University of Chicago Press.

Calhoun, Craig. 2010. "Beck, Asia and Second Modernity." *British Journal of Sociology* 61 (3): 597–619.

Cave, Peter. 2007. *Primary School in Japan: Self, Individuality and Learning in Elementary Education*. London: Routledge.

Chan, Anita. 1985. *Children of Mao: Personality Development and Political Activism in the Red Guard Generation*. London: Macmillan.

Chen Jia. 2010. "Country's Wealth Divide Past Warning Level." *China Daily*, May 12. www.chinadaily.com.cn/china/2010-05/12/content_9837073.htm (accessed February 18 2013).

Chen Xin, and Xu Junqian. 2012. "Record Number of Hopefuls Sit Annual Civil Service Exam." *China Daily.com.cn*, November 26. /www.chinadaily.com.cn/china/2012-11/26/content_15956436.htm (accessed January 31, 2013).

Chen, Shirong. 2011. "Chinese Overseas Students Hit Record High." BBC News Aisa-Pacific. www.bbc.co.uk/news/world-asia-pacific-13114577 (accessed October 10, 2011).

Chen, Weijun, dir. 2008. *Please Vote for Me.* DVD documentary. New York: First Run Features.

Chen, Yangbin. 2008. *Muslim Uyghur Students in a Chinese Boarding School: Social Recapitalization as a Response to Ethnic Integration.* Lanham, MD: Lexington Books.

Cheng Fangping, Liu Yiguo, and Wu Hua. 2009. "2009 Bluebook of Education: China on the Eve of Tremendous Change." In *The China Education Development Year Book, 2009* edited by Yang Dongping, 1–37. Leiden: Brill.

Cheung, Kwok Wah, and Suyan Pan. 2006. "Transition of Moral Education in China: Towards Regulated Individualism." *Citizenship Teaching and Learning* 2 (2): 37–50.

China Education and Research Network. 2011. *2008 nian quanguo jiaoyu shiye fazhan tongji gongbao* [Report on national educational statistics from 2008]." www.edu. cn/jiao_yu_fa_zhan_498/20090720/t20090720_392038_2.shtml (accessed October 17, 2011).

China's Ministry of Education. 2010a. "A Blueprint for Educational Modernization—The Birth of the Outline of China's National Plan for Medium and Long-Term Education Reform and Development." July 31. http://moe.eol.cn/edoas/en/level3.jsp?tablenam e=1245221141523299&infoid=1286874547640206&title=A%20Blueprint%20for%20 Educational%20Modernization (accessed October 15, 2011).

———. 2010b. *Guojiazhong changqi jiaoyu gaige he fazhan guihua gangyao 2010-2020* [National Outline for Medium and Long-Term Education Reform and Development 2010–2020]. July 29. www.gov.cn/jrzg/2010-07/29/content_1667143.htm (accessed March 10, 2011).

———. 2011. *2010 nian quanguo jiaoyu shiye fazhang tongji gongbao* [A statistical report of regarding national educational development in 2010]. www.jyb.cn/info/jytjk/ tjgb/201107/t20110706_441003.html (accessed March 10, 2011).

Chua, Amy. 2011. *Battle Hymn of the Tiger Mother.* London: Bloomsbury.

Cleverley, John. 1991. *The Schooling of China: Transition and Modernity in Chinese Education.* Sydney: Allen & Unwin.

Croll, Elisabeth. 2006. *China's New Consumers: Social Development and Domestic Demand.* London and New York: Routledge.

Culp, Robert. 2006. "Rethinking Governmentality: Training, Cultivation, and Cultural Citizenship in Nationalist China." *Journal of Asian Studies* (65): 529–554.

Curricula Research Institute. 2007. *Zhengzhi shenghuo: jiaoshi jiaoxue yongshu* [Political life: Teachers teaching manual]. Beijing: Renmin Jiaoyu Chubanshe.

Davey, Gareth, Chuan De Lian, and Louise Higgins. 2007. "The University Entrance Examination System in China." *Journal of Further and Higher Education* 31 (4): 385–396.

De Bary, William Theodore; Irene Bloom, and Joseph Adler. 2000. *Sources of Chinese Tradition,* Vol. 1. 2nd ed. New York: Columbia University Press.

Dean, Mitchell M. 2009. *Governmentality: Power and Rule in Modern Society.* London: Sage.

Dello-Iacovo, Belinda. 2009. "Curriculum Reform and 'Quality Education' in China: An Overview." *International Journal of Educational Development* 29 (3): 241–249.

Deng, Peng. 1997. *Private Education in Modern China.* Westport, CT: Greenwood.

Dillon, Sam. 2010. "In PISA Test, Top Scores from Shanghai Stun Experts." *New York Times,* July 12. www.nytimes.com/2010/12/07/education/07education.html (accessed September 12, 2011).

Ding Fan, Jiujun Yang et al., eds. 2008a. *Yuwen [Language and Literature]*. Vol. 4, 2nd. semester high school. Hangzhou: Jiangsu Jiaoyu Chubanshe.

———. 2008b. *Yuwen [Language and Literature]*. Vol. 1, 1st. semester high school. Hangzhou: Jiangsu Jiaoyu Chubanshe.

Duffell, Nick. 2000. *The Making of Them: The British Attitude to Children and the Boarding School System*. London: Lone Arrow Press.

Dushu 1991 (4):143–147. "Mudi he qianti," abridged translation by Chang Wuneng of Herman Hesse's "Betrachtungen und Berichte."

Dushu 1990 (3):141–145. "Shu de moli," abridged translation by Chang Wuneng of Herman Hesse's "Magie des Buches."

Edwards, Louise. 2010. "Military Celebrity in China: The Evolution of 'Heroic and Model Servicemen.'" In *Celebrity in China*, edited by Elaine Jeffreys and Louise Edwards, 21–44. Seattle: University of Washington Press.

Elman, Benjamin A., and Alexander Woodside, eds. 1994. *Education and Society in Late Imperial China, 1600–1900*. Berkeley: University of California Press.

Fei, Wu. 2011. "Suicide, a Modern Problem in China." In *Deep China: The Moral Life of the Person*, edited by Arthur Kleinman, Yunxiang Yan, Jun Jing, Lee Sing, Everett Zhang, Tianshu Pan, Wu Fei, and Jinhua Guo. Berkeley: University of California Press.

Feng Weiguang. 2004. *Renminwang—xiesheng ganbu shi jiaqiang da xuesheng sixiang zhengzhi jiaoyu de zhongyao yikao nengli* [Student cadres are an important force for strengthening ideological and political thought among university students]. *Renminwang* (webpage of the *People's Daily*). http://www.people.com.cn/GB/jiaoyu/1055/2983160.html (accessed 22 October 2011).

Fong, Vanessa L. 2011. *Paradise Redefined: Transnational Chinese Students and the Quest for Flexible Citizenship in the Developed World*. Stanford, CA: Stanford University Press.

Fong, Vanessa L., and Philip G. Altbach. 2011. "School Achievement: Let's Not Worry Too Much about Shanghai." *Education Week*, January 12. www.edweek.org/ew/articles/2011/01/12/15fong.h30.html?qs=pisa+shanghai (accessed April 14, 2011).

Fong, Vanessa L., and Sung won Kim. 2011. "Anthropological Perspectives on Chinese Children, Youth, and Education." In *A Companion to the Anthropology of Education*, edited by Bradley A. Levinson and Mica Pollock, 333–348. Hoboken, NJ: Wiley-Blackwell.

Foucault, Michel. 1982. "The Subject and Power." *Critical Inquiry* 8 (4): 777–795.

Fu Jing. 2010. "Urban-Rural Income Gap Widest Since Reform." *China Daily*, February 3. www.chinadaily.com.cn/china/2010-03/02/content_9521611.htm (accessed June 10, 2011).

Gao, Yang, Li Ping Li, Jean Hee Kim, Nathan Congdon, Joseph Lau, and Sian Griffiths. 2010. "The Impact of Parental Migration on Health Status and Health Behaviours among Left Behind Adolescent School Children in China." *BMC Public Health* 10 (1): 56.

Gaztambide-Fernández, Rubén A. 2009. *The Best of the Best: Becoming Elite at an American Boarding School*. Cambridge, MA: Harvard University Press.

Giddens, Anthony. 1991. *Modernity and Self-Identity: Self and Society in the Late Modern Age*. Cambridge: Polity Press.

Goossaert, Vincent, and David A. Palmer. 2012. *The Religious Question in Modern China*. Chicago: University of Chicago Press.

Greene, T. William. 2008. "Three Ideologies of Individualism: Toward Assimilating a Theory of Individualisms and Their Consequences." *Critical Sociology* 34 (1): 117–137.

Greenhalgh, Susan. 2005. *Governing China's Population: From Leninist to Neoliberal Biopolitics*. Stanford, CA: Stanford University Press.

———. 2008. *Just One Child: Science and Policy in Deng's China*. Berkeley: University of California Press.

———. 2010. *Cultivating Global Citizens: Population in the Rise of China*. Cambridge, MA: Harvard University Press.

Griffiths, Michael B. 2012. *Consumers and Individuals in China: Standing Out, Fitting In*. London and New York: Routledge.

Grimshaw, T. 2007. "Problematizing the Construct of the 'Chinese Learner': Insights from Ethnographic Research." *Educational Studies* 33 (3): 299–311.

Guo Daohui, Mingan Jiang, Dingjian Cai, et al. 2011. *Xuezhe huyu cujin gaodeng jiaoyu jihui gongping de gongkaixin* [An open letter from scholars calling for the promotion of equal opportunities in higher education]. In *Bluebook of Education: Annual Report on China's Education*, edited by Dongping Yang and Chunqing Chai, 320–323. Beijing: Social Sciences Academic Press.

Guo, Zhenyi, and Stephen Lamb. 2010. *International Comparisons of China's Technical and Vocational Education and Training System*. Heidelberg, London, New York: Springer.

Han Sang-Jin, and Shim Young-Hee. 2010. "Redefining Second Modernity for East Asia: A Critical Assessment." *British Journal of Sociology* 61 (3): 465–488.

Hannum, Emily, Xuehui An, and Hua-Yu Sebastian Cherng. 2011. "Examinations and Educational Opportunity in China: Mobility and Bottlenecks for the Rural Poor." *Oxford Review of Education* 37 (2): 267–305.

Hannum, Emily, and Albert Park, eds. 2007. *Education and Reform in China*. London and New York: Routledge.

Hannum, Emily, Albert Park, and Kai-Ming Cheng. 2007. "Introduction: Market Reforms and Educational Opportunity in China." In *Education and Reform in China*, edited by Emily Hannum and Albert Park, 1–25. London and New York: Routledge.

Hansen, Mette Halskov. 1999. *Lessons in Being Chinese: Minority Education and Ethnic Identity in Southwest China*. Seattle: University of Washington Press.

———. 2005. *Frontier People: Han Settlers in Minority Areas of China*. London: Hurst & Company.

———. 2008. "Organising the Old: Senior Authority and the Political Significance of a Rural Chinese 'Non-Governmental Organisation'." *Modern Asian Studies* 42 (05): 1057–1078.

———. 2012a. "Recent Trends in Chinese Rural Education: The Disturbing Rural-Urban Disparities and the Measures to Meet Them." In *Towards a New Development Paradigm in Twenty-First Century China: Economy, Society and Politics*, edited by Eric Florence and Pierre Defraigne, 165–179. London and New York: Routledge.

———. 2012b. "Learning to Organize and to Be Organized: Student Cadres in a Chinese Rural Boarding School." In *Organizing Rural China: Rural China Organizing*, edited by Stig Thøgersen and Ane Bislev, 125–141. Lanham, MD: Lexington Books.

———. 2012c. "'More Matriarchal Than the Moso': When Kids in the Field Provoke

Reflections on Gender, Education and Cultural Relativism." Unpublished paper presented at the American Anthropological Association, San Francisco, November.

———. 2013. "Learning Individualism: Hesse, Confucius, and Pep-Rallies in a Rural High School." *China Quarterly* (213): 60–77.

Hansen, Mette Halskov, and Cuiming Pang. 2008. "Me and My Family: Perceptions of Individual and Collective among Young Rural Chinese." *European Journal of East Asian Studies* 7 (1): 75–99.

———. 2010. "Idealizing Individual Choice: Work, Love and Family in the Eyes of Young Rural Chinese." In *iChina: The Rise of the Individual in Modern Chinese Society*, edited by Mette Halskov Hansen and Rune Svarverud, 39–64. Copenhagen: NIAS Press.

Hansen, Mette Halskov, and Rune Svarverud, eds. 2010. *iChina: The Rise of the Individual in Modern Chinese Society*. Copenhagen: NIAS Press.

Hansen, Mette Halskov, and T. E. Woronov. 2013. "Demanding and Resisting Vocational Education: A Comparative Study of Schools in Rural and Urban China." *Comparative Education* 49 (2): 242–259.

Hayhoe, Ruth, ed. 1992. *Education and Modernization: The Chinese Experience*. Oxford: Pergamon.

He, Baogang, and Stig Thøgersen. 2010. "Giving the People a Voice? Experiments with Consultative Authoritarian Institutions in China." *Journal of Contemporary China* 19 (66): 675–692.

Heimer, Maria, and Stig Thøgersen, eds. 2006. *Doing Fieldwork in China*. Copenhagen: NIAS Press.

Hoffman, Lisa. 2010. *Patriotic Professionalism in Urban China: Fostering Talent*. Philadelphia: Temple University Press.

Hou, Zhi-Jin, and Naijian Zhang. 2007. "Counseling Psychology in China." *Applied Psychology* 56 (1): 33–50.

Howard, Cosmo. 2007a. "Introducing Individualization." In *Contested Individualization: Debates about Contemporary Personhood*, edited by Cosmo Howard, 1–25. New York: Palgrave Macmillan.

———., ed. 2007b. *Contested Individualization: Debates about Contemporary Personhood*. New York: Palgrave Macmillan.

Institute of International Education. 2010. "Open Doors 2010 International Students in the U.S." Press release: "International Student Enrollments Rose Modestly in 2009/10, Led by Strong Increase in Students from China." October 15. www.iie.org/Who-We-Are/News-and-Events/Press-Center/Press-Releases/2010/2010-11-15-Open-Doors-International-Students-In-The-US (accessed October 10, 2011).

Iredale, Robyn, Naran Bilik, and Wang Su, ed. 2001. *Contemporary Minority Migration, Education and Ethnicity in China*. Northampton, MA: Edward Elgar.

Jeffreys, Elaine. 2004. *China, Sex and Prostitution*. London and New York: Routledge.

Jiang Xueqin. 2010. "How Shanghai Schools Beat Them All." *Diplomat*, January 8. http://the-diplomat.com/2011/08/01/how-shanghai-schools-beat-them-all/ (accessed December 9, 2011).

Jin Zhu. 2010. "Rural Population Could Drop to 400m." *China Daily*, February 25. www.chinadaily.com.cn/business/2010-02/25/content_9502683.htm (accessed June 10. 2011).

Jing, Jun. 2000. "Environmental Protests in Rural China." In *Chinese Society: Change,*

Conflict and Resistance, edited by Elizabeth J. Perry and Mark Seldon, 197-214. London and New York: Routledge.

Johnson, Kay Ann. 2004. *Wanting a Daughter, Needing a Son: Abandonment, Adoption, and Orphanage Care in China*. St. Paul, MN: Yeong & Yeong.

Jones, Alisa. 2005. "Changing the Past to Serve the Present: History Education in Mainland China." In *History Education and National Identity in East Asia*, edited by Edward Vickers and Alisa Jones, 65-101. London and New York: Routledge.

———. 2012. *History and Citizenship Education in Post-Mao China: Politics, Policy, Praxis*. London and New York: Routledge.

Kennedy, Kerry J., Gregory Fairbrother, and Zhenzhou Zhao, eds. 2012. *Citizenship Education in China: Preparing Citizens for the "Chinese Century."* London and New York: Routledge.

Kingdon, Geeta. 2007. "The Progress of School Education in India." *Oxford Review of Economic Policy* 23 (2): 168-195.

Kipnis, Andrew. 2001. "The Disturbing Educational Discipline of 'Peasants.'" *China Journal* 46: 1-24.

———. 2006. "Suzhi: A Keyword Approach." *China Quarterly* 186: 295-313.

———. 2008. "Audit Cultures: Neoliberal Governmentality, Socialist Legacy, or Technologies of Governing?" *American Ethnologist* 35 (2): 275-289.

———. 2011. *Governing Educational Desire: Culture, Politics, and Schooling in China*. Chicago: University of Chicago Press.

Kipnis, Andrew, and Shanfeng Li. 2010. "Is Chinese Education Underfunded?" *China Quarterly* 202: 327-343.

Kleinman, Arthur. 2011a. "Quests for Meaning." In *Deep China: The Moral Life of the Person*, edited by Arthur Kleinman, Yunxiang Yan, Jun Jing, Lee Sing, Everett Zhang, Tianshu Pan, Fei Wu, and Jinhua Guo, 263-291. Berkeley: University of California Press.

———. 2011b. "Remaking the Moral Person in a New China." In *Deep China: The Moral Life of the Person*, edited by Arthur Kleinman, Yunxiang Yan, Jun Jing, Lee Sing, Everett Zhang, Tianshu Pan, Fei Wu, and Jinhua Guo, 1-36. Berkeley: University of California Press.

Kleinman, Arthur, Yan Yunxiang, Jun Jing, Lee Sing, and Everett Zhang, eds. 2011. *Deep China: The Moral Life of the Person*. Berkeley: University of California Press.

Kuai Pengzhou, and Quan Jiang. 2011. *Renkou biandong yu jiaoyu geju de bianhua qushi* [Demographic changes and trends in the transformation of educational patterns]. In *Bluebook of Education: A Report of the Development of Education in China*, edited by Dongping Yang and Chunqing Chai, 39-50. Beijing: Social Sciences Academic Press.

Kwong, Julia. 1983. "Is Everyone Equal before the System of Grades: Social Background and Opportunities in China." *British Journal of Sociology* 34 (1): 93-108.

———. 1988. *Cultural Revolution in China's Schools, May 1966–April 1969*. Stanford, CA: Hoover Institution Press.

Kyung-Sup, Chang. 2010. "The Second Modern Condition? Compressed Modernity as Internalized Reflexive Cosmopolitization." *British Journal of Sociology* 61 (3): 444-464.

Kyung-Sup, Chang, and Song Min-Young. 2010. "The Stranded Individualizer under Compressed Modernity: South Korean Women in Individualization without Individualism." *British Journal of Sociology* 61 (3): 539-564.

Lafraniere, Sharon. 2009. "China's College Entry Test Is an Obsession." *New York Times*, June 13, sec. International/Asia Pacific. www.nytimes.com/2009/06/13/world/asia/13exam.html (accessed January 28, 2011).

Langfitt, Frank. 2013. "In China, Beware: A Camera May Be Watching You." First broadcast January 29, 2013. National Public Radio. www.npr.org/2013/01/29/170469038/in-china-beware-a-camera-may-be-watching-you (accessed April 8, 2014).

Latham, Kevin. 2007. *Pop Culture China! Media, Arts, and Lifestyle*. Santa Barbara, Denver, and Oxford: ABC-CLIO.

Lee, Thomas. 2000. *Education in Traditional China: A History*. Leiden: Brill.

Lee, Wing On, and Chi Hang Ho. 2005. "Ideopolitical Shifts and Changes in Moral Education Policy in China." *Journal of Moral Education* 34 (4): 413–431.

Levin, Dan. 2011. "Coaching and Much More for Chinese Students Looking to U.S." *New York Times*, May 29. www.nytimes.com/2011/05/30/business/global/30college.html?_r=1&pagewanted=all (accessed May 5, 2012).

Li Rui. 2007. *Guanzhu xuesheng wenhua—jiaqiang xuesheng tuanjie jianshe* [Pay attention to student culture—Strengthen the building of student communities]. *Jiaoyu Guanli* [Educational Administration] 1: 20–21.

Li, Wen, Albert Park, and Sangui Wang. 2007. "School Equity in Rural China." In *Education and Reform in China*, edited by Emily Hannum and Albert Park, 27–44. London and New York: Routledge.

Lin, Jing. 1999. *Social Transformation and Private Education in China*. Westport, CT: Greenwood.

Liu Jiansheng. 2006. *Wen zongli xiang daxue xiaozhang qiujiao ruhe peiyang geng duo jiechu rencai* [Prime Minister Wen seeks advice from university rectors regarding how to foster more outstanding talents]. *Xinhua*, November 28. http://news.xinhuanet.com/school/2006-11/28/content_5400168.htm (accessed January 25, 2013).

Liu, Fengshu. 2012. "'Politically Indifferent' Nationalists? Chinese Youth Negotiating Political Identity in the Internet Age." *European Journal of Cultural Studies* 15 (1): 53–69.

Liu, Judith, Heidi A. Ross, and Donald P. Kelly, eds. 2000. *The Ethnographic Eye: Interpretive Studies of Education in China*. New York and London: Falmer.

Liu, Melinda. 2009. "Back to Basics: China Rediscovers the Benefit of Vocational Schools." *Daily Beast (Newsweek)* August 9. www.thedailybeast.com/newsweek/2009/08/09/back-to-basics.html (accessed January 9, 2011).

Liu, Mingxing, Rachel Murphy, Ran Tao, and Xuehui An. 2009. "Education Management and Performance after Rural Education Finance Reform: Evidence from Western China." *International Journal of Educational Development* 29 (5): 463–473.

Liu, Shao-Hua. 2010. *Passage to Manhood: Youth Migration, Heroin, and AIDS in Southwest China*. Stanford, CA: Stanford University Press.

Lomawaima, K. Tsianina. 1994. *They Called It Prairie Light: The Story of Chilocco Indian School*. Lincoln: University of Nebraska Press.

Long, Xiancheng. 2008. *Zuo yi ming chengzhi de xuesheng gangbu* [How to be a competent student cadre]. *Hengyang Normal University News*. November 17. www.hynu.edu.cn/web/1/200811/17163034609.html (accessed August 11, 2011).

Lukes, Steven. 2006. *Individualism*. Colchester: ECPR Press.

Ma Xiangxiang. 2008. *Hangshi xuesheng zizhu Guanli—youhua xuexiao deyu gongzuo* [Improve the students' self-responsibility—Optimize the ideology work in schools]. *Kaoshi Zhoukan* (Examination Weekly, 7): 220–222.

Mallee, Hein, and Frank N. Pieke. 1999. *Internal and International Migration: Chinese Perspectives*. London and New York: Routledge.

McDermott, Ray, and Jason Duque Raley. 2011. "The Ethnography of Schooling Writ Large, 1955–2010." In *A Companion to the Anthropology of Education*, edited by Bradley A Levinson and Mica Pollock, 34–49. Hoboken, NJ: Wiley-Blackwell.

Michels, Volker. 2007. *Sämtliche Werke, Hermann Hesse*. Frankfurt am Main: Suhrkamp.

Milwertz, Cecilia Nathansen. 1996. *Accepting Population Control: Urban Chinese Women and the One-Child Family Policy*. London and New York: Routledge.

Ministry of Education Group (compiling experimental teaching material within the standard curricula of the regular high school subject of Thought and Politics), ed. 2008. *Sixiang Zhengzhi 1: Jingji Shenghuo* [*Thought and Politics 1: Economic Life*]. Beijing: Renmin Jiaoyu Chubanshe.

Ministry of Education of the People's Republic of China. 2012. *Education as Long-Term Priority*. www.moe.edu.cn/publicfiles/business/htmlfiles/moe/moe_2862/201010/109030.html (accessed November 22, 2012).

Ministry of Foreign Affairs of the People's Republic of China, and United Nation System in China. 2010. *China's Progress towards the Millennium Development Goals 2010 Report*. n.p: United Nations.

Mok, Ka Ho. 2009. "The Growing Importance of the Privateness in Education: Challenges for Higher Education Governance in China." *Compare: A Journal of Comparative and International Education* 39 (1): 35.

Mok, Ka Ho, Yu Cheung Wong, and Xiulan Zhang. 2009. "When Marketisation and Privatisation Clash with Socialist Ideals: Educational Inequality in Urban China." *International Journal of Educational Development* 29 (5): 505–512.

Murphy, Rachel. 2004. "Turning Peasants into Modern Chinese Citizens: 'Population Quality' Discourse, Demographic Transition and Primary Education." *China Quarterly* 177: 1–20.

Murphy, Rachel, and David Johnson. 2009. "Education and Development in China—Institutions, Curriculum and Society." *International Journal of Educational Development* 29 (5): 447–453.

n.a. 2004. "China Has More Than 70,000 Private Schools." *People's Daily Online*, March 26. http://english.peopledaily.com.cn/200403/26/eng20040326_138601.shtml (accessed October 22, 2011).

———. 2009. "China's Compulsory Education Policy Covers 160 Mln Students So Far." *People's Daily Online*, December 9. http://english.people.com.cn/90001/90782/90873/6755669.html (accessed October 22, 2011)

———. 2012. "Chinese Students Get IV Drips While Studying for Gaokao Exam." *China Smack*, May 7. http://www.chinasmack.com/2012/pictures/chinese-students-get-iv-drips-while-studying-for-gaokao-exam.html (accessed April 7, 2014).

———. 2012. "Drowning Tops Student Deaths." *South China Morning Post*, February 7. (accessed October 22, 2011).

Naughton, Barry J. 2006. *The Chinese Economy: Transitions and Growth*. Cambridge, MA: MIT Press.

Nie, Hongping Annie. 2008. *The Dilemma of the Moral Curriculum in a Chinese Secondary School*. Lanham, MD: University Press of America.

Nienhauser, William H. Jr. 1985. *The Indiana Companion to Traditional Chinese Literature*, Vol. 1. Bloomington: Indiana University Press.

O'Brien, Kevin J., and Lianjiang Li. 2006. *Rightful Resistance in Rural China*. Cambridge: Cambridge University Press.

Ong, Aihwa. 2006. "Introduction: Neoliberalism as Exception, Exception to Neoliberalism." In *Neoliberalism as Exception: Mutations in Citizenship and Sovereignty*, 1–31. Durham, NC: Duke University Press.

Osnos, Evan. 2011. "Meet Dr. Freud." *New Yorker*, January 10. www.newyorker.com/reporting/2011/01/10/110110fa_fact_osnos (accessed December 10, 2011).

Pang, Cuiming. 2004. *Shei lai zhaokan haizi* [Who will attend the children]. *Shehui yuelan* (Societal Readings) 4: 17–20.

———. 2011. "The Power of Cyber Communities: Building Collective Life in China." PhD diss., University of Oslo.

Pepper, Suzanne. 1996. *Radicalism and Education Reform in Twentieth-Century China: The Search for an Ideal Development Model*. Cambridge: Cambridge University Press.

Peters, Michael, and Tina Besley. 2007. *Why Foucault? New Directions in Educational Research*. New York: Peter Lang.

Peterson, Glen, Ruth Hayhoe, and Yongling Lu, eds. 2001. *Education, Culture, and Identity in Twentieth-Century China*. Ann Arbor: University of Michigan Press.

Pieke, Frank N. 2004. "Contours of an Anthropology of the Chinese State: Political Structure, Agency and Economic Development in Rural China." *Journal of the Royal Anthropological Institute* 10 (3): 517–538.

———. 2009. *The Good Communist: Elite Training and State Building in Today's China*. Cambridge: Cambridge University Press.

Postiglione, Gerard, ed. 1999. *China's National Minority Education: Culture, Schooling, and Development*. New York: Falmer.

———. 2006. *Education and Social Change in China Inequality in a Market Economy*. Armonk, NY: M.E. Sharpe.

Rabkin, April. 2011. "On Your Marks . . ." *South China Morning Post*, October 16, pp. 34–38.

Rawski, Evelyn. 1979. *Education and Popular Literacy in Ch'ing China*. Ann Arbor: University of Michigan Press.

Rohlen, Thomas P. 1973. "'Spiritual Education' in a Japanese Bank." *American Anthropologist* 75 (5): 1542–1562.

Rose, Nikolas. 1999. *Governing the Soul: Shaping of the Private Self*. 2nd rev. ed. London: Free Association Books.

Rosen, Stanley. 2009. "Contemporary Chinese Youth and the State." *Journal of Asian Studies* 68 (02): 359–369.

Ross, Heidi, and Yimin Wang. 2010a. "The College Entrance Examination in China: An Overview of Its Social-Cultural Foundations, Existing Problems, and Consequences." *Chinese Education and Society* 43 (4): 3–10.

———, eds. 2010b. *Chinese Education and Society* (Special Issue) 43 (4).

Scharff, David, and Sverre Varvin, eds. 2014. *Psychoanalysis in China*. London: Karnac Books.

Schoenhals, Martin. 1993. *The Paradox of Power in a People's Republic of China Middle School*. Armonk, NY: M.E. Sharpe.

Schulte, Barbara. 2013. "Unwelcome Stranger to the System: Vocational Education in Early Twentieth-Century China." *Comparative Education* 49 (2): 226–241.

Scott, James C. 1992. *Domination and the Arts of Resistance: Hidden Transcripts*. New Haven: Yale University Press.

Seeberg, Vilma. 2000. *The Rhetoric and Reality of Mass Education in Mao's China*. Lewiston, NY: E. Mellen.

Shan Xiaoqi and Guo Zhanxin. 2011. "Angry Youth of the New Century and the Patriotism of Young People." *Chinese Education and Society* 44 (2): 95–103.

Shandong University Law School. 2011. *Faxueyuan judong xuesheng dangyuan he xuesheng ganbu sixiang jiaoyu he gongzuo peixun* [The law school launch ideological and work training for student members of the party and student cadres]. June 11. http://www.xinwen.wh.sdu.edu.cn/show.jsp?aId=14317&classID=071227170306588162 (accessed August 11, 2011).

Shi Lingming. 2008. *Gaodeng zhiye jiaoyu banxue tixi tansuo* [A study of the system of higher vocational education]. Beijing: Zhongguo nongye kexue jizhu chubanshe.

Shi Yuchang, and Jun Wu. 2011. *Qian Dongnan Zhouzhong zhiye jiaoyu mianfei zhengce shishi qingkuang yanjiu* [A study of the realities regarding the implementation of the policy of providing free vocational education in Guizhou Dongnan Prefecture]. In *Bluebook of Education: Annual Report on China's Education (2011)*, edited by Dongping Yang and Chunqing Chai, 208–218. Beijing: Social Sciences Academic Press.

Shirk, Susan L. 1982. *Competitive Comrades: Career Incentives and Student Strategies in China*. Berkeley: University of California Press.

Shouxi Yehua [Night Talk in the Seat of Honour]. "Zhui meng de laoren" [Old People in Pursuit of their Dreams]." First broadcast May 20, 2012 by CCTV1. Directed by Lai Ali. http://news.cntv.cn/program/shouxiyehua/20120521/100270.shtml (accessed June 18, 2012).

Strickland, Michael. 2010. "Aid and Affect in the Friendships of Young Chinese Men." *Journal of the Royal Anthropological Institute* 16 (1): 102–118.

Student Cadre Net. 2011. *Ruhe tigao gaoxiao xuesheng ganbu suzhi* [How to Raise the quality of student cadres in higher education]. www.xsgbw.com/list.php?id=58. (accessed November 3, 2011).

Su, Zhixin. 1995. "A Critical Evaluation of John Dewey's Influence on Chinese Education." *American Journal of Education* 103 (3): 302–325.

Sun, Wanning. 2009. "Suzhi on the Move: Body, Place, and Power." *Positions: East Asia Cultures Critique* 17 (3): 617–642.

Suzuki, Munenori, Midori Ito, Mitsunori Ishida, Norihiro Nihei, and Masao Maruyama. 2010. "Individualizing Japan: Searching for Its Origin in First Modernity." *British Journal of Sociology* 61 (3): 513–538.

Svarverud, Rune. 2010. "Individual Self-Discipline and Collective Freedom in the Minds of Chinese Intellectuals" In *iChina: The Rise of the Individual in Modern Chinese Society*, edited by Mette Halskov Hansen and Rune Svarverud, 193–225. Copenhagen: NIAS Press.

Thøgersen, Stig. 1990. *Secondary Education in China after Mao: Reform and Social Conflict*. Aarhus: Aarhus University Press.

———. 2002. *A County of Culture: Twentieth-Century China Seen from the Village Schools of Zouping, Shandong*. Ann Arbor: University of Michigan Press.

Thøgersen, Stig, and Anru Ni. 2010. "He Is He and I Am I: Individual and Collective among China's Elderly." In *iChina: The Rise of the Individual in Modern Chinese Society*, edited by Mette Halskov Hansen and Rune Svarverud, 65–93. Copenhagen: NIAS Press.

Thomas, Sally M., and Wen-Jung Peng. 2011. "Methods to Evaluate Educational Quality and Improvement in China." In *Education Reform in China: Changing Concepts, Contexts and Practices*, edited by Janette Ryan, 75–91. London and New York: Routledge.

Tian Er. 2010. *Xin shiqi gaoxiao xuesheng ganbu peiyang fangfa shenyan* [Investigations into the means of training student cadres in higher education in the new era]. www.59up.net/article/7/86/2011060134556.html (accessed November 4, 2011).

Tomba, Luigi. 2009. "Of Quality, Harmony, and Community: Civilization and the Middle Class in Urban China." *Positions: East Asia Cultures Critique* 17 (3): 591–616.

Trafzer, Clifford, Jean A. Keller, and Lorene Sisquoc, eds. 2006. *Boarding School Blues: Revisiting American Indian Educational Experiences*. Lincoln: University of Nebraska Press.

Tsung, Linda. 2009. *Minority Languages, Education and Communities in China*. Basingstoke, Hampsire: Palgrave Macmillan.

Twenty-First Century Educational Research Institute. 2011. *2010 niandu zhongguo zhuyao chengshi gongzhong jiaoyu manyidu diaocha* [A survey of the level of public satisfaction with education in China's main cities in 2010]. In *Bluebook of Education: Annual Report on China's Education (2011)*, edited by Dongping Yang and Chunqing Chai, 252-270. Beijing: Social Sciences Academic Press.

Tyl, Dominique. 2002. "The Formation of New Citizens in China's Secondary School." *China Perspectives* 39: 4–16.

Unger, Jonathan. 1982. *Education under Mao: Class and Competition in Canton Schools, 1960–1980*. New York: Columbia University Press.

Vandermensbrugghe, Joelle. 2004. "The Unbearable Vagueness of Critical Thinking in the Context of the Anglo-Saxonisation of Education." *International Education Journal* 5 (3): 417–422.

Vickers, Edward. 2009a. "The Opportunity of China? Education, Patriotic Values and the Chinese State." In *Education as a Political Tool in Asia*, edited by Marie Lall and Edward Vickers, 43–82. London and New York: Routledge.

———. 2009b. "Selling 'Socialism with Chinese Characteristics' 'Thought and Politics' and the Legitimisation of China's Developmental Strategy." *International Journal of Educational Development* 29 (5): 523–531.

Vickers, Edward, and Xiao-dong Zeng. 2012. *Education and Society in Post-Mao China: Pragmatism and Ideology in the Quest for Modernization*. London and New York: Routledge.

Wang, Dan. 2012. "Workplace Depoliticized: Rural Teachers Under Corrupt Bureaucracy in China." Unpublished paper presented at the European Association of Chinese Studies, Paris, September.

Wang, Danning. 2010. "Intergenerational Transmission of Family Property and Family Management in Urban China." *China Quarterly* 204: 960–979.

Wang, Ting. 2007. "Understanding Chinese Culture and Learning." *International Journal of Leadership in Education* 10 (1): 71–88.

Wang, Yimin, and Heidi Ross. 2010. "Experiencing the Change and Continuity of the College Entrance Examination." *Chinese Education and Society* 43 (4): 75–93.

Wang Guoquan. 2008. *Rensheng shejiwang huiyuan shouce* [Handbook for members in the network for designing human life]. n.p.: n.p.

Wang Xinyuan. 2012. "Local Disposable Incomes See Growth." *People's Daily Online*, July 30. http://english.people.com.cn/90778/7891412.html (accessed April 8, 2014).

Watkins, David A., and John Burville Biggs, eds. 1996. *The Chinese Learner: Cultural, Psychological, and Contextual Influences.* Hong Kong: CERC.

Wellens, Koen. 2010. *Religious Revival in the Tibetan Borderlands: The Premi of Southwest China.* Seattle: University of Washington Press.

Whalley, John, and Ximing Yue. 2009. "Rural Income Volatility and Inequality in China." *CESifo Economic Studies* 55 (3–4): 648–668.

World Bank. 2009. *Gender Gaps in China: Facts and Figures.* Washington DC: World Bank.

Woronov, T. E. 2009. "Governing China's Children: Governmentality and 'Education for Quality.'" *Positions: East Asia Cultures Critique* 17 (3): 567–589.

———. 2011. "Learning to Serve: Urban Youth, Vocational Schools, and New Class Formations in China." *China Journal* 66: 66–77.

———. 2012. "Doing Time: Mimetic Labor and Human Capital Accumulation in Chinese Vocational Schools." *South Atlantic Quarterly* 111 (4): 701–719.

Wright, Daniel. 2005. "The Politics of Private Education in Rich and Poor China." PhD diss., Johns Hopkins University.

Xinhua. 2011. "China Sees High Employment Rate for Vocational School Graduates." *Xinhua, China.org.cn,* June 24. www.china.org.cn/china/2011-06/24/content_22850830.htm (accessed January 9, 2011).

Xinwen diaocha: Ta shi Lei Feng [News probe: This is Lei Feng]. 2012. CCTV channel 1, March 3.

Yan, Yunxiang. 2003. *Private Life under Socialism: Love, Intimacy, and Family Change in a Chinese Village, 1949–1999.* Stanford, CA: Stanford University Press.

———. 2009. *The Individualization of Chinese Society.* London: Athlone.

———. 2010. "The Chinese Path to Individualization." *British Journal of Sociology* 61 (3): 489–512.

———. 2011. "The Changing Moral Landscape." In *Deep China: The Moral Life of the Person,* edited by Arthur Kleinman, 36–77. Berkeley and Los Angeles: University of California Press.

———. 2012a. "Food Safety and Social Risk in Contemporary China." *Journal of Asian Studies* 71 (3): 705–729.

———. 2012b. "Of the Individual and Individualization: The Striving Individual in China and the Theoretical Implications." In *Futures of Modernity: Challenges for Cosmopolitical Thought and Practice,* edited by Michael Heinlein, Cordula Kropp, Judith Neumer, Angelika Poferi, and Regina Römhild, 177–195. Bielefield: Transcript.

———. 2013. "Afterword: The Drive for Success and the Ethics of the Striving Individual." In *Ordinary Ethics in China Today,* edited by Charles Stafford, 263–292. London: Bloomsbury.

Yang, Jie. 2011. "The Politics of the Dang'an: Spectralization, Spatialization, and Neoliberal Governmentality in China." *Anthropological Quarterly* 84 (2): 517–533.

Yang Dongping, and Chai Chunqing, eds. 2011. *Jiaoyu lanpishu: Zhongguo jiaoyu fazhan baogao (2011)* [*Bluebook of Education: Annual Report on China's Education (2011)*]. Beijing: Social Sciences Academic Press.

Yang Zhonghua. 1997. *Chongfen fahui xueshenghui zai xuexiaozhong de jiji zuoyong* [Bring into full play the positive use of student associations in school]. *Jiaoxue yu Guanli* (Education and Administration) 3: n.p.

Ye Jingzhong. 2005. *Guanzhu liushou ertong: Zhongguo Zhongxibu nongcun diqu laodongli waichu wugong dui liushou ertong de yingxiang* [Following left-behind children: The influence of rural labor migration on left-behind children in China's midwest). Beijing: Social Sciences Academic Press.

Ye Jingzhong, and Pan Lu. 2011. "Differentiated Childhoods: Impacts of Rural Labor Migration on Left-Behind Children in China." *Journal of Peasant Studies* 38 (2): 355–377.

Yin Pumin. 2011. "Rural Students Falling Behind." *Beijing Review* 37: September15 www.bjreview.com.cn/nation/txt/2011-09/13/content_389895.htm (accessed November 10, 2011).

Yu, Haibo. 2009. *Identity and Schooling among the Naxi.* Lanham, MD: Lexington Books.

Yu Huiqiong, and Lijun Zhang. 2006. *Toushi nongcun xin "dushu wuyong lun"* [A perspective on the new "idea that studying is of no use" in rural areas]. *Zhongguo Qingnian Yanjiu* [China Youth Research] 9: 66–71.

Zhan Wansheng, and Ning Wujie. 2004. "The Moral Education Curriculum for Junior High Schools in Twenty-First Century China." *Journal of Moral Education* 33 (4): 511–532.

Zhang, Everett, Arthur Kleinman, and Weiming Tu, eds. 2010. *Governance of Life in Chinese Moral Experience: The Quest for an Adequate Life.* London and New York: Routledge.

Zhang Xiaohua. 2006. *Xuesheng zuzhi yu zhongxue deyu de "mutong xiaoying"* [The organizing of students and the "bucket effect" of moral training in high schools]. *Xuexiao dangjiao yu sixiang jiaoyu* [Party Building in Schools and Ideology Education] 7: 42–43.

Zhang Zhengshen, and Hao Bingjun. 1993. *Zhongguo zhiye jishu jiaoyushi* [The history of Chinese vocational education]. Lanzhou: Gansu Jiaoyu Chubanshe.

Zhao, Zhongwei, and Fei Guo, eds. 2007. *Transition and Challenge: China's Population at the Beginning of the Twenty-First Century.* Oxford and London: Oxford University Press.

Zhejiang Provincial Government. 2011. "Zhejiang China: Economy and Society." *Zhejiang China—Government Bulletin.* www.zhejiang.gov.cn/node2/node1619/node1622/userobject13ai697.html (accessed October 11, 2011).

Zheng Ruoling. 2010. "On the Rationality of the College Entrance Examination." *Chinese Education and Society* 43 (4): 11–21.

Zhou Ling. 2011. *2009 nian quanguo ji difang zhengfu jiaoyu touru fenxi* [An analysis of national and provincial educational investments in 2009]. In *Bluebook of Education: A Report of the Development of Education in China,* edited by Dongping Yang and Chunqing Chai, 243–251. Beijing: Social Sciences Academic Press.

Zhu Xiaoman. 2006. "Moral Education and Values Education in Curriculum Reform in China." *Frontiers of Education in China* 1 (2): 191–200.

INDEX

Africa, 90–91
Agricultural University, 22
alcohol, 51
American Idol, 15
Anhui, 20
anime, 170
architecture, 46
Atkinson, Paul, 31
autobiographies, 15, 29, 31, 116, 126, 148, 163, 168

Bakken, Børge, 11
basketball, 112
Battle Hymn of the Tiger Mother, 4
Bauman, Zygmunt, 12–13
Beck, Ulrich, 12–14
Beijing, 20, 69, 132; Normal University, 99
birthdays, 43
blogs, 15, 91, 97–98, 100
boredom, 49, 114, 182

cadre: definition of, 96; student, 96–127
campaigns, 70, 89–94, 102, 112, 128, 145, 179–80
CCTV (China Central Television), 90, 121, 136

celebrities, 88, 121, 136. *See also* heroes
cell phone. *See* mobile phone
censorship, 178
Chen Wei, 97
Chinese Communist Party (CCP), 3, 7–8, 67, 85, 88, 96–97, 144–45, 155, 157, 171–72, 180, 182; Youth League, 3, 30, 52, 95–97, 107–8, 125–26, 136, 180, 192n8
Chua, Amy, 4
civil liberties, 86–87. *See also* freedom
civil service examinations, 74, 174
class struggle, 9, 19, 144
Colbert Report, The, 4
College of Professional Technology, 55
computer games, 61–64, 72, 170
Confucianism, 4, 6, 9, 71–74, 155
consultative authoritarianism, 126
consumerism, 15, 80, 83–84, 100
corruption, 22, 40, 90, 94, 121, 145, 184
cosmopolitanism, 14
creativity, 5–6, 60, 82, 94, 146, 155, 175–76, 181–84
Cultural Revolution, 19, 88, 152

dating, 103, 162, 165, 167; TV programs, 137, 145–46, 151. *See also* love

Declaration of Human Rights, 86
Deng Xiaoping, 4, 19, 87
Denmark, 48, 147–49
depression, 45, 48, 140, 167
Dewey, John, 155
Diary of Anne Frank, The, 72
Die Zeit, 4
Discourse on Teachers, 71–75
divided self, 67, 70, 154, 173
divorce, 39, 47
dress code, 50
dropping out, 106
Dushu, 75

educational standards, 5; international,
    175
elite: schools, 18, 49, 53, 61, 63, 69, 157, 167,
    182; universities, 97, 121
English, 48, 61, 63, 170
Enlightenment, 86
entrance exams: high school, 27, 40, 51,
    56, 122; university, 9, 16, 21–22, 27–28,
    34, 39, 51, 54, 58–60, 79, 81, 109, 122,
    129–38, 167, 192n1
ethics, 8, 32, 35, 93, 171; of the striving
    individual, 156–57
ethnic minority: areas, 17, 22, 25, 38;
    education, 9, 25–26, 79, 181
eye exercises, 111

factory work, 37, 88, 121
fees, 19–20, 40
Feichang wurao, 146
Feng Weiguang, 99
filial piety, 141–42, 150, 159, 168, 171
Finland, 5
Fong, Vanessa, 53
football, 54
fortune tellers, 39–40
Foucault, Michel, 8–10, 96, 188n14. *See
    also* governmentality
freedom, 13, 84–87, 112, 152, 155–56, 177;
    consumer, 84; individual, 85–87; of
    speech, 86–87; precarious, 13; small,
    154, 168. *See also* civil liberties
Fudan University, 137
Fujian, 31, 88

Gansu, 31, 131–32
gaokao. *See* entrance exams
gender, 38; balance, 38; inequality, 143,
    192n6; stereotypes, 118–19, 143
generation gap, 141, 153, 163, 165
Giddens, Anthony, 12–13
Gini coefficient, 18
God, 160
governmentality, 8,11, 97, 154, 166–68,
    177, 179
grabism, 72
grandparents, 31, 34, 41, 43–44, 65, 141,
    170
guanxi, 22, 26, 40, 102, 110, 161

Han Yu, 71–75
harmonious society, 20, 62
hedonism, 32, 76, 91, 94
heroes, 35, 73; among the people, 180;
    sports, 145. *See also* Lei Feng
Hesse, Herman, 71, 73–77
hidden transcripts, 67
holiday, 28, 34, 61, 64, 96, 112
household registration, 18, 22, 25, 37, 131
Hubei, 132
Hu Jintao, 10, 20
humanities, 28, 54, 78–79, 122
hukou, 18, 22, 25, 37, 131

If You Are the One, 146
India, 17–18, 24
individualism, 8, 13, 80, 100–101, 126, 148,
    177–78, 180, 188n17; negative, 152
individuality, 14, 84, 89, 146, 148, 172
individualization, 12–16; authoritarian,
    16, 32, 125, 128, 149, 182, 184; partial, 15
intellectuals, 10, 15, 73, 155, 175–76
Internet, 51–52, 61–64, 72, 87, 112, 144,
    151, 153, 165, 168, 178; cafés, 46, 103;
    communities, 3. *See also* QQ
iron rice bowl, 160

Japan, 13, 24, 79, 145, 149
Jones, Alisa, 70

King, Martin Luther, Jr., 72
Kipnis, Andrew, 11–12, 24

Lao She, 72
Lei Feng, 88–94, 102, 179
Leninism, 95
Liang Qichao, 15
liberalism: philosophic, 155; political, 14
library, 46, 51
Libya, 91–92
Li Keqiang, 23
Liu Xiaobo, 87
love, 142–43, 146, 162, 165, 167, 181
Lu Xun, 72

Mao Zedong: cult, 88–89; education under, 9, 19; thought and Maoism, 9, 15, 19, 87, 93, 144
marriage, 38–40, 161, 168, 171; naked, 39
McDonalds, 72
memorization, 47, 74, 82, 93, 116, 130–31, 154
Mengzi, 72
middle class, 24, 33, 157, 167, 185
mobile phone, 50–52, 62–65, 72, 74, 83, 103, 158, 168–69
modernity, 12–15, 176; cosmopolitan, 14; first, 14–15, 171; late, reflexive or second, 12, 14, 157, 171

nationalism, 79, 144–45. *See also* patriotism
National Outline for Medium and Long-Term Education Reform and Development (2010–2020), 23
natural sciences, 5, 28, 54, 78–79
neoliberalism, 7–8, 13, 149, 176, 180, 182; late-socialist, 7, 154
neosocialist: China, 8, 101, 126, 177, 182; citizen, 16, 95, 125, 129, 149; individual, 16, 32, 70–71, 77, 84, 94; school, 32, 185; subjects, 68; values, 91, 148
new socialist man, 154–55
New Zealand, 24
NGOs, 176, 184
Nie, Hongping Annie, 89
Nobel Prize, 73–74, 87, 190n8
Norway, 47–48

OECD (Organization for Economic Cooperation and Development), 5
Olympic Games, 135, 145, 180
one-child policy, 17, 37–38, 188n13, 189n3
online games, 61–64, 72, 170

patriotic professionals, 157
patriotism, 70–71, 78, 85, 112, 179–80. *See also* nationalism
Peking University, 22
Pieke, Frank, 7–8
PISA (Program for International Student Assessment), 4–5
pollution, 178, 184
post-1980 generation, 153, 184
primary school, 16, 19, 36, 42, 55, 96, 130, 134
private education, 9–10, 36, 43–44, 54, 57, 61, 122, 149, 182
Problem-Based Learning, 6
propaganda, 101–2, 145
psychiatry, 15, 45
psychological problems, 45, 47–49, 106, 139

Qing dynasty, 8
QQ, 60–61, 63, 151, 153, 166
quality: discussion on, 11, 118, 129–30; education, 5, 19, 23; low-quality parents, 160, 166–70; low-quality students, 57, 59, 109, 118, 168; personal 55–56

Red Sorghum, 155
risk society, 13–15, 178, 183

Sa Beining, 121
Schleicher, Andreas, 5
scholarship, 104
science fiction, 64
security, sense of, 151, 159
Shaanxi, 31
Shandong, 8, 24, 49; University, 100
Shanghai, 4–5, 19–20, 26, 49, 69, 121
Shishuo, 71–75
siblings, 25, 36–37, 47, 50, 66, 167
Sichuan, 31, 88

Silverman, David, 31
Singapore, 24
sleeping, 43, 74, 139, 156
smoking, 58, 111,
social mobility, 56, 58, 131, 169, 183
South Korea, 13, 24, 165
spaceship spirit, 73
sports, 48, 50, 54, 101–2, 108–12, 119, 125, 170
stigmatization, 53–54, 56, 59, 125
striving individual, 128, 142–43, 156
student association elections, 7, 29, 95, 101, 107–27, 177, 179
Student Cadre Net, 99–100, 191n3
study abroad, 6, 24–25, 48, 143, 175
suicide, 45, 49, 152, 190n11
suzhi. See quality

Tang dynasty, 73
Teachers Teaching Manual, 85
Teenpower, 147–49
Thøgersen, Stig, 8–9
Tianjin, 20
Tibet, 145
Tiger Mother, Battle Hymn of the, 4
Tsinghua University, 22

unemployment, 39, 145, 175
United States, 4, 6, 18, 24, 79, 149
utilitarianism, 33, 73, 100

Vickers, Edward, 70

Wang Guoquan, 134–36, 139, 143, 145, 148
welfare state, 13–14, 159, 184
Weng Naiqun, 72
Wen Jiabao, 5, 22, 175
Whalley, John, 18
white-collar workers, 38, 157, 169
Woronov, Terry, 10, 182

Xi Jinping, 23

Yang Liwei, 73
Yan, Yunxiang, 14, 142
Yuan Guiren, 22
Yue, Ximing, 18
Yunnan, 26, 31, 65, 79–80, 188n11

Zhejiang, 26–27, 66, 132
Zhuangzi, 72
ziyou. See freedom